D0266416

PRESIDENT
MARY McALEESE

PRESIDENT MARY McALEESE

BUILDING BRIDGES
Selected Speeches and Statements

FOREWORD BY SEAMUS HEANEY

First published 2011

The History Press Ireland
119 Lower Baggot Street
Dublin 2
Ireland
www.thehistorypress.ie

British Library Cataloguing in Publication Data.
A catalogue record for this book is available from the British Library.

ISBN 978 1 84588 724 7

Typesetting and origination by The History Press

CONTENTS

BUILDING BRIDGES

Before Mary McAleese's first term as President of Ireland, before she was elected, even before she was nominated as the Fianna Fáil candidate, she said, 'We have come to realise that the emotional reach of the Presidency is much, much greater than its Constitutional reach.'

This may have been intended as a tribute to the then incumbent Mary Robinson, whose 'emotional reach' to the Irish diaspora had been such an inspiring feature of her seven years in the Presidency. But it was also a foreshadowing of the seven years, indeed the twice seven years, that were to come.

Some months later, in her inaugural address, President McAleese referred to another of her predecessors in the office, the late Cearbhall Ó Dálaigh, and quoted his observation that 'Presidents, under the Irish Constitution, don't have policies. But … a President can have a theme.'

And she went on to announce that her theme would be 'Building Bridges'. At the time the phrase could have been taken as a decent metaphor and a pious aspiration, but fourteen years on it stands out as the expression of courageous resolve and a summary of historic achievement.

That inaugural address was given on 11 November 1997, Armistice Day in Britain and Northern Ireland, the day when Unionists in Mary McAleese's home province of Ulster remembered the dead of the Ulster Division who fell in the carnage at the Somme. Exactly a year later, in the company of Queen Elizabeth II, she built one of the many sturdy arches that would sustain the bridge work throughout her time in office. On Armistice Day 1998, President and monarch officiated at the opening of The Island of Ireland Peace Park at Messines in Belgium, a place dedicated to the memory of those First World War dead, Unionist and Nationalist, Catholic and Protestant, whether of the 36th Ulster Division or the 16th (Irish) Division.

It was an early manifestation of the President's deeds matching her words, reconciliation in action: an outreach towards the Northern Unionist people for whom the sacrifice of those thousands at the Somme represented a hallowing of the ties with Britain; but it was also an inclusive gesture by the Irish Head of State, a reminder to people in both parts of the island that thousands from the Nationalist side also died in British uniforms. Their hope when they enlisted was the same as that advanced by W.B. Yeats – that 'England may keep faith', that their service to the Crown would win independence for Ireland when the war was over. Instead, in the aftermath of the Easter Rising in 1916 and the War of Independence, they became the lost generation, the one the nation was in denial about for most of the twentieth century. The President's attendance at Messines and nearer home at ceremonies in the Irish National War Memorial Gardens in Islandbridge helped to reintroduce them to their proper place in the narrative.

Unexpectedly, however, it wasn't politics but theology that provided a test of strength for one of the earliest arches in the President's bridge. At the end of her first month in office, she made bold to take communion at a Church of Ireland Eucharistic Service in Christ Church

Cathedral, Dublin. This was generally understood to be an ecumenical act by the new President but it soon became clear that admiration for her readiness to cross the reformed divide was by no means universal. Several priests voiced their disquiet, the Catholic Archbishop of Dublin laid down the Canon Law, and the media did their bit to air the issue.

But as a person of devout faith and strong personality, the President rode out what proved to be something of a storm in a chalice.

A year into that first Presidency, however, the omens were favourable. The Good Friday Agreement had been signed, the country's prosperity was on the up, the rising tide was lifting transatlantic planes full of young successful Irishmen and women in business class, beneficiaries of the IT boom, networking and internetting. It was a good time to be President of Ireland, and the vision Mary McAleese had announced in her inaugural address seemed on the verge of fulfilment. There she had spoken of 'the cruelty and capriciousness' of the violent conflict in the North, extolled the example of Gordon Wilson as a man of peace and declared, 'I want to help in every way I can'. Then, as Head of State, she said of Ireland that it 'sits tantalisingly ready to embrace a golden age of affluence, self-assurance, tolerance and peace.' It is sadly ironic to read these words in the wake of the economic collapse that would put paid to that dream of affluence, yet what endured in the President herself were those very qualities she wished for the country: self-assurance, tolerance and unsentimental devotion to peace.

Because of her experience in Belfast as a member of a family forced from their home by loyalist mobs, Mary McAleese has a sure knowledge of the violence of sectarianism – but equally she is, like many Northern people on both sides of the divide, a connoisseur of its velleities. She knows that it is small, almost domestic occasions rather than official declarations which can have the most effect, so when she and her husband Martin host a party on the Twelfth of July for guests from north of the border, it is another arch – an Orange arch all right, but one that can be walked under without unease by people from whatever party or persuasion.

The Peace Process has been a constant concern of Mary McAleese's two Presidencies, and from the start Martin was her stalwart ally in opening paths and minds, North and South. Yet the domestic diplomacy that has gone on at Áras an Uachtaráin, and the several visits paid to destinations on both sides of the North's religio-political divide, have been only one manifestation of Mary McAleese's desire to be a President for all the people. She has proved herself equally caring for the citizens within her jurisdiction, those native to the country and the immigrants who have arrived in their thousands. Her compassion for the disadvantaged and disabled, her sympathy for those who suffer exclusion and her celebration of those who distinguish themselves by service to the community or achievement in sports or the arts – all this is exemplary.

All of which added to the emotional reach of Mary McAleese's Presidency. But it also meant unremitting calls on her physical and emotional energy, thousands of official engagements over the past fourteen years – and that is not counting the visits and State Visits abroad where her vivacious and accomplished presence made emigrants proud to be Irish and made her hosts aware that her country had now indeed taken her place among the nations of the world.

At almost every one of those official engagements and on others, less formal, the President had to speak or make a speech. But in her case the difference was only one of length between brief unscripted remarks and a fully fledged oration. The same substance, conviction, comprehension and passionate utterance were in evidence every time. There have been high public moments during her term of office but I'll always remember the first time I was in an audience when she spoke. She was in her element, a former law professor delivering a lecture at the Kennedy School of Government at Harvard University and taking questions afterwards from the faculty and students. It would have been a testing experience for anyone, but especially for a President who was appearing, willy-nilly, not just as her private self but as representative of her country. And of course, she shone – the main lecture delivered with great intellectual and oratorical verve, the questions answered with scholarly certitude and forensic resource. We left the hall with a new spring in our step.

But the greatest moment in this President's two terms of office was when she welcomed Queen Elizabeth II on her State Visit to the Republic of Ireland, the first in a century by a British monarch. Those three days of hospitality and ceremonies set a crown – almost literally – upon a lifetime's effort. And with the construction of this particular arch, the British–Irish bridge was in place as never before. Again, private and public were fused to dazzling effect: the President's personal friendship with the Queen counting for much in the easy, amicable style of her presence during those three historic days. And it counted for much also in the Queen's readiness to undertake such a busy three days of engagements, including a visit to the Garden of Remembrance where the dead of the Old IRA are honoured and where she bowed her head in silent memory.

The President could rightly and proudly call the visit 'a culmination of the success of the Peace Process' but the rest of us can regard it also as a culmination of the achievements of a great Presidency. A Presidency which saw the Queen begin her speech to an audience in Dublin Castle in Irish and which saw both Heads of State solemnly acknowledge what the poet Wilfred Owen called 'the eternal reciprocity of tears'.

Seamus Heaney, 2011

1

INAUGURATION (1997)

Inauguration Address

Dublin Castle, 11 November 1997

A uaisle,

Lá stairiúil é seo im'shaol féin, i saol mo mhuintire, agus i saol na tíre go léir. Is pribhléid mhór í a bheith tofa mar Uachtarán na hÉireann, le bheith mar ghuth na hÉireann i gcéin is i gcóngair.

This is a historic day in my life, in the life of my family and in the life of the country. It is a wonderful privilege for me to be chosen as Uachtarán na hÉireann, to be a voice for Ireland at home and abroad.

I am honoured and humbled to be successor to seven exemplary Presidents. Their differing religious, political, geographical and social origins speak loudly of a Presidency which has always been wide open and all-embracing. Among them were Presidents from Connacht, Leinster and Munster, to say nothing of America and London. It is my special privilege and delight to be the first President from Ulster.

The span of almost sixty years since the first Presidential Inauguration has seen a nation transformed. This Ireland, which stands so confidently on the brink of the twenty-first century and the third millennium, is one our forebears dreamed of and yearned for; a prospering Ireland, accomplished, educated, dynamic, innovative, compassionate, proud of its people, its language, and of its vast heritage; an Ireland at the heart of the European Union, respected by nations and cultures across the world.

The scale of what we have already accomplished in such a short time allows us to embrace the future with well-based confidence and hope.

It is the people of Ireland who, in a million big and small ways, in quiet acts of hard work, heroism and generosity, have built up the fabric of home, community and country on which the remarkable success story of today's Ireland is built.

Over many generations there have been very special sources of inspiration who have nurtured our talents and instilled determination into this country. Many outstanding politicians, public servants, voluntary workers, clergy of all denominations and religion, teachers and particularly parents have, through hard and difficult times, worked and sacrificed so that our children could blossom to their fullest potential.

They are entitled to look with satisfaction at what they have achieved. May we never become so cynical that we forget to be grateful. I certainly owe them a deep personal debt and as President I hope to find many opportunities both to repay that debt and to assist in the great work of encouraging our children to believe in themselves and in their country.

Among those who are also owed an enormous debt of thanks are the countless emigrants whose letters home with dollars and pound notes, earned in grinding loneliness thousands of miles from home, bridged the gap between the Ireland they left and the Ireland which greets them today when they return as tourists or return to stay. They are a crucial part of our global Irish family. In every continent they have put their ingenuity and hard work at the service of new homelands. They have kept their love of Ireland, its traditions and its culture deep in their hearts so that wherever we travel in the world there is always a part of Ireland of which we can be proud and which, in turn, takes pride in us. I hope over the next seven years there will be many opportunities for me to celebrate with them.

At our core we are a sharing people. Selfishness has never been our creed. Commitment to the welfare of each other has fired generations of voluntary organisations and a network of everyday neighbourliness which weaves together the caring fabric of our country. It has sent our missionaries, development workers and peacekeepers to the aid of distressed peoples in other parts of the world. It has made us a country of refuge for the hurt and dispossessed of other troubled places. It is the fuel which drives us to tackle the many social problems we face, problems which cynicism and self-doubt can never redress but painstaking commitment can. We know our duty is to spread the benefits of our prosperity to those whose lives are still mired in poverty, unemployment, worry and despair. There can be no rest until the harsh gap between the comfortable and the struggling has been bridged.

The late Cearbhall Ó Dálaigh, Ireland's fifth President and, dare I say it, one of three lawyers to grace the office, said at his inauguration in 1974, 'Presidents, under the Irish Constitution don't have policies. But … a President can have a theme.'

The theme of my Presidency, the eighth Presidency, is 'Building Bridges'. These bridges require no engineering skills but they will demand patience, imagination and courage, for Ireland's pace of change is now bewilderingly fast. We grow more complex by the day. Our dancers, singers, writers, poets, musicians, sportsmen and women, indeed our last President herself, are giants on the world stage. Our technologically skilled young people are in demand everywhere. There is an invigorating sense of purpose about us.

There are those who absorb the rush of newness with delight. There are those who are more cautious, even fearful. Such tensions are part of our creative genius; they form the energy which gives us our unique identity, our particularity.

I want to point the way to a reconciliation of these many tensions and to see Ireland grow ever more comfortable and at ease with the flowering diversity that is now all around us. To quote a Belfast poet, Louis MacNeice, 'a single purpose can be founded on a jumble of opposites.'

Yet I know to speak of reconciliation is to raise a nervous query in the hearts of some north of the border, in the place of my birth. There is no more appropriate place to address that query than here in Dublin Castle, a place where the complex history of these two neighbouring and now very neighbourly islands has seen many chapters written. It is fortuitous, too, that the timing of today's inauguration coincides with the commemoration of those who died so tragically and heroically in two world wars. I think of nationalist and unionist, who fought and died together in those wars, the differences which separated them at home fading into insignificance as the bond of their common humanity forged friendships as intense as love can make them.

In Ireland, we know only too well the cruelty and capriciousness of violent conflict. Our own history has been hard on lives young and old. Too hard. Hard on those who died and those left behind with only shattered dreams and poignant memories. We hope and pray, indeed we insist, that we have seen the last of violence. We demand the right to solve our problems by dialogue and the noble pursuit of consensus. We hope to see that consensus pursued without the language of hatred and contempt, and we wish all those engaged in that endeavour well.

That it can be done – we know. We need look no further than our own European continent, where once bitter enemies now work conscientiously with each other and for each other as friends and partners. The greatest salute to the memory of all our dead, and the living whom they loved, would be the achievement of agreement and peace.

I think of the late Gordon Wilson, who faced his unbearable sorrow ten years ago at the horror that was Enniskillen. His words of love and forgiveness shocked us as if we were hearing them for the very first time, as if they had not been uttered first 2,000 years ago. His work, and the work of so many peacemakers who have risen above the awesome pain of loss to find a bridge to the other side, is work I want to help in every way I can. No side has a monopoly on pain. Each has suffered intensely.

I know the distrusts go deep and the challenge is awesome. Across this island, north, south, east and west, there are people of such greatness of heart that I know, with their help, it can be done. I invite them to work in partnership with me to dedicate ourselves to the task of creating a wonderful millennium gift to the Child of Bethlehem, whose 2000th birthday we will soon celebrate – the gift of an island where difference is celebrated with joyful curiosity and generous respect and where, in the words of John Hewitt, 'each may grasp his neighbour's hand as friend.'[1]

There will be those who are wary of such invitations, afraid that they are being invited to the edge of a precipice. To them I have dedicated a poem, written by the English poet Christopher Logue, himself a veteran of the Second World War:

> Come to the edge.
> We might fall.
> Come to the edge.
> It's too high!
> Come to the edge!
> And they came,
> and he pushed
> and they flew.[2]

No one will be pushing, just gently inviting, but I hope that if ever and whenever you decide to walk over that edge, there will be no need to fly; you will find there a firm and steady bridge across which we will walk together both ways.

Ireland sits tantalisingly ready to embrace a golden age of affluence, self-assurance, tolerance and peace. It will be my most profound privilege to be President of this beautiful, intriguing country.

May I ask those of faith, whatever that faith may be, to pray for me and for our country that we will use these seven years well, to create a future where, in the words of William Butler Yeats, 'Everything we look upon is blest.'[3]

Déanaimis an todhchaí sin a chruthú le chéile.

Notes

1   Hewitt, John, 'A Little People', *The Collected Poems of John Hewitt*, ed. Frank Ormsby (Blackstaff Press, 1992), p. 539.

2   Logue, Christopher, 'Come to the Edge', *Selected Poems* (Faber & Faber, 1996), p. 64.

3   Yeats, W.B., 'A Dialogue of Self and Soul', *W.B. Yeats Selected Poetry* (Pan, 1962), p. 145.

2

IRELAND
IN THE WORLD

MILLENIUM ADDRESS TO THE HOUSES OF THE
OIREACHTAS, 'IRELAND OF THE LIFTING SHADOWS'

16 December 1999

A Cheann Comhairle, a Chathaoirligh an tSeanaid agus a chomhaltaí na Dála agus an tSeanaid,

Is mór liom an phribhléid bhunreachtúil labhairt le baill Dhá Theach an Oireachtais cruinnithe le chéile. Agus muid i mbéal na Míleaoise is fóirstineach an ócáid í chun an deis seo a thapú. Míle bliain ó shin scríobh manach Éireannach na línte seo agus é ag smaoineamh ar an Chéad Mhíleaois:

> Ní mhaireann glún den ghinealach
> a chuaigh romhainn siar go hÁdhamh;

mise féin ní feasach mé

an liom an lá amárach.

Is cuí agus is tairbheach dúinn, agus muid ar chuspa ócáide móire, súil a chaitheamh siar ar a bhfuil caite agus caillte, ar a bhfuil déanta agus thart. Murach sin is beag a bheadh foghlamtha againn mar chine. Ach ní miste dúinn fosta aghaidh a thabhairt ar an todchaí; agus, murab ionann is an manach bocht tinneallach, is cóir dúinn é a dhéanamh go hurrúsach, lán dóchais agus dánachta, lán mórtais agus cinnteachta, muid múnlaithe ag a bhfuil imithe ach gan a bheith faoi chuing ag an stair.

Fifteen days from now a page of history will turn and the world will mark the beginning of the third millennium.

We know, of course, that in the natural world, where things change over millions of years, nothing will change on that date. But we human beings measure our brief lives in years, rather than centuries and for us the beginning of the year 2000 is an occasion of great symbolic importance.

Because of this, I think it right to avail, as the Millennium Committee suggested, of the privilege which the Constitution accords the President of delivering an address to both Houses of the Oireachtas meeting in joint session.

On the eve of this new millennium, as one age yields place to another, it seems timely to take a backward glance at the journey we and our ancestors have come and reflect together on the new destinies open to us as a people. For what marks us off most from those who preceded us is the capacity we now have to control our world, to shape our future. More than that, unlike the natural world, we human beings can change ourselves.

In his poem 'Celebration', Michael O'Siadhail talks of:

> Lines with loops of days or months or years
> We don't know how to begin to think of time

Yet a first reflection must surely bring us back to the beginning of these 2,000 years and to the significance for the Christian world of this otherwise arbitrary calendar date.

Throughout history, women and men have sought to make sense of the world, of the transience of human life and the inevitability of death. That quest has led many people, in many cultures and many ages, to a search for the Divine, the transcendent, a search for God. Christians believe that at a moment in time, that search was reversed. God sought out humanity; the Divine took human form in a child born in Bethlehem: God's gift of his son to help us understand the transformative powver of love. Many people on this island are Christian and for them it is this momentous event two thousand years ago that we now celebrate.

There are many among us who are people of deep faith and who are not Christians. There are those who have no faith at all and those who have no time for religion. They will, I hope, understand and patiently respect the importance which Christians, in particular, attach to this great Jubilee.

We can, however, all join together in celebrating the secular significance of this particular New Year, for when we add the new political dispensation in Northern Ireland to our recent economic success and our remarkable cultural confidence, it is evident that for Ireland this millennial moment is not just an important anniversary but a time of genuine and profound change. It is a time of hope, of celebration and joy. The shadows are lifting.

So often we have felt the heavy weight of our past. As the poet Brendan Kennelly put it:

> My dark fathers lived the intolerable day
> Committed always to the night of wrong[1]

We have thought of ourselves so often as the objects and not the subjects of our own history, that we can scarcely believe what has been happening here in recent years. We do not yet perhaps fully under-stand to what extent the weight of the past is now lifting and what new possibilities are opening to us.

The decisions we make now and in the years ahead, the values which imbue those decisions and the use we make of today's opportunities, these will give our future its shape, its depth. They will determine the kind of Ireland we hand on to future generations, for while we have, thankfully, come a long way, we still have a distance to travel before our star stops over an Ireland where all feel truly equal. The choices are ours. Will the old iniquities and inequalities lurk beneath the veneer? Will idealism be dulled by selfish materialism, shrill begrudgery and apathy, or will we bequeath to our children a land of peace, prosperity, equal opportunity and respect for difference?

There was a time in our history, in the middle part of the first mil-lennium, when an Ireland such as this did exist. We speak of it as our golden age. St Patrick, who came to our shores as a stranger, connected in an imaginative way with the Irish people. As Thomas Cahill says, 'Patrick's gift to the Irish was his Christianity – the first de-Romanized Christianity in human history'. It was a Christianity that completely melded itself into Irish life, growing unselfconsciously side by side with the old pagan culture, with no anxiety to obliterate it.

As a result, Ireland was transformed into something new; a place with a distinctive psychological identity, capable of seamless yet radical change. Respect for difference became enshrined in the rulebooks of convents and monasteries. St Bridget declared, 'Different is the condi-tion of everyone.'

The rule of St Carthage said, 'And different the nature of each place'. Columbanus, our first great ambassador to France, must have raised a few eyebrows when he asserted, '*Amor non tenet ordinem*' – Love has nothing to do with order.

Love and respect for difference are the natural precursors of peace and its younger sibling prosperity. Many of the conditions that facilitated that former glorious period of our history are now once again falling into place on our island.

Of course that golden age did not last. It fell victim to the Viking invasion, and indeed much of our subsequent history through the centuries up to recent times is a litany of hopes raised and then dashed, one lament after another. Little wonder that we gained a reputation as a nation of romantic dreamers whose dreams seemed unlikely ever to come to pass.

It is true that the reality of Irish life was often more nightmare than dream; the lives of ordinary people were lived on brinks very different from the one we are privileged to be on. The wars, invasions, rebellions, plantations and plagues they endured brought awful suffering and worse was to come in the Ocras Mór, the unbearable tragedy of the Famine which devastated our country in the last century.

Our senior citizens will remember their own childhoods in the early years of this century, when poverty and deprivation stalked the land. Children died in their thousands. A swelling stream of emigrants, many of them young women, flowed out of Ireland on every vessel from every port. In the words of an American journalist, writing in 1909, 'the Irish in Ireland are kept alive by the Irish who have been driven to other lands'.

And still more grief to come, more cause to lament, as a new generation's bid for freedom from the grip of colonialism gave us the Easter Rising, the War of Independence and a bitter Civil War. Along with the forgotten dead in Flanders, each left behind a legacy of success and failure, of pride and contempt, the scarring inheritance, the unfinished business of the next generation.

Yet even in the darkest days of our chequered past, our unique Irish psychological identity shone through. Edmund Campion, the English Jesuit martyred at Tyburn in 1581, said of the Irish:

The people are thus inclined ... Franke ... Sufferable of paines infinite ... great almes-givers, surpassing in hospitalitie ... they are sharp-witted, lovers of learning, capable of any studie whereunto they bend themselves, constant in travaile, adventurous, intractable, kinde-hearted, secret in displeasure.

These were the qualities which kept and still keep our people going through the good times and the bad – and of the bad times there have been many!

The difficult birth of the new State did not create a magic wand with which its many problems could be waved away. With hindsight, we see the faults and failings of our infant State; its introspection, its economic instability, the limits it imposed on women, its confessionalism, its dark side where vulnerable children suffered dreadfully and in silence, its failure to adequately address the consequences of partition, and much more.

Yet we need to acknowledge the good that was done. Many people worked tirelessly to build that fledgling State out of the chaos of empire. They gave us a democracy – something which had never existed before on this island. They stitched together the tattered and scattered fragments of our cultural heritage, breathed new life into our weary collective Irish psyche, and kick-started what was a third-world country. We owe so much to them. A great many never saw their dreams realised in their own lifetimes, but in very difficult times they used the meagre tools at their disposal to lay the foundations of this Ireland of today.

We owe a debt of gratitude, too, to those who left this island. Some went from the most admirable of motives, as missionaries or as volunteers in healthcare and education. Most went reluctantly, in huge waves, driven out by hunger and lack of opportunity in circumstances no different to those which bring economic refugees from other parts of the world to our own shores today. Their going was more often than not a badge of failure. These were not the celebrated Wild Geese or political refugees of previous centuries. These were poor men and women who ploughed lonely furrows in strange lands. These were the people who, through their lives, globalised the name of Ireland. They brought our culture with them and refreshed it, enriched it with the new energy it absorbed from the varied cultures into which it was transplanted. Our emigrants have done much to help us on our journey. They kept faith with our island's destiny, at the same time giving us a taste of what a multicultural and globally engaged Ireland could look forward to. They gave us that huge Irish family now proudly celebrated and acknowledged in the new Article 2 of the Constitution.

Who could have predicted, even a decade ago, this Ireland of the lifting shadows. The economic landscape has been transformed; the tide of emigration has been reversed; a new and more self-confident generation, neither docile nor xenophobic, has made, as Patrick did, a new imaginative connection with the wider world; our great literary tradition has been built on, making Ireland a centre of gravity for arts and culture; urban and rural communities have found a high-achieving new empowerment based on partnership; old enemies have become friendly neighbours; peace is no longer a rumour, it is real.

Today, where the name of Ireland is spoken, the word success is close behind. We really have taken our place among the nations of the world. Part of our success we undoubtedly owe to our membership of the European Union. Part of our success we owe to ourselves, to the spirit of enterprise, of partnership and common purpose among our people, to the genius and initiative unlocked by widening educational opportunity, to the visionary leadership and public endeavour which together pushed Ireland into a new gear.

Along with the manifest benefits of success have come new challenges. We are the first generation to have the eradication of poverty within our grasp, the first generation to experience Ireland as a land of fresh starts and new opportunity for people from other cultures. We are the first generation to be seriously tested on the *bona fides* of our legendary hospitality, our céad míle fáilte. We are the first generation for centuries to have the opportunity to build and consolidate a lasting peace between this island's two traditions. As the shadows lift, the world looks very different, is very different.

Nowhere is that more obvious than in Northern Ireland. Seamus Heaney's poem 'The Cure at Troy' reminds us:

> Human beings suffer,
> They torture one another,
> They get hurt and get hard.

We know just how hurt, just how hard; so hard that only a short few years ago the Ulster poet John Hewitt was lamenting that the future could find no crevice to enter by.

Miraculously, that crevice has been found, or more correctly crafted, and with immense difficulty by people who are deserving of our deepest gratitude.

We are mindful of the hurt caused to so many, hurts which may never heal, but we take heart from the forgiveness, the generosity, the love and compassion, the willingness to take risks even in the absence of trust, of so many ordinary people who were and who are the very heart and soul of this phenomenon we call the Peace Process. Their story tells us why it is worth dreaming – even when the cynics say it is impossible and the naysayers threaten to make it impossible.

I take great pride in these people, who have committed themselves to overcoming deep divisions and building a humanly decent society, respectful of difference, rooted in human rights, at ease with all who share this island. We now have in place the structures which will allow us to build healthy relationships between these islands and to harness our collective energies to build an Ireland where divisions, whether in the mind or on the map, will be transcended by shared prosperity, a spirit of cooperative endeavour and a new language, much kinder and softer than before. It was a stranger, George Mitchell, whose listening ears heard the soft words we could not hear over the bitter recriminations. It was he who found a way to move hearts weighed down by history's heavy armour. He followed a star of hope, at times no more than a glimmer, and now, like the Magi, he and those he worked with have given us a precious Christmas gift of peace.

Who can predict where this new star will lead us? We know where we have been, we know the laborious road to where we are, and so people of goodwill are following this star for they know there is no other.

On his journey from the outrageous carnage of war-torn Europe, another extraordinary man, Jean Monnet, followed a star which led to the European Union, a partnership of once bitter enemies. Many thought it a fanciful and unlikely dream. Today we are living it. It was fanciful, it was unlikely, but it is real: so real that a long queue has formed to join us in the most exciting adventure in democracy and partnership Europe has ever known. Just as we were helped on our journey to prosperity, soon we in turn will be expected to help others. When that day comes I hope we see it as a badge of honour.

Today's Ireland is a first-world country with a third-world memory, a memory to keep us humble, to remind us of the fragility of it all, a memory to remind us that too many people across the world wake up each day to lives of sheer terror and dread. They too need dreamers to imagine a day when the shadows will lift. They too need friends to help make the dreams real. We have a long and proud history of being such a friend, a champion of the poor, the oppressed, the ignored and neglected.

And for all our success we have them too on our own doorstep. We have our own dark side, the people who watch today's fast-moving, self-assured Ireland from our own margins. The Constitution acknowledges the equality of each of us and recent history has shown the enormous benefits of widening, equalising the embrace of opportunity. The evidence is all around us. Just look what a radical transformation has already been accomplished and still we have not unlocked anything like our full potential. How much talent, how much energy is still waiting to be nurtured and developed into fulfilled lives instead of frittered away in the frustrations and the many social problems of under-achievement?

We get to write a chapter of our country's history. What story will the twenty-first century tell about us? Will it tell of Ireland's new golden age, a sophisticated and intuitive age, rich in imagination, rooted in community, grateful for its prosperity, aware of its frailty, accepting of its responsibility to sustain and develop the economic miracle? Will it tell how we used our resources generously and well, sharing them equitably at home and abroad? Will it tell how we consigned poverty to history, how we created a society that was all centre and no margins, where opportunity was a birthright? Will it tell that we vindicated the rights of others to such a world? Will it tell how a generation freed from the wastefulness of conflict and the burdens of the past galvanised its energy, talents and resources in a determined effort to make Ireland the best, the most egalitarian it has ever been?

All that may sound impossible, implausible, out of tune with the scepticism, the supposed 'realism' of today – a realism fed by revelations of low standards, high places. We live in times when windows open more easily on the unpleasant side of human nature. This is an age of righteous accountability which should serve to make us wiser and warier but may instead, if we are not careful, feed an uncaring indifference, a cynicism which will erode our capacity to dream and to deliver dreams. Just as in this room are gathered today's political leaders, to whom we are grateful for their fidelity to public service and their role in today's success story, so for tomorrow, we need to encourage and nurture an unselfish vocation to public service among our young men and especially among our young women.

As Sr Stanislaus Kennedy has said:

We can all be sowers of our time, people who sow the seeds that will be reaped by the next generation. When we sow, we must not expect instant success, but sow we must if a new world is ever to come to fruit. The purpose of our generation is to make a better world possible in the future and to prepare for it.

Together we will sow, we will write a new chapter for Ireland. Let it begin with a sigh of relief at the weight that has lifted from us, with joyful gratitude for the hope we have and with determination to use well and with integrity the tools we have been given.

These past two thousand years have taught us much about human nature. No child comes into the world distrustful and unloving, bigoted and uncaring. These things, adults teach. These things, adults have to stop teaching. This century has created many incredible images and stories from holocaust to moon landing, from World Wars to the World Wide Web, but one recent image struck me as powerfully symbolic at this Jubilee time. It was the picture of an unborn child's tiny hand reaching out from the womb and wrapping itself around the finger of the surgeon who was operating to save its little life. Another moving nativity; another reminder of how much we need each other, how much we have to offer each other. We have had all the lessons we could ever need in hatred, in neglect, in hurt. We human beings need to be loved; we blossom in love; its absence shrivels us. We get hard.

Every Christmas, Christians gather around the crib, drawn again and again to its innocence. We gather in a world which has long since lost its innocence, but we gather in hope that maybe in this future we are about to live, the story of Bethlehem, so often badly misused, might at last prove true. As the sun goes down on this millennium, just as that page of history turns are we aware at all of the awesome power we each hold in our own hearts, our own hands?

In his poem 'The Cure at Troy' Seamus Heaney says:

> So hope for a great sea-change
> on the far side of revenge.
> Believe that a further shore
> is reachable from here.
> Believe in miracles
> and cures and healing wells.

And so it has come to pass. The great sea-change we hoped for is here. We can reach that further shore. We who can change can cure. We who have hope can heal. This is the age of miracles. This is the age of lifting shadows.

May I thank you and wish you well in all you do on behalf of the Irish people. A very happy Christmas and a peaceful New Year to you all.

Notes

1   Kennelly, Brendan, 'My Dark Fathers', *Collection One* (1966) reprinted in *The Oxford Book of Ireland*, ed. Patricia Craig (Oxford University Press, 1998), p.347.

REMARKS ON THE OCCASION OF SEPTEMBER 11TH

September 2001

On this National Day of Mourning, we take time to reflect on the horrendous events of the past few days in the United States.

These horrible scenes represent an attack on the very foundations of our human dignity.

We are sad, shocked, sickened, grieving, disbelieving, frightened all at once. We are only beginning to hear the human stories, the unbearable stories of final calls of love, the heroism of so many, the loss of so many. These stories will continue to unfold for many days and weeks to come, bringing with them a growing realisation of the full extent of the pain and sorrow – the legacy of these awful acts of hatred.

The people of the United States hold a special place in the hearts of all of us here in Ireland. The roots go down through the centuries and are as strong today as they ever were. Our first thoughts are therefore with the American people, as they try to cope with the magnitude of what has happened in their great country. To the bereaved, the injured and to those waiting of news of their loved ones, we in Ireland send our prayers, our deepest sympathy and our support.

Our closeness, in so many ways, to America and to the American people, means that we cannot but be deeply affected here in Ireland. We only have to look at the photograph of the beautiful faces of Ruth Clifford McCourt and her gorgeous little girl Julianna to see with our own eyes the loss which Ireland has experienced. There are deep worries about the other loved ones missing, yet unaccounted for, and we pray for the Irish families who wait to hear some word, who wait for any possible consolation.

We have watched in admiration as the rescue services work ceaselessly to locate the victims of these attacks, and sadly we know now that many of the emergency personnel have perished in the course of their duties. Historically, many Irish citizens and Irish Americans have contributed significantly to the police and fire services in the United States – this applies particularly in New York. Our prayers go to the relatives and friends of these brave men and women who have sacrificed their very lives for the sake of others. Their heroic, loving care for the stranger stands in sharp contrast to the evil of those who perpetrated these horrors.

Our Embassy and Consulates in the United States and government departments at home are deeply involved in providing caring assistance to our Irish family here and in the United States. We thank them for their efforts; for the spontaneous kindness and sensitivity with which they go about their difficult work.

This National Day of Mourning is a very special opportunity for all of us to show solidarity with our brothers and sisters in the United States of America. It sends a message across the Atlantic and indeed around the globe, that Ireland, too, is grieving at the unconscionable waste of life we have witnessed this week.

God bless those in the United States, those in Ireland and people throughout the world who have been personally, deeply affected by this tragedy. May God guide us safely through these troubled days.

Speech at the *Irish America* Top 100 Awards

Plaza Hotel, New York, USA, 14 March 2002

Honourees, ladies and gentlemen,

Dia dhíobh a cháirde. Is mór an onóir agus is mór an pléisiúir dom bheith anseo libh tráthnóna ar an ócáid speisialta seo. Ba mhaith liom mo bhuíochas a chur in iúl díobh as an cuireadh, agus as an fáilte caoin, cneasta agus croíúil a chuir sibh romham.

I am very moved to be here in New York at such a very special time, and to be with so many Irish and Irish-American friends.

The video clips that we have just seen and the honourees we have heard from remind us – if it were possible to forget – of the heart-break and heroism of September last in New York. It is entirely fitting, therefore, that this year's awards ceremony is dedicated to the many who inspired us with their courageous and selfless actions on that fateful day when hatred broke our hearts and tried to break our spirit.

I thank *Irish America* magazine for hosting this very special event, and in particular Niall O'Dowd and Patricia Harty. Your vision and energy in establishing these Top 100 Awards has helped to expand the network of leaders in all fields with an active interest in their Irish heritage. Your awards ceremony has become a showcase of Irish-American talent and spirit. To all of the honourees this evening, we in Ireland rejoice in your success. We are proud of your stellar contribution to political, community, cultural and business life in your adopted country and I am delighted to see the achievements of the Irish in America receive the recognition they deserve.

It is a singular honour for me to join with you in saluting those who gave their very all in protecting the people of this great city, a city sorely tested, on September 11th. The representatives of the Police, Fire and Port Authority Departments who will receive awards tonight stand for those who faced into that test with no thought for themselves, who came through it to pass into proud legend, their lives surrendered, their families and colleagues left with unbearable loneliness and loss, the future of their city and country changed forever, not by the forces of evil which overwhelmed them, but by the forces of good with which they overcame evil.

I was in Áras an Uachtaráin on September 11th, waiting to receive a new Ambassador to Ireland, when word reached me of the unbelievable events unfolding in the United States. A short time later, I found myself conveying the incomprehension, the sadness and the shock of the Irish people at the tragedy. I admire greatly how well the American Ambassador Richard Egan, who had only himself presented his credentials the day before, coped with those shattering events.

The enormous devastation and loss on that day had profound and far-reaching consequences for all of us. Every home in Ireland stopped in failed comprehension and horror and disbelief. We wondered about sons and daughters, about nieces and nephews, about friends and neighbours, about all of those who had left our shores to seek a new and better life here. Your fear was our fear. And as the enormity of the tragedy unfolded, your grief was our grief.

Given the size of a country like Ireland, no one was far removed from the pain of that loss. Eight Irish-born people perished that day. But we lost many more Irish-Americans who had close ties to Ireland. The litany of Irish names among the dead emergency rescue personnel told its own story. It felt, in the days that followed, that we were all touched personally and profoundly by the loss, so profoundly that the Government declared a National Day of Mourning and Ireland shut down everything except its solidarity and sympathy with the suffering people of the United States.

This morning, with my husband Martin and Minister Tom Kitt, I visited Ground Zero. What we saw was only a pale image of the horror which confronted the heroic uniformed services who lead the rescue effort and I think we would all say that what we felt was enormous pride in the indomitable human spirit which has filled that gaping wounded space with goodness, determination and honour. It was a privilege to be so close to the place where so many deliberately headed into danger because that was their vocation, a calling that insists that care for the stranger in need comes before care for the self.

I was reminded of the words of Abraham Lincoln in his Gettysburg Address, when he said:

> We cannot dedicate, we cannot consecrate, we cannot hallow this ground. The brave men, living and dead, who struggled here, have consecrated it far above our power … The world will little note, nor long remember what we say here, but it can never forget what they did here.

During those days we turned to our friends and loved ones with a more profound appreciation of the comfort they bring to our lives. If we were more aware of our vulnerability in an open and free society to the caprices of evil, we were also much more aware of our need for true and constant friends and their capacity for loving support of each other. It was a time for Ireland to stand with her dearest friends and she did – for America has been there for us through many difficult times and we felt privileged to offer our hands and hearts at a time of unbearable sadness. The wreath I laid today at Ground Zero, in the name of the Irish people put it simply, 'We know that by standing shoulder to shoulder, hope for the future will triumph over the hurt of the past.'

We in Ireland have been privileged, in our own difficult journey toward peace with justice in Northern Ireland, to have had the solidarity, loyalty and support of our many friends here in the United States. You have stood by us, supporting and encouraging us in our bad days as well as celebrating with us in our good. We greatly appreciate the continuing commitment of President Bush and his Administration, and the US Congress, as we continue the important work of implementing the Good Friday Agreement. America's interest in Irish affairs has, to a substantial degree, been generated by the efforts of our Irish community here. It reflects the standing you enjoy at the highest levels of decision-making in this country. It also reflects the spontaneous decency of our Irish family which keeps on caring about the welfare of Ireland, no matter how many generations or miles separate us. That collective interest in Ireland is something to be cherished, for it arises simply out of goodness. It is not mandated by any law and is something one should never, ever take for granted. The fact that it exists and that it is manifestly a powerful, history-changing energy, calls us to both pride and gratitude.

Your energy has been a vital ingredient in forging our template for peace. It has also been invaluable in supporting our efforts to modernise the Irish economy over the last decade. Those great historic bonds of kinship and family that we have shared over the centuries have been deepened, freshened and renewed by a new generation's generous contribution to peace in Northern Ireland and to Ireland's remarkable economic success. Now, that same feisty spirit of engagement is turned to the recovery and regeneration of New York. It does not give up, no matter how hard the struggle. I have been so inspired by the energy and resilience of New Yorkers in the face of this catastrophe and I am proud that there is much Irish blood in the veins and arteries that keep this city's strong heart beating. We are a people who have faced hardship and catastrophe, loss and grief. We have a distilled wisdom, a long, long experience in getting up, getting out, and facing the new day with a steely faith-filled optimism.

Many nations counted their dead on September 11th and many nations have combined to create the unique passion that flourishes in this great city, a passion for life. Evil men thought they could kill that passion; that the ugliness of violence, the awesomeness of wanton deaths, would snuff it out. They were wrong. New York is still passionate about life and now that very passion has been deepened and stretched by the avalanche of grief it has had to struggle through, to find its way back to the future again. Irish men and women can rightly claim to have planted their flags on the landscape of that future and the words those flags bear are courage, fortitude, perseverance and selflessness. The generations who went before them would be proud of a modern generation who have known the easy times and comfort of prosperity but who, when tested, chose the hardest road of all.

We are proud of them tonight.

Go raibh maith agaibh go léir. Guím rath Dé sna blianta atá le teacht.

Speech at the
'Re-Imagining Ireland' Conference

Charlottesville, Virginia, USA, 7 May 2003

Distinguished Guests,

Immediately after the word 'Reilly' in the *Shorter Oxford English Dictionary* comes the word 're-imbark' (var. of re-embark), smack bang in the place where you might expect to find the word 're-imagine'. You may be shocked to hear it does not appear at all. I have to admit there is a deliciously subversive pleasure in doing something the *Shorter Oxford English Dictionary* has not yet imagined. But since there are those who believe that Ireland is now enjoying the once elusive 'life of Reilly' and there are many who once left Ireland's shores who have re-embarked on the journey back to Ireland – precisely because Reilly's life is now more broadly distributed and more easily accessible – it may be that the words 'Reilly' and 're-embark' have, after all, a place in this undertaking of re-imagining Ireland.

The organisers, to whom I am indebted for the invitation to Charlottesville, the Virginia Foundation for the Humanities and, in particular, its President, Mr Raymond Vaughan, Mr Andrew Wyndham and Ms Tori Talbot have worked with a passion to gather this impressive collection of Irish talent, wit and wisdom. This has the makings of a seminal gathering and I wouldn't be surprised if there was the odd modest opportunity for a bit of craic too. But the work comes first and if I don't re-imagine Ireland quickly, the dark clouds of hunger – such a familiar part of Ireland's historical landscape – may well be more than imaginary.

A French nobleman once observed that Thomas Jefferson had placed both his mind and his famous house here in Charlottesville 'on an elevated situation from which he might contemplate the universe'. Hopefully we too will benefit from this 'elevated situation' and from the perspective that distance as well as discourse can create.

You would think that with all the Nobel winning poets we have produced they might between them have penned a helpful starting place with a poem entitled 'Re-imagining Ireland', but the closest we get is Seamus Heaney's 'Seeing Things'. This poem brings us to the Ireland of the horse-drawn potato sprayer – a world away from the convulsively changed Ireland we are conjuring to re-imagine, where you would quicker find a jacuzzi than a spring well. In his poem 'Bean on tSleibhe', Cathal Ó Searcaigh's mountain woman says, 'It's not ageing I am but ripening!' It could be Ireland talking, for the English words carry an ancient Irish syntax which gives us our very colourful and unique particularity, and the description of 'ripening' is as good as it gets of modern Ireland.

Many an Irish man and woman made the journey to Charlottesville before us, and in very different times. They carried a memory of Ireland of the goodbyes, not Ireland of the welcomes. They formed and shared with their children images of possibilities of an Ireland without abject poverty, without most of its population stacked on the narrow margins, a fair and equal Ireland, a free Ireland. They sang laments for that imagined Ireland, the one which, in its non-existence, presented them with choices that were desperate and required courage beyond imagining.

And now things have changed and how they have changed. The third-world Ireland they left is now a first-world country. So many feet have come off the brake that used to be on Ireland's development that it is not always easy to say which moved first or mattered most. One way or another, the door of Ireland opened and let the future in.

The little impoverished island off the west coast of Europe which became an unremarkable member of the European Union thirty years ago has become the symbol of the Union's potential, the place with the economic success story that everywhere else wants to imitate. The country that up to thirty-five years ago offered the liberating key of education to only a small elite has felt the surging energy of its greatest natural resource – the genius of its own people – empowered through widened access to second-level and third-level education. The country that has known outward migration for one hundred and fifty years has suddenly become a place of net inward migration, coping with the complexities of multiculturalism and the challenge of asylum seekers. The genius of Irish women, once corralled into narrowly prescribed spheres, is moving inexorably, if slowly, towards a yet to come flood tide. The politics of peace are transforming the landscape of possibilities within Northern Ireland, between North and South and between Ireland and Britain.

The old vanities of history are disappearing. Carefully hidden stories like those of the Irish who died in the First World War are coming out of the shoeboxes in the attic and into daylight. We are making new friends, we are influencing new people, we are learning new things about ourselves, we are being changed. If 'imagining' carries always the hint of something not yet formed, of a fantasy not yet real, today's Ireland is full of things not yet known with certainty but things which are most certainly different from and mostly better than the past.

We cannot deny that there are casualties. The many excellent nuns, priests and brothers who dedicated their lives to education and healthcare, both in Ireland and around the world, contributed greatly to this ripening Ireland, with its network of friends throughout the globe. Now they are visibly ageing and their future is far from easy to predict. And as the mountain woman of Ó Searcaigh's poem might say, 'In this country the hardest crusts are given to those with least teeth.' The widespread embrace of prosperity has been a wonderful and heartening phenomenon, but if you are still marooned on the beach and the uplifted boats are sailing over the horizon, the space between can seem a frightening, unbridgeable chasm.

More money in pockets has visibly lifted standards of living but it is being badly spent too, on bad old habits that have never gone away. The Irish love of conviviality has its dark side in the stupid wasteful abuse of alcohol and its first cousin – abuse of drugs. They chart a course of misery and malaise so utterly unnecessary that we need to re-imagine an Ireland grown intolerant of behaviour which it has too benignly overlooked for too long.

Our expectations are now high indeed, driven by the successes of the past decade. But we have shown ourselves capable of remarkable change – to be adaptable, to be willing to learn – and while there is still much to accomplish, there is a new-found confidence in our capacity not simply to cope, as in the past, but to transcend, to transform, to reduce the imagined thing to reality.

I am probably in as good a place as any – if not the best place – from which to judge the capacity for re-imagining of the Irish people. Day in and day out I meet the people who are making the crucial differences that are quietly layering up a better future. They are building hospices, day care centres for the elderly, providing respite for carers, bringing the Special Olympics World Games to Ireland, empowering the illiterate, spotting and mentoring potential early school leavers, enabling the disabled, welcoming the stranger, moving from conflict-ridden marches to community-based festivals, breaking down sectarianism, building up communities. I have mentioned only a small part of the voluntary effort that is heaving us forward. The world of business, trade, tourism and investment – for all the untidy capriciousness of the marketplace – has shown a resolve and creativity which still make us one of the most robust and stable economies around, even though the giddy days of 8 per cent growth are manifestly over. If 'ceann faoi' is how we used to imagine ourselves – today it is very definitely 'can do'.

Who could ever have imagined that an Irish Government would purchase the site of the Battle of the Boyne and develop there a heritage site for all the people of the island of Ireland? Someone dared to and its existence changes language and texture forever. Who could have imagined a government in Northern Ireland with Sinn Féin ministers working side by side with the Ulster Unionists? Someone dared to and we fervently hope it will move from the imagination to lived reality again soon. Who could have imagined Gaelscoileanna flourishing right around the country, with Irish-language nursery, primary and secondary schools a growing phenomenon in Northern Ireland? Who could have imagined the cultural exuberance which has made global icons of Irish names in every field of the arts, many of them under this roof, or the technological sophistication that has made Ireland the world's number one exporter of computer software, ahead even of the United States itself?

I should stop this list because there are many other spheres, too many to mention here, which feed the dreams of our imagination. Post September 11th we became intensely conscious of the fragility of our globe, its vulnerability and the urgency of its haphazard struggle against ignorance, hatred, oppression and poverty. Ireland was a member of the United Nations Security Council during those heady days of 2001 and 2002, elected there by an overwhelming vote as a small island with a reputation for having a large voice of integrity and a history of courageous peacekeeping and considerable outreach to suffering – truly a first-world country with a respected and real third-world memory.

This year we celebrate thirty years of membership of the European Union, a forum to which we have contributed much and from which we have benefited enormously. The platform it has afforded us will be showcased to great effect when we assume the EU Presidency, for the sixth time, on 1 January 2004 and when Dublin becomes the scene of the most historic moment in the Union's story since its foundation. Next May, ten utterly unique countries from the Baltic and Eastern Europe will be welcomed back into the European family of nations. We will have to stretch our imaginations around these new colleagues and their stories and their possibilities. The shape of the Union will change and so will we. They will want to know their new neighbours better. They will want to know, who are the Irish? How should they imagine us? Our wandering saints from the first millennium will already have left their imprints on most of their countries, but that aside, they have been largely out of touch with us for a long time.

There are also neighbours closer to home, the neighbours who share the island of Ireland, who need to get to know each other better, to build the trust and friendships which alone can secure peace and partnership. A big investment in friendship-building should be part of our imagining, our planning for the future. Nothing to fear in that, for we are good at that. Friendship-building is our *forte*. Networks are our element.

No other nation holds on to its children and its children's children like we do. Five generations away from Ireland living in Chicago, Kuala Lumpur or Canberra, we meet them and we interrogate them until the parish is found, and the bothárín their emigrating ancestors set out from and the cousins of theirs we know back home in Ireland. We have ties of family so extraordinary that when 15,000 of our young people go off around Australia annually on their year-long working visa, they feel instantly at home in that land 12,000 miles away with its population that is one third Irish. We are a connecting people. It is our strength and our global Irish family is today one of our greatest resources, feeding our culture, expanding its imagination, opening doors, keeping faith with our intriguing homeland.

The very strength of our connectedness, the very ease of our intimacy can itself appear to be a powerful wall of exclusion for some of those who look at us with doubt and mistrust. There can be no hermetic seal on the Irish family and its circle of friends and neighbours, even its reluctant neighbours north of the border. Like strands of a rope they all take their shape from each other and they have an important voice too in the re-imagining of Ireland – for Ireland's future is also theirs. There is an onus on those of us who imagine a reconciled Ireland to actively promote the culture of 'fáilte'.

Ireland is still unfinished business. The Ulster poet Derek Mahon wrote:

> ... Spray-blind,
> We leave here the infancy of the race,
> Unsure among the pitching surfaces,
> Whether the future lies before us or behind.

There have always been pitching surfaces and given a choice I'd settle for the mild turbulence of a modern jet over the stormy seas of an emigrant coffin ship any day. If the men and women of Ireland's past could choose a time to live, there would be a long queue for this one. It is far from perfect but it is as good as it has ever been. Even more importantly, it has a huge, as yet untapped capacity to be better still. Whether the future lies before us or behind us is our choice. We have too often ransacked the past for ammunition with which to booby trap the future. Now would be a good time to ransack it for the values and memories that build us up humanly and pack them for the best journey yet – to a ripened and mature Ireland, an island flying on two strong wings. The bridge to that Ireland lies in the imagination and in the courage it takes to step across it to something not known with certainty but longed for with passion. Isabel Allende says happiness is achieving something you have wanted for a very long time.

We have longed for peace and prosperity, longed for equality and justice, longed for opportunity and reconciliation, longed for an Ireland standing tall in the world, her children's genius revealed and rampant. No other generation has come as close to all those things as ours. A few more bridges and we may well arrive at a happy Ireland. Twenty-first-century Ireland is at least in part living the Ireland imagined in past centuries. Now is a good time to sketch the imagined landscape of tomorrow's Ireland and inspire the champions who will take us to it. I salute you, the artists and the bridge builders, and wish you well as you take us to that Ireland via Charlottesville.

Thank you.

REMARKS ON THE OCCASION OF THE DAY OF WELCOMES

Áras an Uachtaráin, 1 May 2004

Tá muid cruinnithe anseo inniu le lá thar laethanta móra na hEorpa a cheiliúradh; lá a gcuireann muid fíorchaoin fáilte roimh phobal deich baill úra isteach i dteaghlach Aontas na hEorpa.

On this landmark day for the people of Europe, we gather to bid a warm welcome to the ten Member States who are joining the family circle that is the European Union. It is a momentous day of celebration when the past is laid to rest and the future is anticipated with great hope.

We belong to Europe's most blessed generations, for we are witnesses to the unfolding of the future the Union's founders dreamed of. And we are more than mere witnesses, mere spectators. We are called to be the creators, developers, and nurturers of that future.

Our continent is ancient, our Union is young – we are still only at the start of its possibilities. Its potential is limitless. We will build its prosperity with our hands, its peace with our hearts. We will learn about each other and from each other. We will transcend our differences through respectful dialogue, the pursuit of consensus and adherence to a common vision and shared democratic values.

Each member state brings to the Union the unique genius and heritage of its people; twenty-five fascinating faces of Europe's rich history, 450 million people putting their trust in each other. Today we give our children the gift of the biggest European Union ever. Tomorrow we hope they and their children will craft the best.

Guíonn muid rath agus raidhse ar phobal uilig na hEorpa; guíonn muid síocháin agus séan orthu agus ar na glúnta atá fós le teacht. Is é ár mian agus ár rún go dtiocfaidh bláth ar an aisling atá ginte againn anseo inniu.

Speech at the UCD Ireland Diaspora Forum

Belfield, Dublin, 10 November 2008

Thank you for your warm welcome.

As President, I have had the distinct honour to meet with Irish communities throughout the world. My personal encounters with thousands of members of our global Irish family have deepened greatly my respect for their experience and broadened my appreciation of what it means to be Irish. Their hunger for a meaningful connectedness to one another and to Ireland is a recurring theme, and their pride in being Irish no matter how distant the connection is also a recurring and genuine phenomenon.

By organising this conference and through the ongoing work of the Institute for Global Irish Studies, University College Dublin is assisting all of us to better understand and appreciate the powerful resource that is our widely distributed Irish family. I pay tribute to Dr Hugh Brady for his leadership in giving a particular priority to this important issue. I am delighted to see Loretta Brennan Glucksman here today, but not surprised. For many decades Loretta, her late husband Lew and the Ireland Funds have been wonderful builders of a highly effective global Irish network which, among its many contributions, can claim a big role in the development of peace and reconciliation in Ireland.

Good to see here, too, that other great champion of the Irish in America Niall O'Dowd. I know that with *Irish America* magazine he has worked closely with UCD and the Ireland Funds to make today a success.

Thinking of the United States, I cannot let the opportunity pass, particularly in the presence of many proud citizens of that country, to say how impressed and moved we all were by the election last week of Senator Barack Obama as the 44th President of the United States of America. I said in my statement congratulating Senator Obama that his election was transformational in its power and scope, and served as a beacon of hope, not just for America but for the whole world, particularly in the context of these turbulent times of anxiety and uncertainty that we live in. If ever America and the world needed just such transforming experiences it is now and Senator Obama knows he has our support and solidarity as he sets forward on his momentous mission – and not just because his ancestors hailed from Offaly. I also want to pay tribute to John McCain, who, having fought a long, spirited campaign, brought it to a close with a memorably gracious concession speech on Tuesday night. His words augur well for the kind of new unity of purpose and people that President-Elect Obama is seeking to build.

And we too seek a new unity of purpose and people among the Irish at home and abroad. Over 1 million people born on the island of Ireland are estimated to live abroad – a remarkable figure for a population of some 6 million. When people who claim Irish descent are included, the number who can be counted as part of our global Irish family rises to an estimated 70 million. These figures are at once both a frightening testament to the searing legacy of forced emigration and an awesome contemporary resource from which to forge new synergies and opportunities for this still new century.

There are of course enormous differences in culture, outlook and experience between and among our communities abroad. A group of 70 million people spread throughout the world is by its nature extremely diverse and complex. We can truly respect this community and its role in the modern world by avoiding lapses into lazy assumptions and false generalisations.

For instance, our community in Britain – where by far the largest number of Irish-born people outside Ireland live – have had a very different experience to that of the Irish in the United States. Our diaspora includes people as diverse as a third-generation Irish-American steelworker in Pittsburgh; a Dublin-born financial expert working in Hong Kong; an Irish-Australian family in Perth; a Galway-born pensioner in North London; a young Cork-born designer in Paris, and a fifth-generation Irish-Argentinean or Newfoundlander whose lilting Irish brogue is remarkably strong for someone who has never set foot on Irish soil and proof positive of the longevity of the Irish imprint.

In my travels abroad as President, one of the joys has been to encounter pockets of the Irish family in the most unlikely places as well as on the better-known tracks. I will never forget my visit to Butte, Montana, a few years ago, where I encountered an Irish welcome and identity as warm and proud as when their ancestors left the Beara peninsula over a century ago.

Even within this huge dispersion and diversity, certain common threads seem identifiable. Something palpable in the Irish psyche nudges us to be and keep on being community to one another. A deep appreciation of the emigrant experience and an affinity with a sense of Irishness – however that is interpreted – are defining characteristics of the global Irish family. Our culture and heritage are powerful instruments of connection. The music, dance, poetry and stories of Ireland have quite a capacity to gather and to bind this enormous, diverse, scattered Irish family. Of themselves they both entertain and nurture, they showcase and recruit and are effective pathways to linking with our family abroad.

There are, though, subtleties and complexities around the nature of the Irish diaspora that we need to comprehend as well. Sometimes in Ireland we make the mistake of assuming that because so many communities in the United States, Australia or elsewhere celebrate St Patrick's Day or embrace an aspect of Irish culture, that they are automatically affirming a connection to modern Ireland. Yes, some do have a formidable ongoing interest in all things Irish and are well up to speed on what is going on here. Many others have not that same level of interest in or knowledge of today's Ireland. For them, these occasions can often be more a celebration of the Irish emigrant experience in their adopted homeland. Yet, while at times there may be no more than a tenuous affinity to the modern Ireland, they are all an extremely important part of the wider Irish family and part of the ever growing story of Ireland in the world. In building culturally sensitive connections to them, we open up to them an unknown part of their history and they open up to us an unknown part of ours. It's a journey of mutual discovery and rediscovery of great benefit to both of us.

Any discussion of our modern diaspora and how we in Ireland should interact with it in the future must begin with an acknowledgment of the trauma of the past. As President Kennedy observed during his visit to Ireland in 1963, 'no country in the world has endured the haemorrhage which this island has endured'.

Modern Ireland stands today on the shoulders of giants; the men and women who left a land barren of opportunity and built better lives in their adopted countries. Far from ignoring the fate of an Ireland that had failed them, our emigrants kept alive the traditions of home, sent millions in remittances to family and friends in Ireland and worked to ensure that Irish issues featured in the political discourse of their adopted countries.

Out of this awful haemorrhage has emerged the modern Irish global family – unique in its collective experience, its determination to endure and its willingness to engage with and assist a small island on the edge of Europe. They have shown time and again that the heart has room for two homelands and for parallel identities which enhance each other rather than cancelling each other out. Yet today that longstanding image of ourselves as an emigrating nation has been altered dramatically.

A whole new set of dynamics are impacting on us and on our global Irish community. They will bring changes yet to be revealed and some that need to be planned for. Over the past decade we have seen a reversal in the pattern of emigration that plagued so many generations. Ireland relatively suddenly became a place of net inward migration, thanks to a sustained period of unprecedented economic success. New arrivals came from Eastern Europe, Africa and Asia, and many thousands of Irish emigrants and their families decided to return to avail of new opportunities at home. The total number of returned emigrants since 2003 is over 107,000. The return of our people over the past decade has been enormously positive for Ireland in so many ways. However, it has led to a decline in the numbers and vitality of some of our communities abroad, particularly in parts of Britain and the United States, where the vibrancy of Irish communities has depended historically on a largely unbroken flow of emigrants from Ireland. That story has now changed. Also changed, however, is the story of Ireland's relationship with Britain, which has become collegial and warm in recent decades, not least because of the new opportunities for partnership and friendship which have been provided by our common membership of the

European Union, creating quite a different backdrop for Irish emigrants in Britain.

Ireland's relationship with the United States has, at political level, been elevated to an unheard of degree of intimacy with the involvement of successive American administrations in the Peace Process. In every country where we have a substantial Irish presence – Canada, New Zealand, Australia – there has been a heightened engagement with Ireland largely due to efforts at peacemaking. These have sparked renewed interest and a sense of shared success in achieving peace. Ireland's new economic profile as a global exporter of goods and services has created a new class of emigrant, not to mention serious Irish investment in many other countries both inside and outside the European Union.

A further transformative development has been the acceptance on the part of the Irish State and its people of the need to give proper recognition to our emigrant family. The recent amendment to Article 2 of our Constitution now states, 'the Irish nation cherishes its special affinity with people of Irish ancestry living abroad who share its cultural identity and heritage'. Our outreach to Irish emigrants who are in need has grown and developed exponentially in recent years, with new structures and resources now well in place.

In 2002, the Task Force on Policy regarding Emigrants, chaired by Paddy O'Hanlon, provided a comprehensive policy framework aimed at enhancing support for our emigrants. Out of that came the establishment of the Irish Abroad Unit within the Department of Foreign Affairs. Its remit is to focus on our emigrants, to invest in Irish communities throughout the world and to develop strategies aimed at further enhancing the relationship between Ireland and the diaspora. While the Unit has focused primarily on increasing the capacity of Irish organisations abroad to deliver frontline services to our emigrants in need, its agenda has also broadened to include substantial investment in the heritage, social and cultural life of our communities abroad. Irish Government funding for our communities abroad has also reached unprecedented levels, increasing more than fifteen-fold in ten years and now spanning Britain, the US, Australia, Argentina, Canada, South Africa, Zimbabwe, New Zealand, Singapore, the Netherlands, Mexico and France. On my visits to communities abroad, I have seen the practical difference that this funding has made to the most vulnerable and how it has enhanced the relationship with today's Ireland, building connections of visible care.

The impact of globalisation and new technologies has been a further transformative development for our diaspora. Thankfully, the days when an Irish emigrant would leave on a boat never to return are long gone. Relatively affordable air travel has meant that more and more people of Irish descent are able to visit and connect with the place of their birth or the place of their ancestors. Instant communication has also brought Ireland and her far-flung family closer together.

Today, children of Irish background in Chicago or Singapore or South Africa can see and speak with their grandparents or other relatives in Ireland via the internet; Irish people spread throughout Asia can share business knowledge, build connections and network through innovative websites, and people throughout the world with an interest in Ireland can stay fully informed of developments here by accessing the wide range of online media and information outlets.

By the way, I recently experienced at firsthand a wonderful example of technology connecting people across generations and oceans. I had the honour to launch the Galway branch of a great initiative called the Senior Help Line on a day when they had a live link to an emigrant Irish group in New York. This listening service created for older people by older people here in Ireland is soon to be exported to America, for the organisers of the Irish Senior Help Line are about to work with Irish Centres in New York to develop a similar service there – evidence of the new connections and synergies that are growing out of old kinships and longstanding mutual care.

Another example of how a greater engagement with our diaspora can be invaluable is the economic space where both the problems and the solutions are global. Harnessing the amazing power of our people, who are scattered in all parts of that globe, is a key opportunity for us. Emigrants are by nature positive, dynamic, can-do people who face into adversity and who produce their best under pressure. Today, they are to be found in every walk of life and with every kind of wisdom and experience. That is an ideal spirit and resource we can draw on as we seek to chart our way forward in these uncertain and difficult times. Properly harnessed, our diaspora can be hugely helpful to us, and we to them, in that journey.

The technologies of the modern world, with their easy and instant universal communications, offer exciting opportunities for much more creative and sustained development of multifaceted relationships between Ireland and its global family.

Wherever they are, they are marked by the indelible imprint of Ireland and in so many remote places they have showcased Ireland's genius and character, making for us friends among strangers, making us known and respected. Theirs has been a formidable ambassadorship, from our missionaries to our famine poor, to our labourers and our university graduates, this family of ours has a phenomenal capacity for connectedness to one another across the miles of geography and down through the generations of history. At the most human of levels they have given us a fearlessness and a confidence when confronted with serious challenges. We have shared and share an irrepressible joy in life.

The challenges of the twenty-first century are now ours to deal with. Many of those who have gone before us on emigrant ships would gladly swap their times for ours. Facing courageously into the responsibilities our time demands would be a very fitting tribute to our scattered forebears. Another tribute lies in connecting today to their children and grandchildren, as friends and partners who have a spontaneous cultural compatibility and a value system of mutual care which they share with us. We are not all the same, for different histories have shaped us differently, but we are cut from the same cloth and in a very fragmented world, our bonds of kinship, our mutual telepathy and empathy, our ease of mutual understanding are a reassuring resource and a basic building block towards a much more peaceful global human family.

Occasions such as this gathering here today, which bring together a whole range of individuals and groups who understand how exciting and important all of this can be, are vital for the success of the journey of reconnection. My congratulations to all involved in putting the event together and my thanks to each and every one of you for showing your interest and commitment by being here.

Go n-eíri an bothar linn go léir.

REMARKS AT THE CLOSING CEREMONY OF THE DEFENCE FORCES CELEBRATION OF FIFTY YEARS OF PEACEKEEPING DUTIES

Cathal Brugha Barracks, Rathmines, Dublin, 28 November 2008

Dia dhíbh a chairde. Tá an áthas orm bheith i bhur measc ar on ocáid seo.

Chief of Staff, distinguished guests,

This Golden Jubilee of Irish peacekeeping has been celebrated in many different places and ways throughout the year, but always with the same pride in those who have served in our name with the UN and the same sadness as we call to mind those who surrendered their lives or their health so that others might know the gift of peace. Now we gather in Cathal Brugha Barracks to officially bring our mix of celebration and commemoration to an end.

It is of course also a beginning, the start of the next fifty years, and already our troops are on this very day immersed in their vocation as global peacekeepers in no fewer than ten fields of operation that include Lebanon, Chad and Kosovo.

In times of poverty and in times of prosperity, Ireland's fidelity to service with the United Nations has never faltered, thanks entirely to the men and women of our Defence Forces who stepped up and shipped out to so many far-flung and dangerous parts of the world. There they became the bridge to peace for so many victims of conflict. They were and are the answer to prayers of despair that go up wherever the power-less are overwhelmed by violence and left to wonder whether anyone out there in the wider world cares.

In Ireland we subscribe to the view that we are, after all, our broth-ers' and sisters' keepers; what hurts them is our responsibility and we showcase that view in many ways, for example through the work of Irish Aid in developing countries where we invest in the education, health and good governance of millions of the world's poorest peoples. We also showcase our concern and our willingness to share responsibility for others through our peacekeeping service with the United Nations. Importantly, too, we also show very powerfully the challenging and unique moral vocation of a militarily neutral country, with an army that has never since its formation been deployed in the making of war.

In the early 1960s, UN Secretary General Dag Hammarskjöld, when asked, coined the term 'peacekeeping', which was not specifically men-tioned in the UN Charter. He said it belonged to 'Chapter six and a half of the Charter', meaning somewhere between negotiated peaceful resolution of conflict of chapter six and the use of force which could be sanctioned by chapter seven. For Ireland, as a neutral and non-aligned country, this method of military participation has proved itself to be a worthy and invaluable channel for our armed forces to lend their con-sidered, measured and subtle military expertise to calm, stabilise and help to pacify some of the world's most troubled regions.

Instead of making us enemies, our peacekeepers have made friends for Ireland across the world. They have done that not just by doing a first-class job of peacekeeping, but by interesting themselves deeply in the lives of those they protected, volunteering to help in a local orphanage, bringing much-needed support to a local AIDS hospice, looking out for their new neighbours in ways that were well above and beyond the call of duty but within the precious realm of human decency and generosity. They also brought with them their camaraderie, their humour, their music, their faith and their capacity to be community to one another, especially during those inevitable spells of loneliness and homesickness which those who serve overseas face into even as they face into all the dangers of conflict and instability. In the uncertain spaces they were called to work, they brought the certainty of reliability, of trust, of kindness and humanity. They also brought the hope of peace.

This thing we call peace, as a word is simple and innocuous sounding. As a concept it is complex beyond belief and as a process it is frustratingly painstaking and long. We in Ireland have reason to understand that better than many others, for our own Peace Process was the antithesis of an overnight success. Today, Irish peacekeepers are back in Lebanon, the place where we began our service with the United Nations almost exactly fifty years ago. The story of the ebb and flow of our service there underlines just how fragile peace is once it is established after years of volatility and how much nurturing it needs if it is to grow robust and enduring. Our seminal mission to the Congo began in 1960 and while we only have a handful of observers there currently, that tragic country remains an area of significant UN operations.

It was George Bernard Shaw who noted that 'Peace is not only better than war, but infinitely more arduous', and generations of Irish peacekeepers can certainly testify to the truth of that. The words of President John F. Kennedy, when speaking in Dáil Éireann in 1963, have been quoted many times and they still ring true as they resonate down the years, 'from Cork to the Congo from Galway to the Gaza Strip, from this legislative assembly to the United Nations, Ireland is sending its most talented men to do the work of peace'. Of course, I can now add that for well over half of those fifty years our talented women have joined their male colleagues in doing the work of peace, serving in some of the most hazardous overseas environments.

I have been privileged as President and in my constitutional role as Commander-in-Chief to visit our peacekeepers in a number of the countries where they have been deployed. I have seen the austerity of their lives, the absence of home comforts, the menacing environments, the ever-present dangers they learn to live with. I have seen the monuments to those who died, met the comrades and families who have been bereaved. I have been the recipient of wonderful welcomes they have so carefully planned and prepared and I have been moved time and again by their formidable love of homeland and their passion to serve it well. At home I have met their spouses and children who so graciously and generously put up with absence and loneliness so that others can know the peace of heart and mind that comes from having friends who care. I have been privileged to meet the retired veterans who wear the blue beret with righteous pride and I can say without being accused of exaggerating that all those I have met from Cathal Brugha to Camp Shamrock, from Áras an Uachtaráin to Africa, have made me hugely proud to be President of Ireland.

Each and every one of them is entitled to the gratitude of the Irish people for their courage and commitment these past fifty years, when, by their efforts, not alone did they bring the gift of peace to so many strangers but to their homeland they brought the gift of international respect and friendship. In this Jubilee year, we as a nation salute them.

Is iontach an obair ata ar siúl agaibh agus go raibh maith agaibh go léir.

REMARKS AT AN INSTITUTE OF INTERNATIONAL AND EUROPEAN AFFAIRS LUNCHEON

Europe House, North Great Georges Street, Dublin, 26 April 2010

Dia dhíbh a chairde.

I am delighted to be back at the Institute of International and European Affairs, this time under the leadership of its new Director General Dáithí O'Ceallaigh. Dáithí is an old friend, an outstanding Irish diplomat and ambassador who has served all over the world and whose contribution as Ambassador in London during a pivotal time in the Peace Process was utterly crucial to the creation, development and consolidation of peace in Northern Ireland and in recalibrating Irish–British relationships to the level of collegiality we now enjoy. Brendan Halligan and his colleagues at the Institute chose well in their new DG, for his commitment to Ireland and to Europe is underpinned by a rare level of skill, wisdom and insight into a wide range of issues, gathered and distilled over a very distinguished career.

In the relatively short time since I last talked at the Institute, Ireland has gone from being the economic toast of Europe to being excoriated for a champagne lifestyle that was based on unsustainable levels of borrowing. It's a humbler and more chastened Ireland we meet in today, for emergence as a globalised economy exposed us to the damaging consequences of the global recession and the blinkered hubris of our banking and property development sectors inflicted colossal damage on what was and still is a young, emerging economy. The opening chapters of twenty-first-century Ireland have been a rollercoaster. First there was the huge economic and social uplift propelled by the best-educated generation ever on this island and then there was the rapid slide into levels of debt that have sobering consequences for the next generation. We have come face to face with confidence and crises of confidence. We face the reality that there is a huge onus on us, ourselves, to dig our way out of this crisis and that we are fortunate to be members of a Union which is supporting and guiding us through these tough times.

The Single Market proved itself to be a major advantage to Ireland, as we established ourselves, with much success, as a nation with a strong exporting pedigree. It is encouraging that despite the shocks in the external international environment and the self-inflicted domestic wounds, our exports have held up reasonably well and are beginning to start climbing again as we make inroads in regaining lost competiveness.

They say that a good team does not become a bad team over night, and Team Ireland had, and still has, a panel of strengths sufficient to reposition us as a smart, innovative, ethically sustainable and competitive economy. Not least of those strengths is our capacity for solidarity, for pulling together across the diverse constituencies of interest, when to do so is the most effective way of protecting our collective national interest. We are right in the middle of just such a time and so far external expert commentators seem impressed at the realism and sacrifice being brought to bear on our parlous economic situation. The repositioning of Ireland, if it is to be successful, will be largely down to our own efforts and our relationship with the EU and its individual Member States is absolutely critical to that repositioning.

After a protracted and energy-sapping debate on institutional reform within the Union, the post-Lisbon era has to be characterised by the focusing of energies on ensuring that the new EU institutional architecture makes a manifest and positive impact on the lives of Europe's citizens. That means bringing financial stability and jobs, for it is the absence of these things or the threat to them that provokes so much worry in Europe's homes. Ireland stands to benefit considerably from embedded financial stability and from a dynamic but sensible and sound pro-business culture. Ensuring a proper balance between effective regulation and credible entrepreneurialism throughout Europe, and indeed further afield, will be key to our future prosperity. So Ireland has to keep doing what it has always done very well and that is to maintain a high level of engagement with our European partners, not just in Brussels but also bilaterally with our European colleagues and those who aspire to membership so that we are not known simply through the voices of external spectators and pundits but known for who we truly are. To be defined solely by our current economic problems would be a massive injustice to a country which has a civic society and community sector second to none and which has a capacity for transcending adversity by sheer hard slog, also second to none.

For all our current preoccupations, we still have an abiding responsibility to prepare for the future, and for a better future. Our position at the heart of the EU is an important asset, so too is the massive, well-disposed international network we have inherited thanks to the efforts of our extensive global Irish family. The Farmleigh Forum last September demonstrated the depth and breadth of that resource and the newly constituted Global Irish Network creates an opportunity to harness and harvest that resource in much more targeted and strategic ways than we have done in the past. Ireland's new migrant population, though growing much less rapidly than in the early post-Enlargement years, has brought the enrichment of cultural diversity and the momentum of individual ambition. Those who leave and speak well of us are important goodwill ambassadors for Ireland back in their native countries. Those who stay widen our human resource base economically, culturally and civically and they are a vital part of our future recovery.

It is a complex time and world we inhabit. Consensus is hard to find and so too is good, sensible, well-informed and reasoned debate. Tabloidism, anecdote and stereotype fuelling heady moral panics are an inevitable feature of the freedom of speech we enjoy but it is essential to all functioning democracies that there is also space for measured and educated debate, which is why the IIEA occupies such an important role in Irish life. You keep us plugged into the major EU and international issues which strategically affect Ireland, even if their direct impact on us may not be immediately apparent. You are part of the checks and balances we need to understand and interrogate our times so that we can make good, sensible choices in the present and for the future; choices that are good for Ireland and good for Europe. You are unlikely to face redundancy any day soon, for the catalogue of issues which are on the agenda is extensive, from enlargement to the environment, from migration to monetary stability, from third-world poverty to global prosperity, from war to peace.

Europe's context has changed beyond all recognition from the chaos of competing empires which soaked the first half of the twentieth century with the wasted blood of its youth. From the advent of the Treaty of Rome, Europe has known a level of peace and stability that defeated all previous generations. This Union is good at the kind of miracles that come from vision and determination. Likewise, in Ireland, this generation has created a peace which has altered beyond recognition the political and social context of the coming times and which is only in the opening chapters of its potential. Though human beings the world over are clearly capable of mega mistakes, we are also clearly capable of clearing up our messes and making them better than good.

This Institute not only helps us to believe that but it tells us that there is a moral imperative to actively involve ourselves in public understanding of the complex issues we need to address to make our world right. These are noble purposes and I wish the Institute continued success in pursuing and discharging them.

Go n-éirí an t-ádh libh! Go raibh míle maith agaibh go léir.

REMARKS AT A BREAKFAST AT THE NEW YORK STOCK EXCHANGE

21 May 2010

Good morning and thank you all for coming at this early hour. It's so good to be back in New York City, where the Irish always feel completely at home.

My visit gives me a chance to speak about the current economic situation in Ireland. I am pleased to have that opportunity, because under the pressure of real-time news cycles our perceptions are often formed by a simplistic headline or sound-bite. It is therefore very important that an influential and sophisticated audience such as this one has an informed overview of the Irish economy.

I do not need to rehearse in this forum the realities that face the global economy and many national economies, including your own. The past two generations saw Ireland leave behind a protectionist and underachieving past and rapidly enter the world of the global marketplace. It has been very successful in that marketplace, attracting high-end foreign direct investment, much of it from the United States, and cultivating a new indigenous entrepreneurial sector which has returned the compliment by investing significantly here. But the trajectory of growth has felt the temporary braking effect of the global financial crisis and consequent economic downturn. This was exacerbated by domestic factors arising from a heavily over-inflated property market and poor banking practices. These factors have impacted heavily on government revenues, our domestic banking system, on jobs and on every household budget in Ireland. Today we are under no illusion regarding the severity of the correction we have experienced or the scale of the response required to address it.

We have already taken strong steps on the three prongs of our recovery plan: stabilising the public finances, repairing the banking system and improving competitiveness. The Irish Government has taken the tough decisions needed to bring spending under control. Our plan to reduce the general government deficit to less than 3 per cent of GDP by 2014 has been endorsed by the IMF, the OECD and the European Commission. And due to these actions we are on course to do that, with 2010 public spending significantly less than the previous year. These cuts in public spending have had real and very painful effects on families across the country, and people rightly feel hurt and angry that Ireland has been landed in this predicament by once trusted individuals and institutions. However, Ireland is characterised by a remarkable social solidarity and today's sense of outrage is also accompanied by a collective desire and determination to fix the problems and secure a sustainable economic future for our children.

Many of the strengths on which we built our recent success remain with us and will be important foundations for medium and long-term growth. As the only English-speaking member of the Eurozone, businesses located in Ireland have barrier-free access to almost 500 million consumers in the European market. We have a young, highly educated, flexible and competitively priced workforce which is proving its realism and adaptability under pressure, and we have an outward-looking economy which exports 80 per cent of everything we produce. As the global economy picks up, we will feel the benefit.

And we retain the business-friendly framework – including our 12.5 per cent corporation tax rate – that, together with other attractive factors, has led to over 500 US companies establishing operations in Ireland. Already this year, US companies like eBay, PayPal and Hertz have announced new investments and jobs in Ireland. Microsoft, IBM, Texas Instruments and Disney Research have recently established new R&D centres and partnerships. LinkedIn has established its European headquarters in Ireland. We are most certainly open for business, for good successful business, and world business leaders like Google, Intel and Facebook recognise Ireland as the pre-eminent location for doing a high-quality job well. We are also recognised as a hub of fresh thinking, a place where innovative and quality oriented people turn bright ideas into world-class goods and services.

On the banking sector, we introduced a State guarantee for most of our banks shortly after the collapse of Lehman Brothers to support the liquidity of systemically important institutions and to maintain market confidence in the system as a whole. Since then, we have nationalised one bank and recapitalised two more. In order to deal with impaired assets on the balance sheets of the banks, the Government established a National Assets Management Agency which is now in the process of buying the riskiest loans from the banks at a significant discount on their book value. As in the US, reforming and improving financial regulation is high on our agenda and the Government has appointed a new Central Bank Governor and Financial Regulator and is putting in place a new domestic regulatory framework for the effective supervision of financial institutions and markets and to safeguard the interests of consumers and investors. Like many other countries, public trust in banks and the financial world has been sorely damaged and a robust, credible reform of a regulatory system is essential to the restoration of that trust. Slip-sliding back to recidivist risk-taking is not an option. The sacrifices made by the population demand an ethical response from those who, in dealing in money, also deal in the real lives, homes, jobs and opportunities of whole nations.

Our nation as a whole is making sacrifices to get the economy back on its feet and the good news is that these sacrifices are now paying off. Labour costs, energy costs and consumer prices are falling. These adjustments are making Ireland a significantly more competitive and attractive place for doing business. Ireland is already among the highest-performing countries for rate of return on US investment and trends like these will only enhance our appeal. The global outlook is improving and the Irish economy is set to return to growth in the second half of this year. Arising from our increased competiveness and strong export orientation, the

European Commission now projects that Ireland's economy will grow by 3 per cent in 2011 – significantly above the EU average.

Our challenge now is to match improving competitiveness with increased productivity and job creation. There, as in so many things, the watchword is innovation. A decade ago, long before the current economic crisis, we already recognised the value and importance of innovation. We trebled our investment in research and development over the last ten years and we have recently strengthened our R&D tax credit scheme in order to promote innovation within the country. Our vision for the Ireland of the future is a smart, high-value, export-led economy and we are sharply focused on this goal.

The Irish writer Colum McCann won the National Book Award here in New York last year for his novel *Let the Great World Spin*. It is a breathtaking portrayal of the lives of many ordinary people for whom their day-to-day struggle is like walking a tightrope. Colum set out, in his own words, to 'create a piece of art that talks to the human instinct for recovery and joy'. The novel is set here in New York City, a city which, according to Colum, keeps going forward because 'it would dissolve if it ever began looking backward over its own shoulder'. In Ireland, we also have our sights set firmly on the future. We know that if we want to compete in a global economy, and we do, we cannot afford to stand still and that there is little advantage in only looking over our shoulders, though the bitter lessons from the past will undoubtedly guide our path ahead. With economic growth now in sight, we trust that the future will bring to the Irish people the 'recovery and joy' Colum McCann has written about.

We want that same recovery and joy for our friends and partners and markets here in the United States.

It is important to us that the markets fully appreciate the progress Ireland is making, the determination it has and the advantages it has on offer. Our message is clear: the fundamental strengths that drove our economy in the 1990s are being renewed; the frailties that weakened our economy in the last few years are being addressed and corrected; we have a robust plan for recovery and growth, and that plan is working and will yield positive outcomes in the period ahead.

I am very conscious that over the twelve years that I have visited New York as President, mostly when I talked about a plan, it was the plan for peace that I was referring to. One of the major future advantages that Ireland has today is that the Peace Process has defied all the vanities and failures of history to become a remarkable success story and one with huge potential for the future of the island of Ireland. This generation brought to a centuries-old and intractable conflict a new sense of urgency, a capacity for compromise, radical thinking and innovation and a willingness to engage the help of friends in order to set history on a new and more optimistic course. Our remarkable global Irish family, especially here in the United States, made a huge investment in that peace and still does. It is also strongly implicated in our economic and cultural future, both informally and more formally through initiatives like the new Irish Innovation Centre in Silicon Valley, the new Irish Arts Centre here in New York and the Global Irish Network formed in the wake of the Global Irish Economic Forum hosted last year in Dublin by the Irish Government, which brought together a formidable think tank of the most influential and successful members of our global community. Quite simply, we are truly fortunate that thanks to generations of outward migration, at a time of international recession we can call upon the support and ingenuity of businessmen and women who are Irish or of Irish extraction. Their willingness to help has been remarkable and is emblematic of the legendary capacity of the Irish for pulling together in adversity. Many more, we hope, will take up the invitation from Tourism Ireland to make this 'The Year to Come Home'.

As that most famous of New Yorkers President Franklin D. Roosevelt, once said, 'the only limit to our realisation of tomorrow will be our doubts of today. Let us move forward with strong and active faith.' That's what we did together in Northern Ireland with the help of our friends here in the US and elsewhere. That's what we are doing to overcome the economic challenges we face now.

Go raibh míle maith agaibh go léir.

REMARKS AT FORDHAM UNIVERSITY COMMENCEMENT CEREMONY

22 May 2010

Distinguished honorees and guests; members of the class of 2010, congratulations!

It is an honour to be here today as President of Ireland in a place that has meant so much to Ireland and the Irish in America for 170 years. It was, after all, a Fordham alumnus, Thomas Cahill, who wrote a book of depth and insight on the Irish love of learning and then, with a modesty that only the Jesuits can teach us, called his book *How the Irish Saved Civilization*. We of course always knew that but we are grateful to him for telling the rest of the world!

When my countryman the poet Seamus Heaney addressed the Fordham commencement class in 1981, he did so in verse. I am going to stick to the more traditional prose and beg your indulgence for these few minutes when I stand between your years of study and graduation.

Your studies were long and your lecturers many, and no matter what your discipline, somewhere along the way, you will have picked up the fact, possibly from the other Irish President here, Fr Joe McShane, that the Irish love words. The poet Peter Fallon wrote that the islanders who dwelt on the Blasket Islands off the west coast of Ireland had:

> A word for every wave
> that ebbs and flows,
> and wind that blows
> Every day's *memento mori*.
> Everybody has a story.

Even more than words, we Irish love stories, for words are just gateways to stories. We all could tell some stories, the parents and guardians and the faculty members as well as the graduates gathered this morning on Edward's Parade. Today we celebrate your stories. No two the same. Each one utterly unique, a little of what you were given at birth, a little of what you learned and did, what you remember and what you aspire to – and then some ingredients that nobody but you can fully know or understand. And each story is even now a work in progress.

As you write fresh post-Fordham chapters in your stories, you will write the future of this city, this country and the world your children will grow up in until they too stand – as one day all too soon they will – in a quadrangle much like this.

But more of quadrangles later. First I want to share a few stories that I hope will have some resonance for your future lives.

Take the story of John Hughes. He was the son of a tenant farmer, born in Annaloughan in the parish of Clogher in County Tyrone, Ireland, in 1797. Ireland was then a colony of the British Empire with a wealthy, powerful ruling Anglican elite whose oppressive Penal Laws bore down appallingly on Catholics and Presbyterians who were denied equality before the law. Like many of his neighbours to whom the State offered nothing but perpetual poverty, John soon left for America, arriving in 1817. With little formal education he took any work he could get. He was a manual labourer, then a stone-cutter and finally a gardener, before entering a seminary after a year of remedial instruction.

By 1838 he was appointed bishop in the diocese of New York, where he served for twenty-six years. Through his life, John Hughes retained a strong sense of outrage at the injustice he had experienced as a child. 'They told me,' he later recalled, 'when I was a boy that for five days I was on a social and civil equality with the most favoured subjects of the British Empire. These five days would be the interval between my birth and my baptism.'

In John Hughes, outrage was a spur to action, not just a once-off anger, not a raging self-pity, but rather a life of action in which he made common cause with the poorest of the poor and set about providing a good education to New York's poorest. His was a radical project of transformation, a leaven that started in the empowerment of the individual and galvanized the potential of whole communities. The results of his labour, his vision, are everywhere around us. He laid the foundation stone for St Patrick's Cathedral, but, much more important, he built the foundation for Fordham University and – dare I say it at a Fordham commencement, Fr McShane? – for Manhattan College too.

We are all here then, in part, because of the foresight and passion for education of a poor and unschooled immigrant from Tyrone. As you leave Fordham take a part of John Hughes' story with you – the part that was outraged to his very core at a world of gross inequality where the talent and potential of so many was allowed to go to waste. And take with you the passion he had for being himself an agent of change.

In 1846, as the first of 1 million deaths from starvation occurred in Ireland from what we now know as An Gorta Mór or the Great Hunger, a young French Jesuit, Henri du Merle, arrived at Fordham. Just as Fordham received its charter and the Jesuit community settled in, famine took hold in Ireland, changing forever our history and the history of the United States. Within a very short few years, a quarter of the population would be either dead or forced into an emigration of despair which brought them in tattered rags and poor health to New York in their hundreds of thousands.

The Irish poet Eavan Boland writes movingly of a famine road built by the starving on the borders of Connacht in 1847. The rough stone

road peters out in ivy and scutch grass and is forgotten, recorded on
no map:

> Where they died, there the road ended
> and ends still and when I take down
> the map of this island, it is ...

> ... to tell myself again that

> the line which says woodland and cries hunger
> and gives out among sweet pine and cypress,
> finds no horizon

> will not be there.

Even here in this country, the land of desperate hope, the road petered
out for many Irish victims who contracted typhus either on route or
on arrival. How many of them wondered was there anyone out there
who gave a damn, who cared enough to care for them? In 1847, Henri
du Merle left the relative comfort of Fordham to work among the
Irish famine victims then arriving in Canada. There he survived an
epidemic of typhus that took nine priests and thirteen nuns that year
and he returned to New York. Then, despite all he knew, despite all he
had seen, he went back, back to the place he knew spelt more than the
possibility of death, and in 1851, as he ministered to Ireland's famine
immigrants, he contracted typhus and died at the age of thirty-two –
one of two Jesuits from this community to die working among Irish
immigrant communities.

With such selfless sacrifice and heroism embedded in its earliest years,
it is no surprise that Fordham remains committed to training students in
humanitarian work through its Institute of International Humanitarian
Affairs, today under the guidance of Dr Kevin Cahill, and that empathy

with the poor is an abiding part of this university's ethos, the imprint it hopes you will bear and bear witness to throughout your lives.

In 1847, Jacques Judah Lyons served as Hazan or prayer reader to the community of Shearith Israel, the oldest Jewish community in the US. Today that community is found only a few short blocks from Fordham's Lincoln Center campus. In March 1847, the community of Shearith Israel held a special service and charity appeal for famine relief in Ireland. They were not fundraising for friends or family. They had none of the familiar links to Ireland which might have prompted such an interest in Ireland's suffering. However, Hazan Lyons pointed out there was indeed one 'all-powerful and indestructible' link between New York's Jewish community and the Irish famine victims: 'The link, my brethren is humanity.'

As you leave Fordham remember the stories of these men who put their gifts at the service of suffering strangers and who saw in each stranger a brother or a sister.

In 1845, as the first signs of future famine emerged in Ireland, Charlotte Grace O'Brien was born in Cahirmoyle, County Clare. She heard disturbing reports of the conditions experienced by young emigrant women arriving from Ireland through the Port of New York at the turn of the previous century. She was neither young nor healthy and yet she booked passage to New York to see for herself just how dreadful things were. It was an act of extraordinary courage and it changed not only the course of her life but it changed the fortunes of countless emigrant women to this country. Her efforts inspired the establishment of a Mission for Irish Emigrant Women in Battery Park. Over 100,000 Irish women found advice, shelter and in many cases work through the Mission's efforts between 1883 and 1908.

So many disadvantages still bear down on women especially in today's world. In the developing world, hunger and poverty have a disproportionate effect on women and in so many cultures they live lives little short of slavery and certainly well short of access to their full potential.

In our world where women have the chance for education and their choice of fulfilling careers, it is important to remember just how much work remains to be done in the full liberation of women from centuries of exclusion. We are still only in the opening chapters. When I began law school way back in the last century, the first textbook on my reading list was *Learning the Law* by the eminent Professor Glanville Williams. It included a chapter ominously entitled 'Women'. There he opined that since women's voices were too weak to be heard in a courtroom, the only conceivable function of females in a law school was as a source of suitable spouses for their male colleagues. I married a dentist for spite and never regretted it! To the women graduating from this class into a financial world compromised by macho-driven super-hubris, I say that the world really needs the balancing intelligence of your genius. We need to maintain the momentum created by pioneers like Charlotte Grace O'Brien who yearned for a world that flew on two wings instead of limping along on one. We need male and female champions of that world that flies on two wings.

What of the story of Ireland? The eighteenth-century Ireland that John Hughes left was ridden with political and religious oppression, violence and sectarianism. The twentieth-century Ireland I grew up in inherited that toxic narrative, and then free second-level education and electricity arrived and with it, as Seamus Heaney says in 'From the Canton of Expectation':

> ... suddenly, this change of mood.
> Books open in the newly-wired kitchens.
> Young heads that might have dozed a life away
> against the flanks of milking cows were busy
> paving and pencilling their first causeways
> across the prescribed texts. The paving stones
> of quadrangles came next and a grammar
> of imperatives, the new age of demands.

The story of the Northern Ireland Peace Process, which is a story of struggling for justice and equality, is the story of that generation, of those educated young heads who had, according to Heaney, 'intelligences, brightened and unmannerly as crowbars'. They used the crowbars of their confidence, their education to begin bit by bit to construct an end to the centuries-old elitist culture of conflict and to replace it with an egalitarian culture of consensus.

As well as a unique confidence and determination, this generation of peacemakers had huge external support, especially here in the United States where our emigrant children, grandchildren and great-grandchildren had advanced to become so influential and respected. They are co-owners of the peace that is today growing ever deeper in Ireland, North and South. Presidents Clinton, Bush and Obama have nurtured the Peace Process; friends of all political persuasions in the US Congress, State Legislatures and City Halls have united in their commitment to our peace. And among our best friends and greatest champions is one of your own, Bill Flynn, Chairman of Mutual of America, who, with a busy agenda and plenty of other things to be busy with, made peace in Ireland his passion and his priority. Through his efforts and the efforts of others, men and women who could see no other road to justice than through violence were persuaded to try dialogue and democracy.

Today, the Irish Peace Process may be one of the best examples of successful peace-building available to us as we set about similar challenges across the world. You have shares in that story, for the innate hope and optimism within the American DNA kept insisting even through the darkest times that we could trudge through the sludge to a rational and equitable solution. So make that story yours too. Especially on a day sometime up ahead when things seem intractable and you are almost ready to stop trying, remember you have crossed the great quadrangle of Fordham and with every step you have been prepared to be 'the crowbar', to face courageously the 'new age of demands'.

You exit into a chaotic old world. It needs leaders. It needs men and women of integrity who are determined to do their best to make things better and at the very least not to make things worse. Ask yourself whose names do you want to be counted among? The givers or the takers? The carers or the careless? The courageous or the cowed? It is after all simply a matter of choice. Your choice.

John Hughes, Henri du Merle, Jacques Lyons, Charlotte O'Brien all chose what was right in the face of so much that was wrong. May each of you never ever swerve from doing what is right in big things and in small, in private and in public and in the service of all God's magnificent and messy creation.

Go n'éirí libh.

3

THE WORLD IN IRELAND

Address to the Literary and Historical Society

University College Dublin, 11 February 2000

It is a great pleasure to be back once again at the L&H, this time with a bit more protocol attached than on my last visit when I made the promise to return. It's taken me a little while to get here, but thank you to Patrick Smyth and his predecessor as Auditor, Barry Ward, for their invitation and their patience.

Outside these four walls, this Society has a long and distinguished history as a venue for public speaking and debate. Inside these four walls, it has an equally long and terrifying history as a venue where speakers are eaten live and swallowed whole by cannibalistic audiences. The two images are not incompatible. Generations of students have honed their skills of argument, logic and persuasion here, and used them to great effect in their subsequent careers. Others with less impressive powers of persuasion and entertainment faced audiences – to quote a public speaker of many years ago – who not only looked at their watches during the speech, but started shaking them for good measure to make certain they were still going! There are even rumours of audiences running up white flags and surrendering. I'll do my best to stay out of that category.

One great advantage of coming here in the month of February is that we are now a fairly safe distance from the turn of this millennium and all of the retrospections, introspections and pyrotechnics which that event brought with it. We are off all the cusps, over all the thresholds, no longer teetering on all those brinks. This is the third millennium; these are the unscripted days replete with all those much awaited opportunities. We are living it, already shaping it and entitled to wonder aloud how the script we are writing will read, what will it tell.

It is hard to believe that the centenary of independence will probably occur in your lifetime and possibly in mine. Hard to believe that a century could be so short! Hard to believe so much could be crammed into a handful of generations. My grandfather's generation, with its memory of the 1913 Lock Out, the Rising, the Civil War, Independence, Partition, poverty, emigration, frustrated hopes – that generation lies uncomfortably close behind us, its story told in history books or in folklore.

We understand that story only imperfectly as yet, for there is not for the moment sufficient distance or detachment to give us the sharpness of perspective, the generosity of spirit to fully comprehend the mark that generation left on this country, on us. Those of you who are budding historians or political scientists or social scientists, will know the rigorous scrutiny those past lives have been and will be subjected to, their mistakes identified, analysed, endlessly debated, even endlessly derided.

Looking back, it is easy to forget that another generation not yet born will sit in similar judgement on us and when they make comparisons between the generations, they will carefully note the grim hand which was dealt to generation after generation of Irish men and women, until now, until this one. For make no mistake about it, the stakes have been raised and exponentially. This generation has been dealt aces. Now it has to play them. It has the winning of the game but it has the losing of it too. Never before has so much been realistically expected. We have had romantic dreamers, of course, maybe more than our fair share, who kept visions of a dynamic, successful Ireland alive on very thin gruel indeed. Mostly when they woke up they woke up to an absence of that dream. When we wake up, many of us, though not yet all of us, wake up to the living of it.

Today's Ireland is built on a dense complex of things; some fragile and transient, others robust and enduring. The most potent of the latter has been education. Education was the means by which parents, often themselves trapped in under-achievement because of lack of opportunity, could see an escape for their children to a better life, to those elusive opportunities denied to themselves. It was the most important equity they bequeathed to the next generation.

The provision of free second-level education in the 1960s transformed the thinking and experiential landscape of this country, altering it and us profoundly. It provided the confidence and the insight which allowed a struggling young nation to wean itself from an unhealthy over-dependence on Britain, economically, intellectually and culturally; to test itself against new markets, to follow other and better exemplars, to dig deep into our own cultural reserve here in Ireland and within the global Irish family to find new sources of energy to refresh and reinvigorate a tired psyche. At a macro level, it created the knowledge and skills base, the huge equity on which today's economic miracle has been built. But it also created a personal miracle for thousands of young men and women, opening up new ideas, drawing them into the world of knowledge, not as passive recipients but as active contributors, creators, discoverers in their own right. It gave us the tools to re-imagine our world and to believe we could shape it to that new image.

In Seamus Heaney's poem 'From the Canton of Expectation', he describes the avalanche of transformation dislodged by widening educational opportunity, how it engulfed stifled destinies and projected them, plunged them forward into a new unconquered space. But first he describes the world before education:

> ... we lived in a land of optative moods,
> under high, banked clouds of resignation.
> A rustle of loss in the phrase *Not in our lifetime*,
> the broken nerve when we prayed *Vouchsafe* or *Deign*,
> were creditable, sufficient to the day.

The dead hand of history had crippled hope, made intellectual eunuchs of successive generations, or so it seemed. Heaney describes the change brilliantly:

> And next thing, suddenly this change of mood.
> Books open in the newly-wired kitchens.
> Young heads that might have dozed a life away
> against the flanks of milking cows were busy
> paving and pencilling their first causeways
> across the prescribed texts.

> ... intelligences ... brightened and unmannerly as crowbars.

The metaphor of the crowbar is particularly apt, for their pathway was littered with many obstacles that had to be removed – the obstacles of fatalistic resignation from within and resistance to change, inequality and exclusion from without. But those generations were infused with a hunger and determination to break through the barriers, to escape the confines of traditional expectation and destiny. There was an excitement, an exhilaration about challenging the old ideologies and hierarchies, about discovering a new consciousness and a new language of equality and human rights. And all that hunger and newfound confidence energised both a search for personal achievement and a desire to make life more equal, more humanly decent for others.

The great gift that education confers is personal empowerment – the confidence and capacity to choose your own pathway through life, not a route pre-ordained by society, family or circumstance. To choose, also, how to use those talents and abilities which education has honed – whether to use them for purely personal advancement or to take a wider and more generous view of how they might be applied. The educational opportunities and choices we now possess did not materialise by magic. They were crafted slowly and painstakingly over generations by the hard work and personal sacrifice of many parents and the vision, idealism and unselfish dedication of those who chose public service, civic leadership as their vocation.

We owe so much to those individuals who never saw their dreams realised in their own lifetimes, but who sowed the seeds – to use the words of Sr Stanislaus Kennedy – that would be reaped by the next generation and the generations to follow.

The idealism that inspired that ethos of public service is as important, perhaps even more important, than ever today. It may seem at a first glance that no challenges remain. After all, we now preside over a society which has witnessed a reversal of the tide of emigration, the imminent approach of full employment, a surge in cultural confidence and pride, a greater respect for diversity, and the increasing depth and reach of the Peace Process. We can all rest happily on our laurels; hasn't paradise been regained? We know the question is ironic for already we see the downstream consequences, the equal and opposite reaction to so much that is good, the accelerating 'left-behindness' of the marginalised. This is a fast-moving society. If you are stuck and going nowhere, those who are moving disappear from view very rapidly. A society where the stuck and the moving lose sight of each other is not a healthy place.

We see it in some of the racist attitudes to economic refugees. It is of course a relatively new phenomenon for Ireland to be a land of fresh and hope-filled starts, but our experience as an emigrating nation teaches us, or should, that short-term views conduce to prejudice and stereotyping, long-term views see once tragic and confused people, settled, contributing, working, the achievements of their children and children's children a source of pride.

Some kind of earthly paradise is of course still a very long way away for many in our society, those for whom the horizon of expectations is not a five-year career plan, but how to get through the next week. Theirs is a world where the little energy each day brings is spent on basic survival, where the provision of free third-level education is tragically irrelevant to them, and even more tragically out of reach for their children. They look at the prosperity of this country not as participants but as spectators on the sideline, unable to join in, knowing only that this confident society is not their Ireland, their world.

Our very success makes the continuing blight of exclusion and poverty even more intolerable than in previous generations, for it is no longer a question of whether we have the means to tackle such problems once and for all. It now comes down to whether we as a people have the will, the imagination and the determination to address these issues and the new social challenges which have emerged: the tragic deaths of young men through suicide; the despair of drug addiction; growing levels of hostility towards asylum seekers – the list goes on. The unconvinced wonder why they should be bothered, why the lives of the poor or underachieving should be their concern – what is to be gained from trying to change things?

We have seen in the past how the widening of opportunity does not lead, as some feared, to the lowest common denominator or to a dilution of the knowledge equity. The more we expand opportunity the more we release individuals from the prison of under-achievement, the more we benefit from fulfilled, contributing individuals, from vigorous and

achieving communities. Our experience, not least in the field of education, has been that extending the reach of opportunity releases a surge of
energy which benefits the entire society. And we are still nowhere near
our full potential as a people. Our business life, our workforce, our culture, our community sector – every facet of Irish life – can benefit from
creating a society that is all centre and no margins, a society where each
child is given as her birthright effective opportunities to blossom fully.

But that society will not be created by chance, by leaving it to others
to do, or worse, by dismissing those who work in the service of others as
misguided idealists, out of touch with reality. Those who recognise that
the natural symbiosis of life in this society has not yet been achieved,
that it is still scarred by elitism and considerably short of its full potential,
are the true realists. They recognise that the faults and failings of Ireland
in the twenty-first century are not inevitable, that they are amenable to
change, and that there can be no greater challenge or fulfilment than
knowing that their commitment, their actions and their sense of hope
have made a difference to the lives of others. There is a fundamental
difference between a realism which induces cynicism and one which
provokes change. Cynics cast around for someone to blame. Changers,
doers, see not only that something needs to be done, but also that they
can contribute to bringing about that change. More importantly, they
intuit that if they do nothing then it is possible that nothing will be done.

It takes courage and independence of mind to commit to crafting the
new social dispensation which lies now within our reach. But I hope
that some of you will; that you will use the education that you have
gained here, whatever the discipline, as a springboard to participating
in Irish public life, whether in politics, the civil service, local government, social services or, dare I say it, even the Presidency. There is no
doubt that our system of governance was impoverished in past generations by the deliberate exclusion of women. That failure to make use of
so much talent, of the particular insights and perceptions that women
could have brought to bear, resulted in a lopsided and narrow process of

policy and decision-making that is only now, slowly, being reconstructed. We have an opportunity to make this century, from its outset, one which is enriched by the full participation of women in every sphere of society, and especially at the most senior levels of our public service. I believe that the will is now there for this to happen, but it can only happen if women of your generation respond to the challenge.

Our society is only as good as we make it, only as open and dynamic, as inclusive and generous, as we want it to be and work for it to be. And the evidence is all around us that there is a strong public will to make life better for all our people. Whether you look at the results of public opinion polls, or the vibrancy of community and voluntary activity, or the breadth of political discourse, Irish people consistently show a remarkable level of genuine altruism, unselfishness and concern for the welfare and wellbeing of others. They want a society they can be proud of, a place where equality of opportunity is not just an academic concept, where a decent standard of living for all is more than just an aspiration.

We are well on our way to achieving that society. We are nearer than we have ever been. We are starting to believe it is within our grasp. And yet still a small but lingering doubt remains: is it all too good to be true? Can we really make it happen?

Nelson Mandela has written:

Our deepest fear is not that we are inadequate. Our deepest fear is that we are powerful beyond measure. It is our light, not our darkness, that most frightens us … as we let our own light shine … as we are liberated from our own fear, our presence automatically liberates others.

This is a good time to believe in ourselves, in our own power, to let our light will shine, liberating a new generation, creating a decent world to be proud of, to offer its light in turn to the rest of the world. Our descendants will sit in this hall, in these seats. They will debate what we did, what we failed to do. They will apply the hardest of criteria to us and rightly, for we have been given a lot and so a lot is expected from us. We have the doing of it. We can make them proud.

REMARKS AT THE INTERNATIONAL FAMILY GARDEN PARTY

Áras an Uachtaráin, 11 July 2005

Is cúis mhór áthais dom fáilte a chur romhaibh go léir chuig Áras an Uachtaráin inniu.

Martin and I are delighted to welcome each and every one of you all here today to Áras an Uachtaráin. Céad míle fáilte – 100,000 welcomes – to each one of you and especially those who have come from so many different parts of the world.

Irish people have always taken pride in the label 'Ireland of the Welcomes'. You are the test of the strength and sincerity of that welcome and it is my fervent hope that whatever your circumstances, your dignity as a human being is honoured by all those you meet here. Not so long ago, we Irish exported our people around the world because there was so little opportunity for them at home. We have generations of experience of emigration. We know what it is to be uprooted and alone, to be full of hope and frightened at the same time. We know what it is like to live without the support of close family and community. We also have long experience of being excluded and cruelly stereotyped. Today things are different and a modern successful Ireland is now a land of opportunity that attracts men and women from far and near.

It is perhaps our historic experience of emigration and of division on this island that has given all right-minded people a strong attachment to the values of justice and equality and an aversion to bigotry and prejudice. We have witnessed an increase in ethnic diversity in Ireland in recent years. It has brought a welcome, wonderful cultural and social enrichment to this country, which we enjoy in so many ways.

We in Ireland are committed to building a society where diversity is respected, where the rights and interests of all who share our society are upheld and enhanced, and we are committed to upholding human rights and respect for the rule of law.

We especially owe it to our children to play our part in developing an intercultural society where they are comfortable with, and welcoming of, friendships with those from other countries. We want no bigotry taught in our homes or practised on our streets. Our republic honours its founders and honours its future when we insist on celebrating diversity as a way of life.

Your presence here today is precisely that: a celebration of the wonderful diversity which is such a very positive influence on life in Ireland today. Just as we Irish brought our language, music, poetry, literature, values and character as gifts to the countries in which we put down new roots, so you too bring those unique gifts of yours to us. The wells that future generations draw from will be the deeper and the better for the new tributaries that flow into them.

I hope you enjoy this historic house, that you feel welcomed here and that you will leave with happy memories and maybe a new friend or two. So take the time to reach out a hand in friendship to those you don't know – it is the quickest way and the only way to make a caring community out of strangers. The easiest bridge is the bridge of a handshake.

I would like to finish by thanking our wonderful entertainers who have helped make today so very special for all of us: the African drummers, the Kurdish children dancers, the Roma musicians and the Filipino singers, not to mention our balloon modeller and the face painters who have given so much pleasure to the youngsters. I would also like to thank members of St John's Ambulance Brigade, Civil Defence, the Gardaí, the tour guides and the staff of the Áras, particularly the gardening staff who have succeeded in making the garden perfect, just when I thought they couldn't make it any better.

Go raibh míle maith agaibh go léir.

REMARKS AT THE PERMANENT TSB ETHNIC ENTREPRENEUR OF THE YEAR AWARDS

Westin Hotel, Dublin, 6 February 2007

Dia dhíbh a chairde. Tá gliondar orm bheith anseo libh inniu ag an ócáid speisialta seo. Míle bhuíochas as an cuireadh agus an fáilte.

Good evening and thank you for both the welcome and the invitation that allows me to celebrate with you the very first business awards event focused on Ireland's growing ethnic communities. I am very grateful to Denis Casey for inviting me to this showcase of the entrepreneurial talent of those who have made Ireland their home.

And it is an impressive showcase; one which places our new minority communities in the public limelight and sets in front of us the significant and wide-ranging contribution which these communities are now making to Irish life. It is an important part of modern Ireland's story and one that Ireland needs to hear.

Not surprisingly, the idea for the award came from Chinedu Onyejelem, whose advocacy against racism and for tolerant multiculturalism is well known, and who is also the resourceful driving force behind *Metro Éireann*, Ireland's first multicultural newspaper. I want to express my appreciation for Chinedu's tireless efforts and notable achievements and to also thank all the sponsors whose generous support of these awards made them possible.

Not so long ago, Ireland's biggest export was our people who took emigrant boats and planes in their thousands because their homeland offered little opportunity. In an extraordinary shift of fortunes, the remarkable contemporary economic success has reversed the tide of emigration, bringing newfound prosperity and prospects. Many Irish emigrants have returned home and newcomers have come to Ireland from countries around the globe, attracted by the chance to create better lives for themselves and their families by twinning their talents with Ireland's opportunities. Ireland has quickly become a country of many races, languages and cultures. The richness of all that diversity, the freshness of the new talent, the imagination and creativity unleashed by the intermingling of such a variety of different aptitudes and abilities are already beginning to reveal themselves. I see it in the schools, in community organisations, in workplaces, and it is very reassuring to see the role being played in business and commerce by ethnic entrepreneurs. Today's Ireland is characterised by a strong, entrepreneurial spirit, but, as all those involved in entrepreneurial activities know, growing businesses is not for the faint-hearted. All the more credit, therefore, to our ethnic entrepreneurs who, besides the everyday risks and worries associated with self-employment, face additional burdens and face them down so successfully. Gaining access to finance and support services, overcoming language barriers, acquiring skills and knowledge of the local business and regulatory environment, and unfortunately, from time to time, having to defeat prejudice can all be additional and difficult hurdles to surmount, but the entrepreneurs in this room are proof positive that these are hurdles which can be successfully faced down and overcome.

Your determination and vision have not just helped create your own success but your efforts are helping sustain Ireland's economic success and develop our country as a comfortable homeland for all its citizens, regardless of their origin. You bring jobs and create wealth but, much more than that, your lives tell us much about Ireland's journey towards becoming a fully socially inclusive republic where everyone counts and everyone has the chance to make the best lives possible. So while this award event will select one overall 'Ethnic Entrepreneur of the Year', in reality every single participant is a winner and your success makes winners of all those who live in Ireland. You have all come through an exacting selection process in which the merits, potential and sustainability of your business project entries have been subjected to rigorous assessment by a panel of business experts and educationalists, under highly demanding selection criteria. As ethnic entrepreneurs, your success is all the more significant and meritorious given the challenges you have faced in getting your businesses off the ground – a foreign environment, language barriers, information and communication gaps, poor access to funding, unfamiliarity with our State agency system, etc. You have demonstrated an abundance of determination, a can-do ethic and a formidable will to succeed – characteristics which are hallmarks of success in business and are also essential elements in building strong, safe communities and a strong, safe country.

To each and every one of you, therefore, I offer my heartiest congratulations on being chosen to represent a particular category of the five categories of entrepreneurial performance to which this award event relates. I want you to know that the very real contribution that you are making within the economy of Ireland is respected, recognised and valued. So too are the many benefits in cultural and social enrichment which you bring to Irish society and which will continue to reveal themselves over the decades ahead.

I again congratulate all those involved in making this event happen but, most importantly of all, I want to congratulate each of today's finalists and to wish you all every success with your business plans in the future. We are delighted that you have come to share your experience with us and hope that your business life will be as enjoyable as it is productive.

Go raibh míle maith agaibh.

REMARKS AT THE CLOSING
OF ISLAMIC AWARENESS WEEK

Royal College of Surgeons of Ireland, Dublin, 26 February 2010

Good evening, ladies and gentlemen.

Thank you for the welcome to this closing ceremony for Islamic Awareness Week 2010 and a special thank you to Fathima Patel for the kind invitation that allows me to be part of this special event through which the story of Islam and of our Muslim neighbours in Ireland and around the world is showcased, celebrated and explained to a wide audience.

Recent years have seen Ireland change dramatically through a remarkable increase in inward migration by people from all over the world. What once was a tiny trickle suddenly grew to become an important tributary. Ours is now a very culturally diverse place where the citizens of 188 countries make their lives and livelihoods. They have brought a rich mix of languages, religions, customs, traditions, histories and perspectives. They have come to a young republic whose people fought long and hard for the right to a free society where all citizens are cherished equally. They have come to a country whose sons and daughters were often emigrants in strange lands themselves. They have come to a country which knows a bitter thing or two about religious and ethnic intolerance and where even the most recent history teaches us that it is possible for neighbours to live next door to one another and yet live in profound ignorance of one another's culture and identity. We have learnt through the divisions between Christians on this island how vital it is that there is good, respectful mutual awareness and we have learnt the awful cost of failing to invest in that awareness; how fears, stereotypes, hostile attitudes and presumptions can take the place of friendship and informed awareness.

Historically, Ireland's links with the world of Islam have been relatively modest. They have largely been forged by Muslim students from many countries who paid us the compliment of undertaking their academic and professional studies here. They have proved to be wonderful ambassadors not just for their countries, faith and culture, but for Ireland, for wherever they have gone in the world they have spoken well of us, opened doors to us and become voluntary advocates for Ireland. Some made their lives here, contributing greatly to the breadth of Irish civic and political life and implanting in Irish life a growing consciousness of the Islamic faith. And it was in fact Muslim students studying here who established the first Islamic Society in Ireland, far back in 1959. Today Ireland's Muslim population, though still relatively small, has been augmented by inward migration and by a large international student population. It is important to acknowledge here the very positive contribution that Islamic students make to Irish society and to our economy. They are helping to advance the frontiers of science, medicine and research; it is their encouraging experience of Ireland that helps our higher education institutions compete for students and recognition in this globalised world. Islamic and Muslim student societies are very active in colleges across the country, promoting awareness and fostering relationships across different cultures. That investment, which I hope is matched by a curiosity and a welcome from those who know little about Islam, is essential if we are to fully live our claim to be a place of many traditions about one community.

My warmest congratulations to all those in the Federation of Student Islamic Societies who have put such effort into this week of celebration of Muslim faith and culture. Through a large variety of activities and events ranging from seminars to food festivals to charity events, Islamic Awareness Week plays an important part in educating our society about it and its members. The spirit of this week is the path to understanding and I hope that as the week comes to a close, more and more people will have joined the journey of mutual understanding which is so essential for the development of a tolerant, peaceful, safe and nurturing society.

Ireland has been on a steep multicultural learning curve and there is plenty of evidence of a strong willingness to honour our reputation as a place of welcome. At Government level we have a minister with a special responsibility for the integration of our migrant communities. We have State and voluntary organisations and agencies devoted to building a genuinely intercultural society and doing the work at community level which promotes the fullest inclusion of all who share this island. The student societies which have come together to organise this week have made themselves part of that vital civic endeavour. They are terrific examples, inspirational examples of active citizenship. They undertook the work not for personal reward but for the fulfilment that comes from building bridges from person to person, from culture to culture, from faith to faith and country to country. We all benefit when those bridges are strong and when they become the pathway to mutual understanding. Those who organised this week have already busy lives and yet they value both Islam and Ireland so greatly that they put an enormous effort into this week. All those who organised and participated should be very proud of the success of Islamic Awareness Week. I am very proud of them all.

Remarks at the Immigrant Council of Ireland Conference 'Diverse Views on Diversity – A Discussion about Identity and Inclusion'

Royal Irish Academy, Dublin, 3 November 2010

Dia daoibh a dhaoine uaisle. Tá an-athas orm bheith anseo libh ag Acadamh Ríoga na hÉireann. Míle buíochas daoibh as an gcuireadh agus an fáilte cairdiúil thug sibh dom, anseo inniu.

Good morning everyone.

It is good to be back in the Royal Irish Academy for this seminar on 'Diverse Views on Diversity' – not the first time the Academy has hosted an event that invites us to carefully scrutinise the increasingly mosaic nature of our society and how well we are coping with diversity. My thanks to the Immigrant Council of Ireland and particularly to Sr Stanislaus Kennedy for inviting me, and to each one of you for making this issue your business, maybe even your mission.

The American poet Maya Angelou, once said:

> We all should know that diversity makes for a rich tapestry, and we must understand that all the threads of the tapestry are equal in value no matter what their colour.

That is not simply an image, it is a philosophy. It is a way of understanding the individual human person's place in the broader society that is shared root and branch with the founding values of our country. It finds expression in the Proclamation's lovely words about cherishing the children of the nation equally. It finds expression in our Constitution, where every citizen is regarded as equal and where the dignity and freedom of the individual is assured. These words are not just words; they are intended to be a way of living, of acting and of thinking. People are meant to see them at work in their lives, in how they are dealt with by the State and by their neighbours. People are meant to put them to work in their lives in how they treat others. It's a simple philosophy of mutual respect and tolerance that is intolerant of prejudice, bigotry and racism and it is a philosophy that has come into its own in these contemporary times, when its robustness, its embeddedness has been tested by the many newcomers who are now part of our communities and our citizenry. Ireland's future will be crafted by men, women and children whose families have been here for generations and families who are newcomers from all over the world. To the extent that they work well and comfortably together, ours will be a good place, a safe and healthy place for all our children to grow up and to live.

We already know that it is possible for groups of people to live side by side in dangerous ignorance of one another – just look at the story of Northern Ireland. Our history of being emigrants in other countries over generations has taught us about the courage and resilience of emigrants, their invaluable contribution to new homelands, their generosity to their birthplaces, their loneliness and the awful impact on them of deliberate exclusion or demonisation.

Now Ireland has the chance and the challenge to do things differently from those other countries where migrants live in parallel societies, where people are ghettoised, consigned to poverty and feel unwelcome. During our economic boom we became, for the first time, a country of net inward migration, with migrants from almost 200 countries. Through the current economic retrenchment some have left but many have stayed, for they came to make Ireland their home for the long term. Their futures are here. Their children's futures are here and their genius, skill and hard work will impact hugely on that future. I meet the children regularly in our schools, where their full embrace of Irish culture is outstanding. It says a lot about them and about the openness and attractiveness of Irish culture that they are so curious about Irish culture while continuing to value, practise and showcase to the rest of us their own languages and traditions.

In these times of economic retrenchment, where the story of our export sector is a shining light of hope, it is worth reminding ourselves as we work hard to sell goods and services across the globe and to break into new markets, that for the first time in our history we have a cadre of Irish citizens who are steeped in the languages, customs and practices of many of those countries we aim to do business with. That is a very robust platform from which to court those markets and from which to attract inward investors who are looking for a wide variety of skills in today's competitive global economy. Our emigrants strengthen us for the future that we face and Ireland has a vested interest in ensuring that Ireland of the Welcomes is what they experience in their homes, streets, workplaces, classrooms and communities.

A society where people feel they must lose their ethnic or cultural identity in order to 'fit in' does not meet the high standards of tolerance or inclusivity that we have set for ourselves and insisted on for ourselves around the world and indeed even in our own country. Our Irish emigrants took with them their music, language, sport, literature, culture, religion and traditions. Their influence in every sphere of life in many parts of the world is incalculable and phenomenal. The stories of those who have emigrated to Ireland will be no less remarkable.

I hope your deliberations here will help all of us who share this country to prepare the ground well for a shared future of comfortable diversity and easy, organic integration. Each individual has it in his or her hands to prepare that ground by being interested in each other's wellbeing. Each street and community has the opportunity and responsibility to try to draw everyone into friendship and good neighbourliness. We want ours to be a society of people who care about each other, not a society of strangers. It cannot happen if we do nothing but the rewards for getting it right are peace on our streets, peace in our hearts, commitment to one another, commitment to our country and the fulfilment of our ambition to be a republic of equals.

I wish you every success with this important conference and thank you all for the excellent work you are doing in ensuring that all those who come to our shores receive a sustained and a nurturing, traditional Irish céad míle fáilte.

Go raibh míle maith agaibh go léir.

4

INAUGURATION (2004)

A Uaisle,

Is le gairdeas croí, le buíochas agus le humhlaíocht a labhraím libh anseo ar maidin, agus mé ar tí tosú amach ar an dara tréimhse seacht mbliana de sheirbhís an phobail. Is mór an phribhléid dom a bheith tofa arís mar Uachtarán na hÉireann. Is é mo ghuí agus mo rún daingean dualgaisí na hardoifige seo a chomhlíonadh go hionraic, coinsiasach.

I begin this second term as President of Ireland with fresh anticipation, proud to represent one of the world's most successful and dynamic countries, with a rags to riches, conflict to peace story that I know inspires many in a troubled world.

Ireland has vaulted from the despondency of 'ceann faoi' to the confidence of 'can do' in a remarkably short time. With so much changing both at home and in the world around us, today is a good opportunity to take stock and reflect on the Ireland that I will represent in a role outside of politics but inside the lives of our people.

We are a country of newly opened doors instead of emigrant boats, flying on two wings, propelled by the combined genius of our men and our women. We wrestle with our prosperity almost as much as we relish it. We are loudly impatient for many frustratingly inadequate things to be better. We worry about matters that hollow out our optimism like youth suicide, racism, binge drinking, street crime and corruption. We know our current economic success cannot be a destination in itself but a route to one of our primary ambitions as a nation – to bring prosperity and security to every single citizen. We have struggled with that other ambition for the unity of our island, agreeing overwhelmingly to an honourable compromise in which we acknowledged the right of the people of Northern Ireland to decide their own destiny and declared our desire to work with them in peaceful partnership.

Cherishing the best of our past, we turn to our future not knowing exactly what it holds but with a clear idea of the hard work ahead of us – work for all of us as citizens and not simply for government alone.

We are busier than before, harder to please, less heedful of the traditional voices of moral guidance and almost giddy with greater freedom and choice. Our Constitution is an important ethical compass, directing us to a practical patriotism, 'to promote the common good', to choose responsible citizenship over irresponsible individualism. Our population is growing; new neighbourhoods of strangers are springing up. Immigrants bring with them different cultures and embrace the richness of ours, as I have observed in the schools where their children speak to me proudly in Irish. Infrastructure of all sorts is struggling to catch up, including the human infrastructure we offer each other through friendship and community solidarity. The cushion of consumerism is no substitute for the comfort of community. And if our country is to be strong and resilient in the face of its problems and its ambitions in this time of transformation, it needs strong resilient communities.

I have been privileged, as President, to see the colossal work undertaken by the individuals, organisations and partnerships that support and sustain our nation's great heartland of community. Community cannot be created by government and it doesn't happen by coincidence. We make it happen ourselves by unselfishly committing our talents, our money and that precious commodity, time, to the service of each other. It will be my mission to nurture and celebrate commitment to community and to responsible citizenship, and to encourage self-belief among the most marginalised. I intend to reach out to our wonderful young people, willing them on to become good leaders rather than the badly led – problem-solvers rather than problems. When I look at the solid work and great imagination that have created our economic miracle, our Peace Process, our vibrant culture, our respected place in international politics, when I remember the massive effort that gave us the Special Olympics, I am reassured that there is little we cannot deal with effectively if we work together.

If community solidarity is vital to social stability and progress at home, global solidarity is equally vital in world affairs, all the more so in an era when the multilateral ethos of the United Nations has come under strain. Today, 11 November, is Armistice Day – a commemoration of those dreadful years when Europeans killed each other in their millions. How different Europe is now. On 1 May, Áras an Uachtaráin hosted the Day of Welcomes as the European Union grew to twenty-five Member States and their leaders gathered under one roof for the first time since the First World War. Ireland has played a hugely significant role in the development of our Union and its values of democracy, human rights, respect for difference and consensus-based politics. The opportunities created by enlargement are waiting to be harvested and I look forward to promoting our country within the Union and to showcasing our membership of the Union around the world.

Ireland's fortunes are linked to global politics as never before and though we are a small, peripheral island, we have a fascinating and exceptional engagement with the world that spans every conceivable connection, from centuries-old ties of religion and kinship, through championing of the world's poor, to trade in the most sophisticated modern technologies, in which we are market leaders. As President I have a key role in the renewal and development of ties to our global Irish family, Ireland's unpaid ambassadors, who make our name and nature known throughout the world. We have experienced the considerable benefits that flow from those intimate friendships. As one of the world's leading export nations we have also come to realise the vast potential that lies in befriending and trading with countries not so well known to us. I will continue to make it my responsibility to assist in the development of our trade in new markets, to get to know new peoples and their cultures, and so help to secure both our nation's wellbeing and global solidarity.

The great divide between rich and poor nations, already worsened by the calamity of AIDS and knowledge poverty, has become more complex still as East–West divisions sharpen alarmingly and dangerous tensions fester. Neutral Ireland is uniquely qualified for the crucial, painstaking work of establishing understanding and trust across those cultural chasms. We are widely respected. We have a talent for friendship, a history of transition from a third-world to a first-world country and a wholehearted commitment to international institutions and international law. I look forward to playing a part in building the human bridges of mutual respect and care which are so necessary to end the cycle of human misery and to keep our world safe.

Seven years ago, the bridge of peace on this island was a structure in the making. Today, more people than ever are committed to its construction and the once massive gulf of mistrust has been reduced to one last step. I use this occasion to ask the hesitant to muster the courage to complete the journey across and let the bright new landscape of hope reveal itself. For my part, I pledge to do my best to make us comfortable in each other's company and unafraid of a shared future.

Many people are working hard to make ours a country, a people and a time to be proud of. I offer thanks to them and for them. I thank everyone who has helped me these past seven years and who gave me the confidence to stand again. I again ask those of faith to pray for me and for our beloved country so that in these coming years we will leave a legacy of good for our children – a legacy so memorably anticipated by Seamus Heaney on 1 May when he exhorted us to:

Move lips, move minds and make new meanings flare.

Dia dar gcumhdach agus dar stiuradh! Go raibh míle maith agaibh.

5

A CARING IRELAND

Inaugural Amnesty International Annual Lecture

Queen's University Belfast, 17 November 1998

Mr Chairman, Vice-Chancellor, distinguished guests, ladies and gentlemen,

It is always a great pleasure for me to return to my hometown and my *alma mater*. I am particularly pleased and proud to have been invited to deliver this Inaugural Amnesty International Annual Lecture. The theme chosen by Amnesty, 'Rights and Responsibilities: Fifty Years of the Universal Declaration', could hardly be more appropriate and timely as we approach 10 December, the date of the adoption of the Declaration in 1948.

It is also appropriate that I take this opportunity to pay tribute to Amnesty International, which, since its foundation by Peter Beneson in 1961, has investigated more than 43,500 cases of alleged violations of human rights and has succeeded – to its enormous credit – in closing more than 40,750 of those cases.

During most of its history, Amnesty's campaigning has focused on prisoners, but the movement has responded to the changing patterns of human rights violations in the world, and has taken action on behalf of people who are not prisoners. It has worked tirelessly against hostage-taking and arbitrary killings, and for asylum-seekers who are at risk of being returned to countries where they might be held as prisoners of conscience or suffer a worse fate.

For all these efforts, Amnesty was awarded the Nobel Peace Prize in 1977 and the UN Human Rights Prize in 1978, and deserves our eternal gratitude and thanks.

The Amnesty symbol, a candle in barbed wire, was inspired by the Chinese proverb, 'It is better to light a candle than to curse the darkness.' The adoption of this proverb as its motto illustrates the positive and practical approach that Amnesty has taken since its inception towards the vindication of human rights. To mark the fiftieth anniversary of the Universal Declaration, Amnesty launched a campaign to compile the world's largest book, made up of pledges by individuals to do their utmost to uphold the rights proclaimed in the Declaration. I was honoured to be the first person in Ireland to make that pledge and since then thousands of Irishmen and women and millions of people throughout the world have added their names to this book. It will be presented to the Secretary General of the United Nations on Human Rights Day, 10 December.

In addressing you on this evening's theme, you will appreciate the deep pride I – and Irish people everywhere – take in the part my predecessor, Mary Robinson, plays in the vital work of human rights advocacy throughout the world as UN Commissioner for Human Rights. I know you will join me in wishing her well in meeting the formidable challenges she faces.

What, then, of the fiftieth anniversary? Have we cause for celebration? The first ever proclamation by the international community of the rights and freedoms of every human being surely deserves to be commemorated. As too does its fostering of the promotion and protection of those rights. But as we look at the contemporary world scene, many of us might conclude that there can be no cause for celebration while everyday hundreds of millions of people experience some serious violations of their human rights. Many of them are children, women, old people, people with disabilities, minorities, migrants and indigenous peoples. The violations they suffer range from torture and arbitrary detention, to hunger and homelessness, from violence against and trafficking in women and children, to child labour.

However, it would also be wrong to neglect to acknowledge that notable achievements have been registered since the adoption of the Universal Declaration. The United Nations Covenants on Civil and Political Rights and Economic, Social and Cultural Rights have been ratified by most of its Member States. Conventions on racism, torture, the rights of the child and the elimination of discrimination against women are also in place, setting standards for conduct to which individual states can be held accountable by UN monitoring committees.

We could, therefore, conclude that the Universal Declaration has made the world a better place, but much remains to be done. We can never be complacent about the progress made in protecting human rights. It is a sad fact that the norms of civilised behaviour are not being respected in many parts of the world.

Against this background, the Universal Declaration stands as a beacon; one of inspiration to those who seek to surmount the darker side of the human condition and one of reproach to those who trample on the rights of their fellow men and women in their search for political, economic or personal gain.

Today, there are some hopeful signs that our definition of what it is to be human extends to a growing sense of international community and solidarity. Almost all civilised people regard it as wrong that millions should die in famines. They would see it as unacceptable that tyrants should violate the basic rights of their people. They would also support policies to bridge the gap between abject poverty and deprivation in developing countries and affluence in developed countries. Yet, all these violations of basic human rights continue. Could it be that – for all our horror or outrage over the atrocities and disasters that make up too many of the media headlines – a sense of numbness or impotence has caused us to lose faith in the capacity of human beings for good? How do we muster and sustain the global improvements needed to tackle these issues and make a difference?

The lamenters and cynics sound and look concerned but accomplish little. It is the doers who make the real difference, and it is the doers like Amnesty members that we need. Lamentation and cynicism are the easy ways out.

The responsibilities mentioned in the title of this lecture refer to the obligation on us all to use the fiftieth anniversary to give new impetus to the promotion and protection of human rights. On a global level, the High Commissioner for Human Rights has been using this benchmark year to examine the progress of the Member States of the UN in the field of human rights.

All UN Member States and UN agencies were required to submit a report earlier this year outlining the implementation of human rights standards within their jurisdiction. All were found wanting – some more than others. How could it be otherwise? The subject of human rights is not one for governments. The promotion and protection of human rights requires constant attention and no Government or bureaucracy can be counted on to remain consistently vigilant. This is why so much responsibility rests on civil society, non-governmental organisations and other activists to continue to press for respect for human rights whenever or wherever they see the need.

What should be the guiding principles which give meaning to rededicating ourselves to the principles of the Universal Declaration? Many of these appear self-evident but they should never be passed over in silence. In trying to put these ideas into practice, we should 'think global and act local'.

The Good Friday Agreement, which offers so much hope to everyone on this island, also represents a major advance in the protection of human rights throughout Ireland. It was agreed by all sides on 10 April that any new institutional arrangements must be complemented and underpinned by the systematic and effective protection of human rights. The issue of human rights is not part of any nationalist or unionist agenda – it is the preserve of all citizens of this island.

The United Kingdom will shortly complete the incorporation of the European Convention on Human Rights into their own domestic legislation. In our jurisdiction, the Government will bring forward measures to strengthen the constitutional protection of human rights – taking account of the work of the All-Party Oireachtas Committee on the Constitution and the Report of the Constitution Review Group. The measures brought forward will ensure at least an equivalent level of protection of human rights as will pertain in Northern Ireland.

The two Governments have agreed to the establishment of new Human Rights Commissions in both jurisdictions on this island. This is an exciting new development. The new Human Rights Commissions will be among the first of their kind in Western Europe. However, institutions such as these cannot be expected to address all the human rights issues which are currently occupying Governments and the international community. Nor are such bodies intended to replace the human rights organs of the United Nations or NGOs working in the field.

There are some who see no good reason for establishing special machinery devoted to the promotion and protection of human rights. They may argue that such bodies are not a wise use of scarce resources and that an independent judiciary and democratically elected parliament are sufficient to ensure that human rights abuses do not occur.

Unfortunately, history has taught us differently. An institution which is in some way separated from the responsibilities of executive governance and judicial administration is in a position to take a leading role in the field of human rights. By maintaining a real and perceived distance from governments of the day, such bodies can make a unique contribution to countries' efforts to protect their citizens and to develop a culture of respect for human rights and fundamental freedoms.

In Ireland, there will be a further unique feature in that the agreement also envisages that there will be a joint committee linking the two new commissions. This joint committee will act as a forum for considering human rights matters throughout the island of Ireland.

In our justifiable enthusiasm following the ending of violence and the arrival of a new, more peaceful era, there is a danger that the victims of violence could be overlooked. However, the agreement acknowledges that the provision of services that are supportive and sensitive to the needs of victims is a critical element in any process of reconciliation. So often it can appear that the victims are expected to do all the forgiving. They need our understanding, encouragement and help to come to terms with what happened to them and their loved ones. They, perhaps more than anyone else, are entitled to enjoy the rewards of peace. Here again, our responsibilities and their rights must be invoked.

So here at home we have some grounds for believing that things will be better – that respect for the human rights of all can soon be taken as a given.

Fifty years on, there is a need for an acknowledgement of the role played by human rights in restoring fully functioning and legitimate democratic systems in Europe. There is a need for a renewed commitment to human rights, since the task of honouring the person does not have any logical endpoint and must continue. New problems are emerging – problems that require the civilising and humanising influence of human rights. New roles need to be found for rights to meet the kinds of challenges posed by social and economic change over the next fifty years.

The politico-legal architecture of Europe has, for a variety of historical reasons, segregated two sides of the one coin: the pursuit of common economic development and the policing of moral limits on State power. This phenomenon has been exemplified in the mandates and roles played, up until recently, by the then European Communities and the Council of Europe. We are presently witnessing a trend (perhaps historically necessary) whereby these two supranational tasks are beginning to merge. In one sense, the European Union is returning to its roots, which had more to do with political goals than with economic goals. In another sense, we are moving beyond purely economic goals, because this is the natural result of the success of the economic venture. The economic dimension to the Union is ultimately a means and not an end. The end is self-evident after two bloody World Wars, with their epicentres in Europe and their legacies the miles of young graves and the gas chambers of Auschwitz: the end is peace through partnership. Today we are witnessing a return to those humanitarian ends (or a progression forward to new ends) that makes this moment in time so unique, exacting and intriguing.

The development of the human face of the European Union, as is to be expected with a changing institution, will be highly problematic. This will be so on several counts. First, it will have to be seen if the legal base of the EU endows the institution with the competence to act in this field. Second, the margins defining the sovereign rights of the Member States and their relationship to the Union will be called into question. Third, the role of the Council of Europe in this new situation will have to be examined.

There are a number of considerations facing Europe today which cannot be left out of the reckoning in any debate on the new directions it may take.

Equality

Equality is fundamental both to human rights and to efficient and rational economic markets. Furthermore, equality contributes to the task of building more inclusive societies, which is one of the most pressing concerns of Europe today. Where gender equality pointed the way, other applications of the equality principle must follow (such as race, the elderly, people with disabilities, sexual orientation). One cogent idea might be to use human rights to animate the notion of a 'Europe for All'. Equality is a core concern because wrapped up in it is some sense of the inherent worth of each person and – just as important – a sense of the equal inherent worth of all persons. Modern trends already being experienced in Europe are likely to put this concept under incredible pressure. These trends, regrettably, can often work in the direction of exclusion. The language of human rights must be deployed to keep pathways into public life open to all.

Social Change

The development and modernisation of the European Social Model (social protection systems, healthcare systems) is taking place because of demographic trends and fiscal constraints. This process of change has obvious implications for social cohesion. Underpinning changes with the language and normative content of human rights (including, obviously, economic and social rights) – in other words mainstreaming human rights, putting it into every policy area – adds a vital dimension to the process.

The Information Society Revolution

This revolution carries with it much more than the old familiar concerns about data protection. For one thing, the Information Society will change the nature and organisation of work. The economic base of our lives will be transformed and this will have social implications that cannot be fully predicted. In short, it will offer both opportunities for the advancement of humanity and much cause for concern. What is critically important is that the construction and regulation of the Information Society should be closely tied to human rights and the values that inspire them. This technology is a tool at the service of humanity – not the reverse. We need to enhance democracy through the advantages bestowed by technology and use it to build a more inclusive society and economy. We must also take care to tackle and regulate effectively the misuse of the Information Society. This is particularly urgent in relation to the protection of children from open, indiscriminate, 'web-flooding' abuse of freedom of use of the internet while maintaining a balance with freedom of expression.

Scientific and Technological Change

Without any doubt, the advances to be made in science (in genetics, for example) and technology over the coming fifty years will be stunning and even frightening. These advances will come whether we like it or not. They are ours to cope with and to be ready to deal with ethically. The problem with such scientific change is that it tends to nurture the viewpoint that people and society are best organised along rational and scientific lines. This has been a danger ever since the Industrial Revolution and will press heavily into the next century. That's why we need confident voices reminding us that the human person is the heart of the matter; the valued, respected human person. As President John F. Kennedy said in his inauguration address, 'the rights of man come not from the generosity of the State, but from the hand of God'.

These are some of the considerations which, in my view, should inform our approach to promoting and protecting human rights in the Europe of 2000 and beyond. We live in exciting times; whether that is our good fortune or misfortune, our Eden or Gethsemane, I will leave to your own judgement. Of one thing we should be certain: fifty years after the adoption of the Universal Declaration of Human Rights, it is now time for us all to try to make a difference. We cannot change the past but we can use today well to write a new script for the future.

Thank you.

Toast at the Franklin Delano Roosevelt International Disability Award Dinner

5 May 1999

Mo bhuíochas libh arís as an onóir mhór seo.

Once again may I thank the Franklin and Eleanor Roosevelt Institute and the World Committee on Disability for the great honour they have done in presenting the Franklin Delano Roosevelt International Disability Award to Ireland.

It is greatly appreciated, not only as recognition of the efforts which we have been making in recent years to develop a fully inclusive society, a society in which people with disabilities, indeed in which all of us can reach our full potential, but also as a spur to us to continue to invest every effort in this important task in the years ahead.

Finally, may I express my deep appreciation for the warm welcome which I have received here today – it has truly been a most memorable occasion – and conclude by wishing the Roosevelt Institute every success in its vitally important work.

Go raibh maith agaibh go léir. Guím rath agus séan ar bhur gcuid oibre san am atá ag teacht.

REMARKS AT THE LAUNCH OF THE COMBAT POVERTY REPORT 'WOMEN AND POVERTY IN IRELAND'

27 May 1999

May I begin by thanking the Combat Poverty Agency and especially its Director, Hugh Frazer, for their kind invitation to launch 'Women and Poverty in Ireland' – a valuable and incisive examination of the causes and effects of female poverty in Ireland today.

It is a subject in which I have a keen interest and which the authors have presented clearly and comprehensively. The report takes as its starting point the results of the 1994 Living in Ireland Survey, which show that the risk of poverty for women remains higher than that for men. Ominously, it also shows that the poverty risk for female-headed households is increasing relative to male-or couple-headed households.

We need to ask ourselves how this has arisen. Ten years ago, our present prosperity as a society would have seemed a utopian but impossible dream. We can justifiably take pride in all we have achieved, not least as a result of the contribution made by women in this country. For I believe that the broadening of educational, training and employment opportunities for women, which released so much pent-up energy and locked-up talent, has played a significant role in our current economic success and cultural confidence. The experience of women is proof that the more we broaden opportunities for other marginalised groups – the disabled, the poor, the socially excluded – the greater economic and social rewards we can expect to reap as a nation.

Yet this report demonstrates that we still have some distance to travel, not least in the case of women. We cannot afford to let pride in our achievements hide the reality of the poverty that still faces so many women. We cannot count ourselves as a total success unless all our people are enabled to share the benefits of that prosperity. We need to know why it is that the risk of poverty among female-headed households, far from declining, actually rose between 1987 and 1994.

Perhaps this report's greatest success is in the way it isolates the causes for this position and pinpoints factors such as household composition, the economic status of household members and dependency on welfare payments as major contributory factors in the relatively declining position of women. If we know the causes, we can create informed solutions, and this has been one of the major achievements of organisations such as the Combat Poverty Agency and the Economic and Social Research Institute. Their primary research on poverty and social exclusion issues, as well as careful analyses of existing data, sheds light both on the problems that we face and potential solutions. It then boils down to whether we, as a society, possess the will and commitment to make equality and the elimination of poverty, in all its facets, the goal to which all our energies are directed. I believe that we do. More importantly, this generation, more than any other, has the resources of money and insight to ensure a new script is written.

There are some who would wring their hands and tell us, 'the poor are always with us' or 'if you lived in my day, you'd know what hardship really was!' There are others who know that nothing is impossible if we have enough goodwill and determination – look at our economic and cultural success. They know, too, that poverty is always relative, not an absolute, because it relates to the way we experience our world and the resources and opportunities we can offer our children in relation to the children of others. We must look at the figures, but also beyond the figures to the reality of the lives they describe.

This report shows us that we cannot afford to become complacent. But I do not see this as a report that simply offers us bad news. In fact, it offers hope to poorer women and women in general in the sense that it identifies the relevant issues and presents us with opportunities for action.

And one must think how much worse the situation might be were it not for the numerous women's groups, working in both rural and urban areas, who provide support for women in all circumstances. I have visited many of these groups since becoming President, and their dedication and commitment to improving the lives of women – particularly those from disadvantaged areas – is an example to us all and one which deserves the utmost praise. Community groups have a unique role in the sense that they experience the problems of poverty and exclusion on a day-to-day basis, in a real and living environment, and as such can effectively contribute to tackling these problems at their roots. They cannot do so on their own. They can only be truly successful if the system within which they operate identifies and tackles inequality. But they are a major component in finding and implementing solutions.

Finding solutions and making them work here in Ireland offers hope not just to the women of Ireland but to the many women worldwide who are still waiting, waiting in quiet despair and desperation for their own liberation from cultures of stultifying oppression and hardship. I think today of the women of Honduras who carry an unequal share of the burden of rebuilding their poor, devastated country. Eighty per cent of their households are headed by women alone – women who have to find the heart and energy to get up in the morning, make the bricks which will give them a home and cope with a culture of domestic violence which further robs them of hope and self-confidence. Let us hope the efforts that are made here will be successful and be a witness to a better world.

We speak, perhaps exhaustingly so, of new approaches and outlooks as we approach the year 2000. Yet each unlived day ahead offers a place to start anew. This report can help us make that start. Once again, may I congratulate Brian Nolan and Dorothy Watson, the authors of 'Women and Poverty in Ireland'.

MILLENNIUM LECTURE
ON THE MARGINALISED CHILD

28 February 2000

It was with great pleasure that I accepted the invitation from Fr Ken McCabe and his colleagues to join you here this evening and to deliver the fourth in this series of lectures on the 'Marginalised Child' for the Lillie Road Centre Group.

The list of previous speakers in this series suggests that I have some fairly hard acts to follow – people such as my good friend Professor Tony Clare, who is of course Chairman of tonight's proceedings. It is doubly intimidating to hear that the Lillie Road Centre Group received enough sponsorship and inspiration from its first lecture here in Dublin to help fund the purchase of a new house in Edenderry. I am not quite sure what sort of value accountants place on Presidential speeches these days, but in case of disappointment, I intend to do the predictable lawyer thing and enter a disclaimer by pleading rising house prices.

A good starting point in any discussion about the marginalised child is to define, or at least explore, what we mean by 'marginalised'. Definitions of that word include, 'relegated to the fringes', 'out of the mainstream' and 'made to seem unimportant'. Those definitions capture something of the lopsided relationships set up by marginalisation, the remoteness from power, the sense of abandonment, the downstream demoralisation that any human being feels when he or she feels or is made to feel inconsequential or left out, left behind.

There are aspects of marginalisation which are easily measured and visible: low incomes, poor housing, early school-leaving, problems with literacy, family dysfunction, and so on, down a line of cause-and-effect manifestations which spin into a complex web. There are aspects of marginalisation which are not so easily measured but which are dire in their consequences because they arise from the insidious psychology of being excluded and feeling excluded.

There is an expression in the Irish language which captures it and which used to be used to describe a national attitude – the ceann faoi. We know how destructive nationally that was, how it insinuated its way into hearts and souls, de-energising them, demotivating them. We also know the radical transformation that comes when a nation looks out to the world with its shoulders back, its head up – when success begins to breed success. It looks at itself differently and others look at it differently. A whole new set of relationships is established, new energies and synergies are released.

The marginalised child still lives with the ceann faoi syndrome; low self-esteem, low self-worth, under-achievement, little lives slowly closed down by the weight of internal and external pressures. And in this world where we are beginning to recognise that failure to properly support, encourage and develop human potential is like throwing away a fortune, the marginalised child has to be for us a particular centre both of economic gravity as well as a natural place for the egalitarian impulse of a republic of equals to challenge itself and chart its future. This is a country now hungry to achieve its full potential. We have seen the remarkable downstream advantages of widened educational access, of greater social mobility and of the release into the national knowledge grid of the energies of constituencies previously held hostage by the dead hand of history and bias. The case of women and their huge contribution to this dynamic Ireland makes the point particularly well. Seamus Heaney makes the same point in his poem 'From the Canton of Expectation' when he contrasts two generations, beginning with that of his parents, accepting, almost acquiescing in their second-class citizenship, living, as he says, 'under high, banked clouds of resignation'. Then comes the next generation, who have free education offered to them, and:

> ... next thing, suddenly, this change of mood.
> Books open in the newly-wired kitchens.
> Young heads that might have dozed a life away
> against the flanks of milking cows were busy
> paving and pencilling their first causeways
> across the prescribed texts ...

That new generation flooded into schools, colleges, institutes and universities, expanding the national knowledge equity while simultaneously expanding the reach of both the individual and community. Knowing what we now know – knowing that we can say emphatically that widening access does not dilute this thing called knowledge, does not divide into smaller parts this thing called opportunity but in fact does the very reverse – we must surely have a sense of urgency and excitement about unlocking the potential of those whose lives are still 'dozed' away.

Those whom we identify as the marginalised are a large part of our national unlocked potential. Without the full value of their contribution we will always, as a society, be operating below par – economically, culturally and socially.

But unlocking that potential is itself problematic. How do we get this marginalised child to the centre? How do we secure a decent future for the children we know will be born tomorrow and the next day, and whose place and circumstances of birth will allow statisticians to predict with some accuracy that this child will probably never see the inside of a college, will probably never hold down a decent job?

Those of us who are the first generation of our clans to go on to university, those who come from poor or modest circumstances, who went to school along with people and are perhaps related to those who today are described as the marginalised, have some particular experiential insight to offer into this complex web of circumstance and structure, of the personal, the familial, the bad luck, the good luck, the community

weaknesses and strengths which made the difference between a successful human outcome and an unsuccessful outcome.

One thing we know is that some stories defy the statisticians' logic
– that predictions do not always get it right. We all know the success
stories that flew in the face of a battery of adversity, we know people
who have escaped from the margins – we may even be those people
ourselves. The wall between margins and centre is not as impenetrable as
it looks, but sometimes you have to get in very, very close to see where
the bridges are; into the life of grandma and grandda, the relationship
between mother and father, the mental and spiritual health of the home,
the homemaking skills, the involvement with the community, the effec-
tiveness of the school, the maturity of the peer group, the strength of
character of the individual – a myriad of accidental, coincidental, plan-
nable and unplannable, foreseeable and unforeseeable facts, changeable
and unchangeable events and circumstances which weave themselves
into the web in which each of us is held – whether as spider, free to
come and go, to shape and reshape, or as fly, trapped, lost in a landscape
not entirely of our making.

Life teaches us that some of those webs are more robust than others;
some are better places for children to grow and develop. Where they
do not develop organically or spontaneously, can we manufacture them,
replicate them or create an effective equivalent? Where they are weak
can we do things to make them stronger? These are the questions which
exercise and have exercised politicians, educationalists, social scientists,
the care service, and anyone who ever wanted a more humanly decent
society. Those who have pursued this Holy Grail professionally know
that we have been engaged in a process of revelation through trial and
error, and we still see through the mists only dimly.

Webs are curious things to mess about with. Pull one bit and the
whole fragile edifice can shudder. It isn't even easy to see an obvious
entry point, but as good a place as any to begin in the life of a child is the
place which dominates the early landscape: the home, the family. In that

part of the web – and it is only part – lie insights which, coherently used, can provide us with the kinds of signposts to comprehension we will need if we are ever to draw the margins to the centre.

The twentieth century seems to have been one long debate about the family, often shedding more heat than light on the topic. Discussion always seems vulnerable to ideological jousting. What is beyond doubt, however, is that the family, however defined, plays a significant role in a child's development. As Robbie Gilligan has remarked:

> … what happens to children within their families, both in the home and in
> the web of wider relationships, is of major influence, if not decisive, in shap-
> ing a child's experience and destiny.

The power to shape destinies is an awesome power indeed. Families matter. They come in all shapes and sizes, from *The Little House on the Prairie* to *Angela's Ashes*, from those with virtually no internal or external support structure to those with a robustness which sees them relatively unscathed, or at least coping remarkably well, through a lot of life's perils.

Few animals in the world of nature take as long as human beings to grow to a level of maturity sufficient for independent living. The level of reliance of child on parent, the privacy of that relationship, its intensity, the ignorance of the child of other models of relationship – these mount up the vulnerability of a child who is unfortunate enough to be born into a family with poor parenting skills, compounded by an adverse social context in which there are no adequate compensating mechanisms or safeguards.

No single model of family is a sure guarantee of a child's safe transportation from the womb to a fulfilled adulthood. We know that the traditional model of a mother and father in a lifelong marriage, successful as it is in incalculable ways, did not always protect a child from the damaging consequences of physical or sexual abuse, from the family turbulence caused by alcoholism or other drug abuse, or the life-skewing consequences of the kind of grinding poverty which provokes low expectation and poor motivation. We also know that shifting those damaged children out of that model into institutional care was also no guarantee of safety or a passport from the margins.

The traditional family model based on marriage certainly has its fair share of fallout and failure, and we have seen increasing numbers of people turn their back on it, dismissing it as old-fashioned and out of step with the demands of modern individualism and freedom of choice. But then there is the fallout, too, from the increasing number of alternative models characterised by single-parenthood, large numbers of births outside marriage and many couples setting up home together outside of marriage.

It is remarkably easy to convince ourselves that these alternative lifestyles are part of some quintessentially modern, futuristic and unstoppable dynamic. Unstoppable it may be, but many a student of modern history could point out the similarity to eighteenth-century England, where half of all births were outside marriage and a complete absence of divorce law, allied to liberal social attitudes, facilitated a plethora of irregular partnerships. Victorian England did not emerge out of nowhere! Tonight's chairman has himself raised serious questions about the growing number of children in whose lives fathers play a negligible or marginal role.

The whimsical nostalgia which would defend the traditional model of family, even to the extent of denying its vulnerable side, and the uncritical assertion that modern flexible domestic arrangements are intrinsically better because they are new and modern, don't take any of us far in our attempts to understand what it is that makes a childhood, safe, secure and developmentally effective in terms of intellect and emotion. Children need families, however constituted, that work well for them and families need to know the truth or truths about themselves. The harder those truths, the more they need to be known, discussed intelligently, and owned.

Part of that debate inevitably involves reflecting on these old and new, conventional and unconventional models of family, identifying what works well and what works badly, what works for and what works against the child. As it happens, the one I know best, the traditional extended family is now being revisited by policy-makers, academics and practitioners involved in the field of family support, ransacking it for those things which are its strengths, working out if they are model-specific or if and how they can be transplanted into other models of family or childhood support experience to bolster and strengthen them in turn.

We didn't use terms like 'social capital', 'secure bases', 'arenas of comfort' and the jargon of social science to describe the safety nets and safety valves which our traditional, extended family and close-knit community provided. But they existed all the same. Yes, they could be patchy from family to family, even on the same street, even within the same clan, and they could be patchy from community to community and sometimes, tragically, familiarity gave an obscene cloak of invisibility to the abuse of children. But when the structures worked well, and for many thousands of people they did, they produced a tolerably steady handrail to adulthood. Its apparent random, rough-and-tumble nature often masked its subtleties, its successes, its foundation on generations of lived life, of distilled, even bitter, wisdom, its capacity to absorb change, to mutate and to adapt.

Every child is entitled to a safe passage to adulthood and too many adults have looked back with regret and anger at lives in which the steady handrail was missing or damaged. They need the world of the expert to be unafraid in charting a course for the future in which the lessons of the past and the emerging present have been well studied and well applied. That is why the work of family-support experts, and in particular the work of those contributing to the debate here in Ireland, will be so critical as we attempt to chart a future that is margin-free. It is particularly encouraging to see so much of this work being done on a North–South axis, maximising the available knowledge and experience.

But although family is a crucial determinant of destiny, it is not the sole determinant, nor does it exist outside a context of some sort or another – a context which can conduce to its health or conduce to its dysfunction. The role of education and of community also impact deeply on destiny. Effective partnerships between parents, teachers and communities can be a crucial factor in discouraging children from the early school-leaving/poor literacy/inadequate skills syndrome widely recognised as the most significant indicator of later disadvantage and marginalisation.

We pride ourselves that we now have a good system of education, and we have. It is a system many other countries would envy. It is a system our parents envy, growing up as they did in an era when they knew the powerlessness that came from poor educational opportunities. This system, which we are growing all the time, is their legacy to the kind of empowered future they wanted for their children and, through them, for their country. The evidence is in – that their faith in education as a liberator is paying off well.

And yet for so many Irish people, that same system has been anything but a source of liberation. It has failed to equip them with the basic building blocks of a fulfilled and successful adult life. I am thinking in particular of the thousands of individuals who have gone to primary and secondary schools and are unable to read and write, either at all or only very poorly. I have met quite a few of them. The shy man who was too terrified to ask his bad-tempered teacher anything in class; whose working life on the building sites was a misery because, as he said himself in the first thing he wrote after adult literacy classes gave him power over his life:

> I loved the buildings but I had terrible problems with reading and writing. Sometimes the men would have a newspaper, so I would always get out of the hut quickly in case I was asked to read. When you can't read you live in fear always. Many times I could be out for a day and go hungry because I wouldn't go into a restaurant. I was always afraid people would look down on

me. When you can't read and write you feel you can't talk to people who are more educated than you.

Or the woman who told me lately that she dropped out of school at thirteen because as a slow learner, made to feel she was irredeemably stupid, she felt she could never catch up. She described how, rather than write a letter of explanation about her child's absence, she would walk down to the school to tell the teacher verbally, in order to cover up the fact she could not spell properly and was ashamed to admit it. A woman with a bright, lively intelligence and marvellous original wit, her life has been lived under a shadow of self-doubt, in low-paid jobs where a high level of literacy is not needed.

For her, and thousands like her, the education system has led not to a release of potential as it should, but to a frustration of it. Out of that frustrated, destroyed potential have comes lives lived unhappily at the margins.

We know the best time to intervene, if we are to break that cycle of misery, is when children are very young, when their inherent capacity and need to learn has not yet been damaged, when their minds are still like sponges, capable of absorbing a world of knowledge. But to have the best chance of success, such interventions must extend beyond the child to his or her parents and wider community. It needs to recognise that a parent may have been scarred by a bad school experience, that education may not be valued in the home – indeed that it may be positively denigrated because of the parent's own bad memories. It needs to recognise that such parents may lack the knowledge and literacy skills to help a child with homework or reading; that conditions in the home for studying may be less than ideal. It needs to recognise that the system works best when parents are involved in the circle of education and feel that they are listened to and valued.

One of the most interesting and encouraging aspects of recent initiatives such as the Department of Education's Breaking the Cycle

Programme, is the way that parents are so centrally involved in the process. It may take a long time to win the trust of parents, even to get some of them inside the school gates, if their own memories of school and of teachers are filled with fear, humiliation and inadequacy. But each small step can help to build up a causeway of trust. It may start with something as simple as encouraging them to come along to their children's art classes, not just to watch, but to participate. Small steps which bring them into contact with teachers, which help to demonstrate that learning need not be based on fear, that school can be enjoyable – a place where their children's self-confidence is built up, not torn down. A place where they are made to feel welcome and which may encourage them to consider their own options, perhaps to re-open a window of hope in their own lives through adult education, or becoming involved in community groups based in or around the school.

In building fluent working partnerships between parents and teachers, we are making much better use of the available energy sources which help empower a child. There are others out there still waiting to be tapped. We talk a lot about our ageing population, sometimes forgetting that in preparing ourselves for the problems associated with ageing, there are also new resources emerging. There are, in particular, so many older and retired people who have huge reservoirs of experience, knowledge and skills that they are only too happy to pass on to younger people, if only the opportunity presented itself. And they possess that most important of all commodities in today's world: time. Sometimes, just spending time with a child, listening to their problems, showing them some new activity, showing them that someone cares, can be the most valuable gift that child can receive. But older people can also help in practical ways, perhaps with a child's reading or homework. Those who are already involved in voluntary adult literacy work or in pilot projects with schools or libraries testify to the huge benefits for both the helper and the helped. Such fresh new ways of looking at and using our national knowledge equity, seeing the ending of marginalisation as a team – and a national team – effort at that, could be an important key to unlocking the potential of the marginalised child in the future.

The building of that team approach is already evident in the success of integrated local partnership initiatives in community development. Time and again I have seen examples where a local volunteer committee, starting from a blank sheet of paper, has drawn in the help of local and central government, voluntary social services, business and industry, local schools, FÁS, and of course the Churches. It has tapped into the sources of available grant funding, has leveraged additional funds from the community and other sources, and out of this amazing patchwork of little successes and achievements, has built up to a radical and benign reversal of the destiny of that community. Communities acting together have found sufficient strength in joint endeavour to tackle tough issues from drug abuse to unemployment, from care for the elderly to self-development and training for young mothers, from combating racism to healthcare for Travellers, to mention only a few. They have shown that seed-bedding a culture which supports local initiative and acknowledges its integrity, its entitlement to equal partnership with the world of the expert, is a winning combination. The days of marginalised communities having things done to them or for them are over. Today, things are done with them and through them, by their leave, so that each step, each little bit of movement towards the centre is theirs to take pride in and to take heart from.

Graham Greene once wrote:

> There is always one moment in childhood when the door opens and lets the future in.

There may also be a moment in a nation's history when a door opens and the future enters. This moment has that feel about it. In one generation, the national ceann faoi has been consigned to history and with it new destinies have been scripted for many of our people. Now we are called to write the next chapter, probably the best chapter of all, where a confident and successful generation, accelerating into the sophisticated world of high-tech and high achievement, decided it would not be comfortable, could not be content, until this country was all centre and no margins. If that is what we want, and the ethos which founded this state says that it is, then the destiny of the marginalised child is our problem, our responsibility. We are his family. He depends on us.

'HOPES FOR THE NEW MILLENNIUM' ADDRESS

St Patrick's Cathedral, Dublin, 11 June 2000

It is always a humbling experience to know that you are following in the footsteps of a Nobel Laureate – doubly so when that person is Seamus Heaney and the task on hand is to speak on a topic as wide-ranging as 'Hopes for the New Millennium'. But then, I am no stranger to the terrors of the pulpit; a number of years back I was asked to preach in a particular cathedral – the first ever woman to do so. Lacking the humility to say no, but devoid of inspiration when it came to writing the address, I turned, like a good Christian, to the Bible for assistance. The New Testament fell open at that part of St Paul's First Letter to the Corinthians so familiar to all women, and to far too many men:

> Women are to be silent in church ... they are not permitted to speak ... that a woman should make her voice heard in church is not seemly.

I was inclined to find the Lord's sense of humour less than helpful in the circumstances, but I am glad to see that the dean does not share St Paul's view of women preachers. I am most appreciative of his invitation to speak to you today.

From the perspective of a human being with a normal lifespan of considerably less than 100 years, a millennium, 1,000 years, seems a long time to plan for, even to dream for. Yet in this great church dedicated to the name of St Patrick, we are reminded that he and the Master he served dared to have hopes for all time and for eternity. Against the changing, chaotic backdrop of history, they insisted there was a linear and purposive journey which offered a profound reconciliation between human beings and between human beings and God.

Not everyone looks at human existence in that way. Not everyone sees God, or purpose, or love as significant issues for this millennium. But no matter what our perspective, we each know that if we have hopes and dreams for ourselves, our children and grandchildren, this moment, the present, the now, is our opportunity to plant them – our only sure opportunity.

For those of us who dare to dream of life in all its fullness, for all of creation, we know we have to get a serious move on. We are privileged to live in an Ireland of unprecedented prosperity, peace and opportunity. Many of us are its beneficiaries and we have good lives. Yet all around us, in our own country and across the globe, lives are being shut down by hatred, fear, neglect, greed, violence, poverty, loneliness and by the sheer corrosive energy of the dark side of human nature.

These past few years have taught us forcefully that we are capable of creating and absorbing the most remarkable changes; that we can generate those changes; that we do not have to accept the dead hand of fate, the paralysis of history. Here in Ireland we know it is essential to have hopes for tomorrow and essential too that we begin the work of making those hopes happen.

Who could have believed, even a generation ago, that Ireland would now be the economic success story of Europe? That we would be encouraging emigrants to return and coping with an influx of refugees to our own shores? That Irish culture would be so vibrant and so globally recognised? Or that the seeds of peace would take root to such miraculous effect in Northern Ireland?

Who would have dared hope, either, to see the human impact of that great sea change: the dawning pride and self-respect in the eyes of a father who has found a job after years of despair; the joy of an illiterate parent who, after half a lifetime of frightened secrecy, finally learns to read; the self-confidence of a poor and marginalised community which has built a new heart for itself through its own efforts? These are our true successes, these men and women who now see themselves through different eyes. Their pride in self allows us to take great heart and hope from what has already been achieved.

But if these last years have brought great hope to many, they have also had a darker side. It has been said about human beings that they have three lives: past life, present life and their secret life. The same could be said of institutions and of societies. Now the sordid side of our country's secret life is under the spotlight and we are deeply challenged by the evidence of many different forms of corruption. We see their collateral damage to public confidence in political, civic and spiritual leadership. They have contaminated the wells of hope that we draw from, poisoning the atmosphere with cynicism and doubt. Yet cynicism builds nothing up. It drains energy, leaches acid into hope. And so we need voices which insist on hoping in humanity's ability to be noble, to be decent, to live authentic lives which can withstand the searching scrutiny of the spotlight. So here is one of my hopes: that this will be a chastening period of purging and purification, radically calling us to higher values instead of providing self-justification for low standards, whether in business, the Church, politics, the street or the home.

Realising that hope may provide the anchor that so many people are seeking in today's Ireland. The extent of social, economic and cultural change has been so radical and so fast that it is little wonder that many are left with a sense of being, in the words of Mexican writer Octavio

Paz, 'dislodged from the present'. There is a feeling of dislocation and unconnectedness, of being swept along by an uncontrollable and unpredictable current, which some find frightening. Others are exhilarated by the freedom of abandoning what they see as old and destructive baggage. There are many who find in the gadgets, gizmos and technological wizardry of this generation an adventure in progress enough to consume them. There are others who want to remind us that piped water is not the same thing as the water from the spring well and that we need the memory of the taste of the spring well water – we need a modern world which is not in the vice-like grip of the past but which is also not amputated from that past. So there you have another hope: that we will find the right relationship between what has gone and what is.

If there is some degree of impatience with looking back to the past in this era of rapid leaps forward it is hardly surprising. So often we have been prisoners of history. So often the past was an arsenal to be ransacked for weapons to confirm our sense of victimhood and to identify the enemy. The wounds of both ancient and recent history are still raw; the scars of emigration, discrimination and poverty, the low self-esteem caused by centuries of colonisation, those 'high, banked clouds of resignation' described by Seamus Heaney – these we can still touch and feel. But our relationship with the past has been problematic, and the core problem is how we have remembered it. The truth is that our memories have been selective and all too often they have served not to illuminate our present, but to disfigure it. Today we have an opportunity to remember it differently, with more generosity and forgiveness, and in that fresh remembering to liberate our present so that we can create the future we hope and long for. It is a journey already started and I have a deep hope it is a journey many more will commit to as we attempt to build new friendships and partnerships between North and South, between unionist and nationalist, Catholic and Protestant, between Ireland and England, Scotland and Wales. Just a few days ago, in Greysteel, I saw that hope translated into reality. I saw how a community devastated by tragedy chose to honour their dead, not by vengeance or withdrawal into tribal bunkers but by working together to build greater unity. The past, even when it has brought us pain, can make us stronger, kinder, more sensitive to the pain of others.

Our past is full of that potential. It has been said that Ireland is a first-world country with a third-world memory – a memory to keep us humble amidst our current prosperity, to remind us of how recently we were the ones in need of help, to remind us too of our responsibility to those who still suffer hunger, poverty and social injustice today in other parts of the world and in our own. That memory has equipped us with a particular insight into what it is to feel alienated and undervalued. It has given us a rare understanding of what is needed to give a people their freedom, their dignity and self-belief. Today's generation is the first generation to have available to it an extensive and complex array of tools and resources to turn the tide of history comprehensively against poverty at home and to be champions of the marginalised abroad. Many poor countries look to us today as witnesses to the triumph of hope over adversity. They see in Ireland's story the seeds of their own possibilities, the energy which fuels their own hopes. Many poor people arrive on our shores seeking a new start in the same way that many of our own families set out on lonely emigrant journeys across the world. We are new to this issue of asylum seekers on our own doorsteps. We are struggling to deal with the issues it provokes. Like so many unforeseen problems in life, how we cope on day one is not how we cope on day 101 – we grow in knowledge, in wisdom, in experience, in acceptance. We begin to see things differently. That which seemed strange gradually becomes familiar and, please God, while many of our neighbouring countries are also coping with the same issues, we in Ireland will, in the days ahead, become a country justifiably proud of how it treats and reassures the vulnerable stranger. So I hope we give each other the space to change and the acknowledgment and encouragement due when those who are today frightened of the stranger, tomorrow find the courage to become the stranger's friend and protector.

There are many here in need of reassurance that this wealthy Ireland, this self-confident Ireland, this Ireland of the new millennium which seems so distant from their reality, is still their home. I am reminded of a Traveller child I met some time back, a child who knows all about poverty and hardship, a child whose life to date had given her little reason for hope. And yet, her ambition in life is to be a doctor. That hope had not yet been drummed out of her by the smug disbelief of others, by their casually cruel, snide remarks or by the harsh reality of a society which has not yet achieved its ambition of treating all its children equally. She is not alone. There are thousands like her in our inner-city schools, in our poor neighbourhoods. I meet them week in and week out, hear them talk out loud of their ambitions for themselves, and know the struggle they do not yet know that they face. Their teachers know it, their parents know it, we know it. And we know a good start is half the work and we are trying in so many ways to reach deep into these little lives and give them that good start. We have a long, long way to go and I hope we can shorten the journey, and soon.

I hope too that we will use these blessed days well – that they will not simply enrich us financially but enrich us humanly, making us more generous, more big hearted, so that we will be genuinely a welcoming people, a courteous people, a people who strive for excellence in all things, whether selling a packet of sweets to a five-year-old or providing hospice care for the dying. I hope our newfound prosperity and self-assertion will not disintegrate into smugness and strident egoism but will help us focus on creating an affirming and reassuring environment of decent human relationships. To have prosperity without kindness, affluence without compassion makes for a hard-edged world, hard-edged hearts. Not a world Patrick would have been proud of. I hope for the world he would smile on with satisfaction.

I also hope that we find a new level of optimism, energy and impetus in relation to religious belief and practice. These past few years have been difficult ones. The traditional well of spirituality, the role of prayer and even the role of Christian hope itself in Irish life have suffered serious damage. Some are inclined to blame forces arrayed outside the Churches, from the media to secularism, yet in truth much of the damage has been self-inflicted. Many opportunities have been missed to bring the Good News and the cost has been high. Failure to champion gender equality, failure to make the professional ministry attractive to a new generation, failure to deal with sectarianism, failure to keep the worlds of the spirit and politics in their proper perspectives, failure to enter the Jubilee year with the unity Christ desired – these things and many more have put distance and doubts between institutions and people.

And yet in Ireland today there still a hunger for the spiritual, a search for the transcendent, for meaning, which crosses all age groups and backgrounds and which has not been quenched by the faults and failings of the Churches. The question is how that yearning is to be satisfied. My hope is that this new millennium will see a more humble, radical and relevant community of Churches, actively promoting joyful and respectful curiosity about each other, champions of social inclusion, radical voices calling us to forgiveness, to reconciliation and to love. In this week alone the voices of the new Moderator of the Presbyterian Church Trevor Morrow and the new President of the Methodist Church Ken Todd have sounded a fresh and energising note, challenging sectarianism and racism. Allied to the Pope's recent call to forgiveness, his admission of Church failings, and mindful of the voices from within the Catholic Church and the Church of Ireland hierarchies challenging racism and urging generosity, we dare to hope for an Ireland where Christians are at last known by the way they love one another and by the way they joyfully welcome the stranger as a brother or sister in Christ.

It was Cardinal Newman who said, 'to live is to have changed, but to be perfect is to have changed often.' Is it too much to hope that we might seek, in this millennium, some sort of profound perfection of the human condition? W.R. Rogers, in his poem 'Nativity', is scathing about our times:

> Lord in this wintry interval we send
> Our indolent regards
> And grey regrets. Make fluent all the pens
> Of all the frozen bards.

I dare to hope the wintry interval is over and the spring is almost upon us.

ADDRESS ON THE OCCASION OF THE ANNUAL TRÓCAIRE LECTURE

St Patrick's College, Maynooth, 11 March 2002

Your Eminence Cardinal Desmond Connell, Monsignor Farrell, ladies and gentlemen,

I am delighted to have been invited to deliver this year's Annual Trócaire Lecture. Being here today gives me a very welcome opportunity to acknowledge the hugely important work done by Trócaire for the over-looked people of our world – the millions, whose talents and energies are ground down daily by the relentless forces of poverty, corruption, war, disease and hunger. The world is waiting for those talents to blossom. We are cursed by so much waste, so much unnecessary misery, but we are blessed in those who bring hope, who refuse to accept the inevitability of the squandering of so much human life. Your response to the needs of the world's poorest gives us much to be proud of and it strikes a particularly deep chord with Irish people, who can speak still of great-grandparents and indeed grandparents who knew the agony of living in a third-world country, where their lives were disregarded and where hunger was familiar company. That memory keeps us alive to the transcendent power of the helping hand; how it nurtures ambition and determination, how it gathers the energy to have faith in the future and belief in the self.

There are many different models of outreach to the developing world but Trócaire has pioneered its own uniquely effective charisma. Fundamental to your work is the promotion of a culture of independence in which both the dignity and life-opportunity of the individual is enhanced by building up personal skills and local capacity – a hand up, not a hand out. Your programmes are guided by a deep respect for human rights, an unshakeable belief in the effective harnessing of the potential of each human being. Trócaire rightly places great emphasis on participation and empowerment as the key to unlocking that potential. Yours is difficult work because your agenda sees far beyond today's hunger to a radically reshaped political, economic and social landscape where people exercise choices they never dreamt they would have, where the overlooked people create their own forces of relevance and make themselves an unmistakeable centre of gravity. You reach in to their dreams and tell them the impossible is possible. The poignant and well-known words of W.B. Yeats seem apt:

> But I, being poor, have only my dreams;
> I have spread my dreams under your feet;
> Tread softly because you tread on my dreams.

These are people whose dreams have been trampled on for so long that you may even have to introduce people to them anew. Trócaire has been a champion of those who dream of social justice, equal opportunity, of an end to slavery, of a real childhood for children, of regular food on the table, a school to go to, fresh water to drink, affordable medicines, a sustainable livelihood, a permanent home, a life with real meaningful choices. Each year your Lenten Campaigns remind us how distant those things are from the lived reality of millions of lives. It is a time to reflect on how lucky we in Ireland are to have so much, and among the many marvellous things we enjoy today is the opportunity to share what we have so that others may know a time when abject poverty and power-lessness are consigned to history.

Like all opportunities, it can be used or it can be thrown away. Each generation is custodian of its own opportunities and as the parable of the talents teaches us, to be confronted with opportunity is to be tried and tested. Because the work of outreach to the poor has been under-taken so often by people of heroic unselfishness, and, in our own case, undertaken for generations by talented, well-educated missionaries who turned their backs on more comfortable lives at home, who deliberately chose discomfort, who drew no salaries, who never dreamt of thanks, it has become deceptively easy to see this work as essentially altruistic, as work of giving rather than receiving. Today that myth is dangerous, for investment in development work is not an optional extra; it is not some-thing which has ring-fenced consequences for people many miles away and little or none for us. UN Secretary General Kofi Annan put it well in a recent speech when he compared our planet to a small boat driven by a fierce gale through uncharted waters, with more and more people crowded on board, desperately seeking to survive. In his words:

> None of us can ignore the condition of our fellow passengers on this little boat. If they are sick, all of us risk infection. And if they are angry, all of us can easily get hurt.

Somehow that message seems easier to comprehend after that grim day on September 11th, when the baleful hand of terrorism shocked the world to an extent few had seriously contemplated. An avalanche of emotions followed, with an outpouring of grief for the dead, the injured, the bereaved and the frightened, and an uneasy wobble which ran through the pillars of global commerce and global politics.

Today, that overwhelming wave of horror is provoking many questions about the root causes of such inhuman violence and about effective responses to it. Our vulnerability to each other has been sharply and appallingly highlighted, our parochial blinkers have been removed and the sweep of our gaze now embraces parts of the world only dimly acknowledged before September 11th. We now know, with a dramatic clarity from which we cannot hermetically seal ourselves, the effects of things that happen thousands of miles away. We are a global human family – and most of that family is living in great pools of poverty and hopelessness, fertile breeding grounds for political or religious fundamentalism, for ignorance about transmissible disease, for chronic corruption that corrodes the rule of law, for the frustration of talented men and women who never know the joy of their own talents revealed and whose anger ferments into distilled hatred, the most powerful weapon on the planet.

1.2 billion people live on less than one dollar a day, while just across the way, the 1 billion people living in developed countries earn 60 per cent of the world's total income, have over 70 per cent of global trade and attract almost 60 per cent of all foreign direct investment. That is one very unbalanced seesaw, looked at in cold statistical terms. Day in and day out, in the slums of Kenya, or the bare hillsides of Honduras, or the bloodstained streets of Palestine, or in any number of lowlights on the spectrum of the contemporary human condition, it is lived by human beings with hearts to be broken by the unfairness of it all and heads to wonder at how fairness can ever be achieved. We in Ireland know those human beings well. In another generation they were our people and we know the many, many ways in which they adapted. Some simply gave up, caving in to despair. Others embraced stoicism and unquestioning acceptance. Yet others found the courage and energy to use what little they had to make achingly slow progress. Some chose principled, purposive resistance and still others the frightening path of obsessive resentment. Today, all over the world, men and women are waking up in circumstances of appalling misery which confront them with a limited range of choices and a limited range of responses. What is more, while the range of choices for those of us in the developed world widens exponentially, the exact opposite is the case in the world's poorer places.

It is as telling as it is sickening that over the last decade the overall volume of development assistance from rich countries has fallen to a historic low. Instead of increasing to meet the UN target of 0.7 per cent of GNP, aid has fallen back to an average of just 0.22 per cent of GNP for all donors. This sharp decline in development assistance is having enormous effects on the peoples of those countries most in need of direct assistance, particularly in Sub-Saharan Africa. While many countries in Asia and Latin America have managed to compensate somewhat for the decline in development assistance through increased flows of private investment, this has not been the case in that part of Africa. The region attracts just 1 per cent of total global foreign direct investment. It has been bypassed by the information and telecommunications revolution and it remains critically dependent on the generosity of rich-country governments and on the support of NGOs.

One of the lessons beginning to emerge from the search for explanations in the aftermath of September 11th is that development assistance should not be and must not be seen as an entirely altruistic phenomenon. Yes, our development aid support is a crucial expression of concern and solidarity, but it is also an essential investment in our own security. Every human being who is helped to grow strong and self-sufficient is a person whose harnessed talents build up the fabric of global civic society. Every person who is helped to avoid AIDS, who is given a chance for a decent education, whose skills attract credible employers who pay proper wages, is a person who is a leaven in a community helping it to transcend the deficit of history's legacy and to build a better future. Every country helped to close the income gap and put on the road towards participation in international trade and investment, every country nudged towards democracy and respect for human rights, increases the stability of our globe and lays the foundations for both peace and shared prosperity.

What makes the historic decline in levels of international development aid even more frustrating is the clear evidence that aid works. Infant and under-five child mortality rates fell by more than half over the past thirty years. It is remarkable that a child born today is expected to live eight years longer than one born thirty years ago and many more will know the liberation of education as literacy rates increase apace around the world. These and many other reassuring statistics show that globally there has been a steady and welcome improvement in human development. Properly targeted aid does give enormous value for money. The evidence is in that it works and so we now face both the challenge and the opportunity in our generation to keep driving those statistics in the right direction.

The UN Millennium Summit in September 2000 adopted a set of simple targets – the so-called Millennium Development Goals based on the work of a series of UN Conferences throughout the 1990s. The over-arching development goal is the relatively modest ambition to cut the number of people living in extreme poverty by half by 2015, with others relating to improvements in the spheres of health, education and the environment. It would be profoundly wrong to characterise such goals as the kind of thing we aspire to without expecting to achieve. The World Bank has now costed the Millennium Development Goals, suggesting that a doubling of international development assistance (that is an additional $50 billion of aid per year) would provide the necessary financial basis. It sounds a lot until you contrast it with current levels of international expenditure on armaments, or even expenditure on non-essential consumer goods in the developed world. Suddenly it seems like a reasonable price to pay for a world where talent is unlocked, not wasted, where we begin to see our true strength and worth as a species, as country after country delivers real opportunity to its people and where a self-confident people harvests that opportunity with enthusi-asm and imagination.

Ireland has already given a strong international lead on the question of increased resources for overseas development aid through its commit-ment to meet the UN target in relation to Overseas Development Aid expenditure by 2007, and of course little Luxembourg, the smallest and wealthiest country in the European Union, no bigger than Limerick, whose Head of State was here last week, has given us all a lead by meet-ing the 0.7 per cent target two years ago. This work needs champions, for the forces of narrow self-interest are powerfully seductive and the home demands on national funds grow ever-greater year on year. At the same time though, the man or woman whose hard-earned taxes or donations are sent abroad as development aid are perfectly entitled to query the ways in which the money is spent, to demand open account-ability and to insist on evidence that the money is being used effectively.

The international community has reached a broad consensus both on the fundamental political and economic requirements for develop-ment progress and on how to deliver aid effectively. These requirements include good governance, the protection and promotion of human rights and a clear commitment to democracy, the rule of law and the fight against corruption. There is also now an appreciation of the need for donors to co-ordinate, to avoid the proliferation of projects and to engage with partner Governments in support of nationally owned development plans.

Ireland is a much wealthier country today than it was twenty years ago. Our people have seen this country blossom in ways many would have thought impossible even a generation ago. We have come to expect that things will get better year-on-year and that prosperity will continue to widen its embrace on an upward linear track. We have an expectation that we can and will eliminate poverty, not just sometime this century but sometime soon. That expectation is not pie in the sky. It is realisti-cally within our grasp. We have work to do to achieve it but there is an energy in our self-belief that comes from the level of success already achieved and the manifest signs of that success all around us.

Pity, then, the people of Sub-Saharan Africa who are today almost as poor as they were twenty years ago and who watch as the scourge of AIDS wipes out decades of development progress. Of the 40 million people infected with AIDS in the world, 28 million are in Sub-Saharan Africa. In some southern African countries, one adult in three is infected and even in a country like Uganda, which is making a real effort to tackle the problem, 2 million children out of a total population of just over 20 million people are AIDS orphans. The damage to family and community structures, the wipe-out of income earners, the lostness of so many children – these are already today's bitter legacy to the future. Those of us who believe so powerfully in the role of education would do well to ponder the fact that in Zambia more teachers are dying of AIDS than are emerging from teacher-training colleges, while in Kenya eighteen teachers die of AIDS each day. Africa's near future is already utterly compromised and anyone who believes the downstream consequences stop at that continent's shores is sadly misguided.

The spread of HIV/AIDS has been assisted by levels of extreme poverty, ignorance and by conflict. As the UN Security Council has recognised, the spread of the epidemic is, in itself, a new security threat, both to the most affected countries and to the rest of the world. It is contributing to the destabilisation of states, to the perpetuation of conflict and to a deepening of the sense of hopelessness and lack of power which lies at the root of conflict and violence. In the worst-affected countries, life expectancy has plummeted in recent years because of the HIV/AIDS crisis. Health facilities are stretched to breaking point and communities are forced more and more to rely on themselves. It was heart-rending to see, in Uganda, the little AIDS clinic set up in a very poor little local house in which the family continued to reside, to see the sufferers make long journeys on foot to get tiny amounts of painkillers, to see nothing in their eyes at all except the crushing weight of sorrow.

And then to meet the grandmothers raising their grandchildren and to wonder at the fact that almost three in every four households have taken at least one orphan into their care. These are families that can barely look after themselves, let alone take care of orphans and yet they do.

We owe them the best energy we can muster, for there are enough others who preach the counsel of despair or neglect. Kofi Annan has rightly identified both local and global political leadership as the key to the success in the fight against HIV/AIDS and indeed where that leadership has been forthcoming we have seen considerable progress. In Uganda, I saw at firsthand how committed political leadership supporting a well-developed national prevention campaign has reduced the rate of adult infection from over 20 per cent to less than 10 per cent. In Senegal, where the Government acted at a very early stage in the epidemic, HIV/AIDS infection has been contained at 2 per cent, and recently talking to those involved in Irish Government-sponsored work on AIDS education in the Gambia, the story was one of measurable success. A sign that the AIDS wake-up call is beginning to work came in January, when, after just six months of preparation, a new Global Fund to fight HIV/AIDS was established. Already it has pledges of over $1 billion and is ready to take applications for support from the most affected countries. Here, too, Ireland has shown international leadership, both through our Development Assistance HIV/AIDS Strategy and our commitment of an additional $30 million per year to the fight against HIV/AIDS.

While the statistics on HIV/AIDS are shocking, the reality is humbling and unforgettable. During my visits to Uganda and Kenya, I had the privilege of witnessing the work of care done by Irish men and women who have invested their skills and their lives in bringing to the poor the comfort of immediate relief or the hope of long-term development assistance. Their work evokes righteous pride at home, but they cannot sustain their work on pride. The test of it, the test of us, is the level of support we give both financially and morally in promoting a culture of voluntarism, a culture of generosity and of visible concern for all of God's human family. It's a baton of a value system carefully handed to us from generations who had much less than we have but who had big hearts and small egos. That baton has been the bedrock of missionary and NGO activities in Africa for generations. As a wealthier nation with infinitely greater opportunities for self-indulgence, it is essential to the health and vibrancy of our own communal civic sense that we retain and indeed enhance our strong tradition of solidarity with the poor of the developing world.

There is nothing abstract about human solidarity. There is nothing easy about it either. It takes effort to seed-bed and sustain. Some day and in some way or another, we all need it, and because we do, the best way of guaranteeing it is there for us when we do need it is to make our own contribution to the great reservoir of human goodness while we can.

Few countries are as fortunate as Ireland in the many champions we have produced whose lives have been given to creating and promoting not just the idea of human solidarity but the lived reality of it. It is their relentless focus on the poorest and most marginalised of peoples and countries which provides a soft human counterpoint to the impersonal hand of the markets. Their hands, voices and smiles are the conduits to hope. The transfer of their skills gives people a new-found control over their own destiny. Their lobbying fosters international debate about the key issues facing the developing world and it integrates the developed and developing world into the dialogue about solutions. The civic conscience of the developed world is being challenged about its responsibilities just as the civic imagination of the developing world is being introduced to its own latent possibilities. An agenda is being set for a global conscious-ness which is driven by the values of the gentle human heart and not the tight fist, by a thirst for justice and equality which cannot be quenched while so many people live lives of manifest and unnecessary grimness.

Trócaire's Lenten Campaign, with its spotlight on the fight against child exploitation and child labour, is a good case in point. In May

2002, the UN General Assembly will hold a Special Session to review progress since the UN Summit on Children last year. Last year's story will not be good enough for those who care. This year's story has to be better and next year's better again. Trócaire's campaign is part of that dynamic that is nudging a wider audience to care passionately about these issues and making a personal quest of their resolution. There is a job to do in forging a functioning global constituency which promotes and supports increased overseas aid and sees it as an investment in our common future. NGOs have an important role to play in fostering the growth of that constituency and feeding the agenda already set by the Millennium Development Goals, ensuring that we meet those goals and move beyond them in a meaningful time frame.

Trócaire's partnership of endeavour with the Irish people tells us a lot about ourselves. There are proven wells of compassion and generosity which are tapped into every year and which never dry up, thankfully. The work undertaken in fifty countries around the world could not happen without the certainty that Irish people will always come through for Trócaire and for the poor. Time and time again they do, and when they do, the pervasive unease we feel about so much of what goes on in our world ebbs a little and we begin to see a light shining through the darkness.

The reassurance of that light is needed all the more in these days when immigrants from poor parts of the world arrive in Ireland seeking the chance to live a decent life. They test us just as others have been tested by the arrival of needy strangers on their shores. It's a story we know well, precisely because, for generations, we were the arriving strangers; the poor, the destitute arriving in the hope that in this foreign land we could find the space to put our talents to work. Out of the distilled wisdom of the bitter experience of our own history of emigration, the Irish should have little to learn about the dangers of racism, of malicious stereotyping, of slammed doors, of being alone. Yet we know that there are those in our society on whom those lessons have been lost. Ireland is sadly not immune to those base human instincts that conduce to bullying, to contempt and hatred, to jealousy and conflict, but there has always been a much stronger, much more resilient instinct for good, an instinct which has drawn deeply on the forces which oppressed so many of our ancestors and out of which has come a rock-solid faith in the human rights and dignity of all human beings, a manifest solidarity with the suffering people of the world and a history of championing the underdog which has earned us respect worldwide. That is precisely why instances of racist behaviour are so utterly offensive. In a well-to-do Ireland they mock and replicate the suffering of our own ancestors driven by poverty from an Ireland which was a forgotten and neglected third-world country, they offend the sensibilities of the majority of our people whose strongest instinct is towards kindness and who prove that year in and year out by their willingness to dig into their pockets, not just for Trócaire but for the many other good causes which rely on the consistency and constancy of that instinct.

The people of today's third world take hope from Ireland's rags to riches story. They take hope from the fact that we continue to make their future our concern. They want to work with us to make a new future for all of us. There is a pathos in their gratitude which should not blind us to the fact that our outreach to the developing world is an investment as much in Ireland's future as it is in the future of Africa or South America. The tangible benefits of peace, stability and prosperity need no enunciation, but the intangible benefits of stretching the reach of human conscience, of linking human beings from one side of the globe with those on the other in a network of human solidarity based on mysterious things, like mercy and love, are miraculous gifts to all of us. They multiply and fill the earth with things which hearten us, things which smooth the raw jagged edges of life, which reconcile us to the chaos and chart a pathway through its perplexing vale of tears to a future not yet arrived at but held in our imaginations. In that world, the work of Trócaire would be over. I would sorely like to be around for such a day but I'll settle for being on the bumpy road to it – a long journey ahead but at least a journey started. There is an Irish saying that 'Two shortens the road.' Trócaire has been the steadfast travelling companion on life's journey to many, many suffering people and I wish it well in shortening the road to the final triumph of love.

Thank you.

REMARKS AT THE OFFICIAL OPENING OF THE SERENITY GARDEN AT AISLINN ADOLESCENT TREATMENT CENTRE

Ballyragget, County Kilkenny, 15 April 2003

Tá lúcháir orm go bhfuair mé cuireadh bheith anseo libh inniu agus ba mhaith liom mo bhuíochas a ghabháil libh go léir as fáilte fiorchaoin a chur romham.

I am delighted to be here with you today to officially open this Serenity Garden and to see at firsthand the wonderful work done here by the dedicated team under the guidance of Sr Veronica Mangan at the Aislinn Centre. I had the pleasure of meeting Sr Veronica and hearing about her hopes for this project at the AIB Better Ireland Awards in Kilkenny two years ago. It is therefore an honour for me to share the realisation of her vision with you today. My thanks to Breda Cahill for inviting me to celebrate this special occasion with you and also to each and every one of you for your very warm and generous welcome.

The fact that there are so many people here today is testament to the very high esteem in which the centre is held both here in Kilkenny and further afield. Since its doors opened in 1998, the Aislinn Centre has provided an impressive, indeed vital, range of treatment services to so many young people, adolescents who have suffered the ravages of alcohol and drug dependency. And as this centre casts a lifeline to those young people, it also plays a hugely important role as a source of great support for the families of young substance abusers as they travel the road – an often bumpy and uncertain road – towards recovery.

Addiction, in all its forms, is a terrible affliction with a grim legacy of waste and misery for the individual addicts and for those whose lives are hurt and disrupted by the addiction of others – families, friends, neighbours, victims, communities and indeed society as a whole. Ireland has always had a ridiculously unhealthy attitude to alcohol. Today we are paying a high price for a culture in which excessive drinking plays such a prominent part. With more money in our pockets, more is being spent not just on alcohol but on drugs, and we know the consequences in street crime, in the highest European consumptions of cannabis among fifteen- to sixteen-year-olds and the highest increase in alcohol consumption within the EU in recent years.

Too many people make a connection between fun and alcohol, socialising and drugs. It is a sinister, cynical and deceptive connection. Here, in this place, the other side of the story can be seen in the damaged lives and wrecked hopes abuse inevitably produces. As a nation, we need to wise up and make the changes to our attitudes and our behaviour which will give our vulnerable young people the leadership and witness to better, healthier and happier alternatives. If we make that change – and we are well capable of doing it – we will give our country the gift of a much better quality of life to match the better opportunities and economic achievements created over the past decade. Homes will be happier, streets will be safer, individual lives will be more fulfilled. Instead of struggling individuals we will have strong individuals, and strong individuals build a strong community and a strong country. So the investment here in these young people is an investment ultimately in Ireland itself and its future. Aislinn has a special vocation to our young people and in particular to those at risk from addiction. Here you help them to believe in themselves again. You help them to find the inner resources to build better lives. You refuse to give up on them. You guide them towards their own empowerment, with sensitivity, patience and faith. We are very grateful that you do and we are grateful to the young people who come here. Their courage gives us hope that there is a good life to be created beyond addiction. Their commitment gives energy to the Aislinn Centre itself and reassurance to families and to the community who want so badly to see our young people flourish free from the trap of addiction. We are very proud of these young people's openness to help and their curiosity about the life they could be living beyond addiction and beyond whatever demons, real or imaginary, feed abuse.

This Serenity Garden is another important tool in Aislinn's repair kit. Its twelve symbols, based on the 12 Step philosophy of Alcoholics Anonymous, reinforce the message that, with addict and treatment centre working wholeheartedly together, there is a roadmap to freedom from addiction.

I love gardening, particularly at my grandfather's cottage in Roscommon where I spend my holidays. I planted a tree there many years ago and came back after one storm to discover it had broken in two and was manifestly dead. I was only down for a short time and decided to leave it until the summer to dig it out by the roots and dump it. When I arrived in July I was astounded to see six new green shoots growing up from the broken stem and today the tree is flourishing even better than it did before the storm damage. So it is with the human person. We are often bent and bowed by life, but with a bit of patience and faith we can stand tall again.

I congratulate Sr Veronica and her staff, and everyone involved this day. I thank all those who have given Aislinn the gift of the Serenity Garden – the Department of Health and Children and the South Eastern Health Board, who provided both financial and other very practical support, the VEC in Kilkenny, which generously provided the wonderfully gifted and talented artists to work on the project, and the Art Therapist and residents of Aislinn. You are entitled to take pride in what you have accomplished and on behalf of all of those who will enjoy the fruits of your labour in the years to come, I say thank you. I now take great pleasure in declaring this Serenity Garden officially open.

Go gcúití Dia bhur saothar daoibh. Go raibh maith agaibh.

Address at the Opening of the Céifin Conference 'Filling the Vacuum'

West County Hotel, Ennis, County Clare, 8 November 2005

Dia dhíbh a cháirde. Tá an–áthas orm bheith i bhur measc anseo ar an ócáid speisialta seo. Míle bhuíochas díbh as an gcuireadh agus an fáilte a thug sibh dom.

Good afternoon and thank you for the welcome to the 2005 Céifin Conference. Thanks also to Fr Harry Bohan for the invitation and for setting a provocative and timely agenda. 'What,' he asks in the introductory brochure, 'is filling the vacuum left by our over-emphasis on commercial values?' He acknowledges that much of the economic and social change Ireland has experienced in recent decades 'has been for the good'. Our people have education, opportunities, jobs, choices and self-confidence which were lacking in the past but there are, he says, 'some aspects of this change which are less positive and with dire consequences for some individuals, families and communities'. These words are strongly reminiscent of Goldsmith's famous couplet:

> Ill fares the land, to hastening ills a prey,
>
> Where wealth accumulates and men decay.

That couplet was, of course, written in a different era, an era when wealth accumulated in the bank vaults of the very few on the backs of the slavery, poverty and political exclusion of the many. It was the righteous anger of the poor which distilled into a strong egalitarian and democratic impulse, the founding spirit of our nation – the very bedrock of our shared value system as a people. The preamble to our Constitution sets out our collective ambition in simple language:

> ... to promote the common good, with due observance of Prudence, Justice and Charity, so that the dignity and freedom of the individual may be assured [and] true social order attained ...

Long after independence was won for this part of Ireland, the indignity of poverty remained intractable and the only freedom, it seemed, was the freedom to emigrate. Until recently, Ireland was a place where you could have had a conference every day of the week on filling the vacuum because there were so many vacuums to be filled.

Seamus Heaney describes that bleak landscape brilliantly in his poem 'From the Canton of Expectation':

> We lived deep in a land of optative moods,
>
> under high, banked clouds of resignation.
>
> A rustle of loss in the phrase *Not in our lifetime* ...

And then remarkably the tide turned. The vacuum created by emigration was filled. The vacuum made by endemic high unemployment vanished. The vacuum of a dwindling population disappeared. The airtight vacuum of monoculturalism – that went too. The vacuum that narrowly corralled the talents of women has gone. The vacuum of poor diet and early mortality was consigned to history. The vacuum in which no Traveller child transferred from first- to second-level schooling disappeared. The vacuum of widespread poverty has manifestly been filled in. Twenty years ago, one in five of us lived in poverty. Today that number has reduced to one in twenty. The vacuum in which corruption festered has been tribunalled into the airy light of day. The vacuum of silence in which children were the tragic victims of physical and sexual abuse and of the suppression of the criminal consequences of that abuse – that is being filled.

In so many aspects of life, the dreadful pervasive void of the 'ceann faoi' has given way to a surging assertive 'can do'. The landscape has filled up with new industries, new houses, new truths, newcomers, new hope. We have been filling historic, longstanding vacuums at a breathtaking pace and at a level of success no other generation could have imagined, and yet we hear talk of a creeping malaise, as if we have arrived at a long-yearned-for destination only to find it disappointing after all. Is it possible that, in the heady excitement of these past short years of phenomenal change, we have somehow drifted out of sight of the fact that ours is a journey only started, not a journey completed; that our wealth is a means to a long-desired end, and not an end in itself?

A conference like this offers us necessary breathing space to stop and look closely at the choices we are making, individually and collectively, which will shape Ireland's future for good or for ill. We have the choice of roads that can either continue the noble adventure of bringing about true social order, which I understand to mean full social inclusion and an end to poverty, or we can become so wrapped up in attachment to the indulgent self that we become indifferent to the completion of that journey and deaf to the voices of the excluded.

It is simply unthinkable that our final destination could be the cul-de-sac of complacent consumerism when we are the first generation to have within our reach the great destination of an egalitarian republic where the strong are driven by a restless and unselfish duty of care for the weak and where every life is given the chance to fully blossom.

For those who seem to have missed the boat named the Celtic Tiger, modern Ireland can be a very scary place, where all you can see in front of you are the far-off backs of those who are making rapid headway in this new time of opportunity. The long-term unemployed, the chronically ill, disabled, elderly, lone parents, carers, children born into dysfunctional or cyclically underachieving families, those overwhelmed by addiction, Travellers, the illiterate, the vulnerable foreign worker in insecure and poorly paid employment – they can each tell what it feels like to be in a race where all the other runners have disappeared from view and you cannot get past the starting line because of the obstacles that stand in your way. Those who are running the race reasonably well, they can tell too of the pressures the race puts on even those who got off to a good start – housing costs, childcare, long commutes, two-job households, high debt, shortage of quality time ... And we have the fallout that comes when a society vaults so rapidly from an era of frugality to an era of plenty. We have senior citizens, to whom the cheque book is still an innovation, struggling to make sense of the credit-card kids with their mobile phones, designer clothes, computers, iPods and whatever the latest must-have is. We have young people, the best educated in our history, with more money in their pockets and more freedom than any generation before them, and sadly some of them, though thankfully not all, fail to see the ugly wastefulness, the obvious dangers and sheer irresponsibility of binge drinking and of experimenting with drugs. Nor are they fully alive to the dangers of settling for becoming simply active consumers rather than active citizens. Their civic formation, which is our responsibility, is crucial if they are to have the courage to set their sights on higher things, to take personal responsibility for the trajectory of their own lives and the future trajectory of their communities and their country. They will, after all, be the makers as much as the inheritors of twenty-first-century Ireland.

And yet for all the cynicism and complaint that is around, I find it hard to believe, on the basis of the evidence that I am privileged to see day in and day out, that the Irish people would ever settle happily, or be let settle happily, for Destination Complacency – for a greedy, selfish, soulless society, a place of strangers rather than neighbours, of individualised cocoons rather than community. Even in these busy times, when we hear anecdotally that it is getting harder to find volunteers for all sorts of community work, my daily life uniquely takes me right into the heartland of the people who are the doers, to the people who are looking out for and looking after one another. There is an army of them out there of all ages and backgrounds. The odd time they might make a local newspaper – more rarely still the national media – but their lived lives go largely unremarked. And yet their side of the story, when told, puts quite a different complexion on modern Ireland and the state of its heart and soul. They are the people who gave us the World Summer Special Olympics Games, who invented a million ways to part people from their money last December when between them they raised almost €75 million for victims of the tsunami at the other end of the earth. If you need a bone marrow transplant tomorrow and no member of your family is a match, over 19,000 Irish citizens have volunteered as stranger donors for an operation that is dangerous to them and that will cost them two weeks of not insignificant discomfort. If you suffer from depression, Aware volunteers will find you. If you are a lonely older citizen, someone in your community will have set up a day care centre or a helpline to bring you into the company of friends. If you are the parents of an intellectually disabled child, you are probably already involved in self-help groups, in carers' lobby groups and the Special Olympics to an extent that would put the cynics to shame. If you are a sick child in Chernobyl, a bunch of Irish people have made you their concern.

Anti-social behaviour among teenagers is often in the news, but I also see thousands of fantastic young people active in their communities through things like the President's Awards, Foróige and innumerable other initiatives.

In a cramped portacabin this week, I met a group of mothers of addicts, whose exasperation led them to set up a support service for each other and for addicts. Like many of the groups I have come across, these wealthier, more confident and open times have made them ambitious, determined and armed with an agenda they intend to see through. They are plugged into the State services, to local businesses, the local community, the Churches, the professions and the media, and they are painstakingly creating, developing and sustaining the part-nership-driven web of mutual care and support that it takes to get through a tough life with dignity. They leverage extraordinary amounts of money from their own pockets and the pockets of the wider com-munity and Government, and they put that money, along with their freely given time, skill and commitment, to knitting all of us together as a caring community and not just a bunch of indifferent strangers. They teach our kids sports, they give their blood to our sick, house the homeless, comfort the bereaved, counsel the troubled, feed the hungry, welcome the stranger, care for the environment, get involved in poli-tics. This very day they will do a million good things that will bring joy and comfort, hope and opportunity, courtesy and kindness into the lives of others, and they will listen with sinking hearts as their massive contribution, their sacrifice and their considerable faith in humanity is overlooked yet again in discussions about the future direction of our country. They are our hope and our reassurance. Their value system, their work and their leadership keep us faithful to the agenda we set ourselves as a nation and which we are challenged to complete. They also know something that those who have never volunteered don't yet know: that it really is in giving that we receive; that amidst the many frustrations there is fun, friendship and fulfilment that no shop can sell, no gadget can generate.

We are fortunate to live in a high-achieving, wealthy Ireland, where so many such men, women and children are not content to be solely mere consumers but where they are impatient for these good times to be shared and experienced more widely still by all our citizens. That impatience and the restlessness it generates is the antidote to selfishness. It is the outward sign of an inward spirit of generosity and deep-rooted egalitarianism. It builds strong communities and makes us resilient in the face of predators who would rob these successful times of their best meaning and fullest potential. That ambition to complete the journey to 'a true social order', where no life is wasted if we can help it – that is and should be our most important gift to our children. It needs even more recruits; it needs a steady supply of champions. Maybe with Céifin's help and the debate it will provoke, we will learn how to carry our shopping bags in one hand and our consciences in the other; how to fill the vacuum with vision and virtue.

REMARKS AT THE INTERNATIONAL ASSOCIATION FOR SUICIDE PREVENTION XXIV BIENNIAL CONFERENCE

Irish National Events Centre, Killarney, County Kerry, 31 August 2007

Dia dhíbh go léir a chairde. Is mór an onóir agus pléisiúir dom bheith anseo libh inniu agus ba mhaith liom mo bhuíochas a chur in iúl díbh as an chaoin-chuireadh agus as fáilte fiorchaoin.

Thank you all for the very warm welcome. I would especially like to thank Dr John Connolly, a founder member of the Irish Association of Suicidology, of which I am patron, for the invitation to speak at this, the twenty-fourth biennial conference of the International Association for Suicide Prevention.

I am particularly delighted to welcome the many delegates who have travelled from all over the world to explore all aspects of suicide, including the latest research programmes relating to self-harm, suicide prevention and mental health. The panels look both fascinating and relevant, and I hope that you have found them useful. Already it has generated considerable media interest and public debate, and helped inform new understanding, fresh consciousness, and to focus renewed commitment.

The issues surrounding suicide, in all their painful, heartbreaking reality, have lately become horribly familiar in Ireland. In particular, the plight of young men, who comprise 40 per cent of all suicides here, is striking. For this segment of society, suicide is now the biggest killer. After them, elderly men living alone comprise the second highest at-risk group. The theme of this conference, 'Suicide Prevention across the Lifespan', could not, therefore, be more apposite to modern Ireland.

If these statistics paint a stark overall picture, then you, more than most, understand that hidden behind the figures lie uniquely personal, often untold stories of loss, depression, social dislocation, breakdown in relationship, substance abuse, distress or some combination of these experiences. We have been reminded of this fact all too often recently with stories of teenage suicides, filicide-suicides and familicides, as well as internet-prompted suicides, which have brought a new and worrying dimension to your work.

Behind the headlines, however, there are encouraging signs of progress in Ireland. The publication of two important strategy documents, *Reach Out: National Strategy for Action on Suicide Prevention for Ireland* in 2005 and *Protect Life*, a strategy for Northern Ireland in 2006, were key achievements. Both strategies set out milestones ranging from general approaches intended to improve awareness and education to specific plans for specially targeted at-risk groups. The establishment in 2005 of the National Office for Suicide Prevention in Ireland gives us a key centre for developing and progressing suicide prevention policies.

The action areas identified in *Reach Out* have led to the implementation of national training programmes, the availability of self-harm services in Accident and Emergency departments throughout the country, a review of bereavement services and support for voluntary organisations working in the field of suicide prevention.

In light of the increased information about suicide and self-harm, an interim target of a 10 per cent reduction in suicide by 2010 has been set. I know that tackling this problem will not be easy but if we are to prevent further tragic loss of life, we simply must continue our efforts in this area. Those efforts will soon be measured and found either wanting or successful. With your help, with the help of Government and of all of us, I believe we can be successful.

Looking at the island of Ireland, work is underway at delivering the actions outlined in the all-island action plan on suicide prevention, in the hope of reaping the benefits that can be achieved through North–South collaboration. Collaboration, I firmly believe, provides us with a key to multiply our efforts to combat suicide. Across the island, a plethora of individual initiatives, often driven by the tragedy of one particular family or community, is evident. The energy behind each of these initiatives is fantastic and would be greatly multiplied if they were able to work with other similar initiatives plugged into a national network, which, while not impinging on the independence of individual initiatives, would ensure that they are sustainable and that they have access to best-practice as it is disseminated by conferences such as this.

In March 2005, I hosted the first ever suicide forum at Áras an Uachtaráin, where people gathered to share insights and experiences in relation to dealing with suicide. The National Office for Suicide Prevention now hosts an annual forum for all those working in suicide prevention. These fora help to consolidate and validate ongoing work in this area, and serve to keep the focus fresh and the determination sharp.

I have been heartened to learn of the valuable research work being carried out into suicide prevention. A major benefit of this research is that valuable information on suicidal behaviour can be obtained and at-risk groups can be identified early. Data from research projects forms an important resource for the development of prevention and intervention programmes. In Ireland, the National Suicide Research Foundation is recognised by the World Health Organisation as a centre of excellence and the Irish focal point for sharing information regarding suicide and its prevention.

Suicide is an issue which affects every element of our society. In particular, the frequent clustering of suicides leaves not just individuals bereaved – families, friends, neighbours and colleagues – but also devastates entire communities, leaving a legacy of hurt, confusion, insecurity and fear.

Reducing suicide rates requires a collective, concerted effort from all groups in society: health and social services, other professionals, communities and community leaders, voluntary and statutory agencies and organisations, parents, friends, neighbours and individuals. It also requires the careful nurturing of a culture in which people in psychological distress don't hesitate to seek help from family, friends, health professionals and community leaders; a culture that recognises the signs and signals of distress and is willing to help, and that focuses early in life on developing good coping skills and avoiding harmful practices – in short, a sensitive culture that cherishes human courtesy and takes responsibility for our own and the mental health of others. Suicide occurs in many diverse contexts but there are recurring patterns and elements that research is revealing to us, and the more we are learning the better we are able to devise strategies and take action.

We already know, for example, that alcohol abuse plays a very significant role in suicide and features prominently in youth suicide. Research has also established that cannabis increases the risk of depression and psychosis and that it reduces normal inhibitions against suicide. Since marijuana is the illegal drug most used by those under twenty-five, a critical factor in suicide prevention must be to inform young people as to its dangers and counter the erroneous impression that it is a benign substance.

We know that bullying sometimes features in the story of suicide. Our young people need to know just how damaging, just how unacceptable, bullying is. Education and access to support structures, whether at work, school or home, are essential parts of protecting the victim of bullying, not just from the bully, but from their own downward spiral into suicidal thoughts.

A less discussed but nonetheless important issue worth raising is the issue of dealing with sexual identity. Although Ireland is making considerable progress in developing a culture of genuine equality, recognition and acceptance of gay men and women, there is still an undercurrent of both bias and hostility which young gay people must find deeply hurtful and inhibiting. For them, homosexuality is a discovery, not a decision, and for many it is a discovery which is made against a backdrop where, within their immediate circle of family and friends, as well as the wider society, they have long encountered anti-gay attitudes which will do little to help them deal openly and healthily with their own sexuality.

So next time we shake our heads in both horror and despair when we hear of another suicide story, it is worth remembering that the answers do not lie exclusively with healthcare professionals or politicians. There are things we need to do and to be vigilant about as a community that cares about its citizens and especially its vulnerable young. Among the things we could do as individuals, as families and as a community that would impact significantly on our suicide statistics and indeed our overall mental health are: we could and should, as a matter of urgency, decommission our culture of binge drinking, of tolerance of alcohol abuse and of drug abuse, and we could and should decommission attitudes that encourage bullying of all sorts, and in particular attitudes that are deeply hurtful to those who are homosexual.

The holding of this conference in Ireland is very important for us; it provides an opportunity to share best practice with practitioners worldwide, it raises the profile of a rapidly evolving problem in Ireland and it shows our determination to fight this scourge. I am delighted to hear from you that this conference has been so productive in sharing ways in which we can address the task which lies ahead.

This event has benefited from the support of a number of organisations including: the Department of Health and Children; the National Office for Suicide Prevention; the Department of Health, Social Services and Public Safety, Northern Ireland; Fáilte Ireland; Console, and the Samaritans. I wish to give special mention to the Irish Association of Suicidology and the International Association for Suicide Prevention for the hard work which went into organising this conference and indeed for your continued commitment to suicide prevention. I would also like to honour the vital work that all of you and the many, many other individuals and voluntary groups in our society do for the cause of suicide prevention.

Finally, I thank you all for attending this conference. May your efforts be vindicated by those lives you touch and bring comfort to.

Go n-éirí go geal libh agus go raibh míle, míle maith agaibh.

REMARKS AT A DINNER IN SUPPORT
OF THE SYMPOSIUM ENTITLED
'A DIALOGUE ON PHILANTHROPY'

21 February 2008

Good evening, and on behalf of Martin and myself, a very warm welcome, céad míle fáilte, to Áras an Uachtaráin. We are delighted to be able to host this timely gathering of stakeholders from both sides of the Atlantic and I am very grateful to my good neighbour, the American Ambassador Tom Foley for helping Ireland to focus on the potential here for a much more structured culture of philanthropy. I hope the discussions over dinner will provide a convivial follow-on to your discussions of earlier today.

There is quite an air of interest around the link between Ireland's contemporary wealth and the possibilities offered by philanthropy. Charitable giving is part of our DNA. It has been from time immemorial and it has been the hallmark of the Irish at home and abroad even in times of great poverty. We also have considerable experience of the collective power of the pennies of even the poorest, for it was those pennies which seed-bedded history-changing organisations like the Land League, the GAA and the Credit Union movement. It was those pennies that built churches, schools and community centres in every corner of Ireland and many a corner of Africa, and today the euro generation is still digging deep into its pockets for causes close to home and around the world. It is a culture of spontaneous generosity to be proud of.

We also have very recent experience of the impact that focused and intensive generosity can have in the resolution of problems once considered intractable. We only have to think of Northern Ireland, where the centuries-old sectarian and tribal divides were bridged by the judicious application of considerable funding from the Ireland Funds, the International Funds for Ireland and EU funding. The incremental but real changes wrought by that funding delivered deep into the heart of communities and were of immeasurable value to the development and ultimate success of the Peace Process. We think of the changes wrought in our education sector by Atlantic Philanthropies and many other donors whose investment in our knowledge equity has utterly changed our prospects.

Ireland is set to write an utterly new chapter in her history. For the first time, we have a peaceful island, with a rapidly growing cross-border culture of good neighbourliness to match the Dublin–Westminster friendship, which is the warmest it has been in possibly a millennium. For the first time we have behind us a generation of economic success and from it the growth of a wealthy, high-achieving indigenous entrepreneurial sector.

Many of those who have earned considerable wealth in recent years are already deeply implicated in charitable outreach, both in Ireland and among the poorest of the world's poor. Not all might agree with Andrew Carnegie that, 'he who dies rich, dies disgraced', but we can understand him to be raising the question about how best to utilise, in the interests of humanity, the resource that is wealth.

In our population of some 4 million, by one reckoning there are some 30,000 euro-millionaires, and at least 300 persons worth more than €30 million. This remarkable cohort has an opportunity to do extraordinary good, with a reach and on a scale that is quite simply unprecedented. If that scale can be harnessed to a strategy which facilitates a culture of planned giving and which targets that giving towards outcomes that are manifestly life-enhancing, we could not only advance much more quickly our ambition to be an egalitarian republic which is only truly complete when no one is on the margins, but could also advance our ambition to live in a world where everyone has access to decent education, healthcare, employment opportunity and environmental stability.

The United States is, of course, a leader in philanthropy, and indeed it was the US which led the way in applying philanthropy to the deep-rooted problems that led to conflict in Northern Ireland.

This is a debate other countries would love to be having. It comes precisely at the confluence of peace, prosperity and partnership. Importantly, it comes just as we are at the very start of a journey through which we will reveal, for the first time in our country's long, troubled history, what kind of Ireland can be built by people, first of all, who stay, people who come as emigrants, people who once ignored each others' true potential, people who wasted so much time mired in the vanities of history that their future was eaten away one miserable day at a time.

Now a confident, well-educated generation has the surging energy that comes from many sources in today's Ireland. They have already shown a talent for global entrepreneurialism and enviable achievement. They still have the Irish heart for helping others.

My neighbour now asks whether it is time to learn new, more exciting, more ambitious ways of giving and to contemplate altogether grander scales of outcomes. Among the privileged elite of past generations there were similar debates. They built workhouses, soup kitchens and funded famine ships. Our entrepreneurs are the children's children of an overlooked poor people deemed worthless in the eyes of the rich. They are the people who transcended that grim past, proved their worth, revealed their genius in a kaleidoscope of ways.

They are sharp, clever and they are problem solvers *par excellence*. They are perfectionists, dreamers, and they possess today not simply wealth but financial power, which, when it is allied to moral responsibility, when it is harnessed to philanthropy, can move mountains. I hope that we will see that power used and used well in writing the next and most exciting chapter in Irish history.

Enjoy your time here at the Áras and thank you for caring about the next chapter and the people in it.

Remarks at the opening of the 12ᵗʰ Annual Conference of the European Network of Ombudsmen for Children

3 September 2008

Dia dhíbh, a cháirde go léir. Tá mé iontach sásta bheith anseo libh inniu.

Good morning everybody and thank you for your warm welcome to your conference. It is my great pleasure, in turn, to welcome all of you, and in particular those of you who have travelled great distances to be here today. It is quite a privilege for Ireland to be your hosts and I am delighted to offer each of you the traditional Irish welcome, céad míle fáilte – 100,000 welcomes. My thanks to Emily [Logan, Ombudsman for Children] for inviting me to the opening of this important conference.

The words conference, network, ombudsman, are three relatively workmanlike, professional words which gather huge meaning and momentum when gathered around the words 'for children'. The more high-powered this conference, the stronger this network, the more ombudspersons there are in this field, the better are the lived lives and the prospects for good lives of our children, Europe's children, Europe's future.

We have high hopes and high ambitions for those children and we desire for them a secure childhood where they are loved, nurtured, protected, educated and supported safely through those years of dependency to adulthood. We know that is not how life pans out for many children. From their earliest moments in the womb they can be unwitting victims of the avoidable actions of others and the unavoidable ups and downs of nature at work in the world; from the children born with foetal alcohol syndrome or HIV, to children born with disabilities or into families where illness makes them worn-down carers before their time, or where poverty or dysfunction reduces their life's chances even before their little lives are launched. Some will transcend adversity with remarkable resilience; others will sink into half-lived lives.

We build many different kinds of fortification around our children to protect them and in particular to protect the most vulnerable. We have a host of laws, institutions, voluntary and State organisations, government departments, international treaties and the UN Convention on the Rights of the Child – the most widely ratified international human rights instrument – and the network they create between them is those children's safety net. The smaller and tighter its mesh, the less are the chances of any child slipping through to that underworld of vulnerable silence, where their lives can leach away, cruelly and unnoticed.

The truth is that children need adult champions, courageous advocates, accessible defenders and vindicators of their rights. Your vocation is to be such champions, to pierce that membrane of silence, to shape the adverse childhood experience into words and actions that lift their lives out of the shadows and into the light. You work in a complex world where children can be in one continent this morning and another this afternoon.

Here in Ireland, our once relatively homogeneous society has been opened up very rapidly in recent years by inward migration from all over the world. Families have come here in the hope of better lives and they have made huge contributions to our economy and our civic life. Among them are many children trying valiantly to cope with a new homeland, new language, new schools, new friends, different attitudes and customs. They may be desperately homesick or lonely for old friends and family left behind. Their sheer courage and determination is often overlooked or simply taken for granted. We have children who arrive alone on our shores, children who are vulnerable to trafficking and abuse.

All these new children are now our care, our kith and kin, for they are the human building blocks of tomorrow's Ireland and we need them to be strong, healthy, educated, confident and fulfilled. We already know only too well the appalling price paid over a lifetime for a childhood mired in abuse. The story has been told and retold through the tragic lives of many children abused in what were meant to be caring institutions. We know too that for many children the family home can be a place of relentless misery rather than refuge. We know the awesome capacity children have for suffering in silence.

The Convention on the Rights of the Child requires more of us than that we merely protect children from harm or vindicate them when abused. It talks about listening to children, respecting their views and ensuring that, in all matters concerning them, their best interests are a primary consideration – that their voices and views are given a chance to be coherently articulated and developed. There is a very telling phrase used by disability groups on the subject of inclusion: 'nothing about me without me'. It is a principle that pervades the approach and work of the Children's Ombudsman here in Ireland, for Emily, in her work, is advised by a Youth Advisory Panel of twenty-two young persons ranging from thirteen to eighteen years of age. The establishment of Offices of Ombudsman for Children across Europe holds great hope that Europe's children and young people, especially those most marginalised, will be drawn meaningfully into the mainstream, where their problems and perspectives will be taken seriously.

The words of our own Irish Proclamation of Independence that dates from 1916 speaks of our resolve as a Republic to guarantee religious and civil liberty, equal rights and equal opportunities to all our citizens and to cherish all the children of the nation equally.

To achieve this core goal, this test of us as a people and as a Republic of equals, we need the best of advice and the best of support from you, Europe's experts in the area of children's advocacy and protection. You in turn need each other and forums like this conference so that you can share experience, wisdom and insight, and at the same time strengthen the base of friendship, mutuality and collegiality that any integrated network needs to be fluent and effective. The more effective your network, the more all of us can have faith in our capacity to cherish our children equally.

I wish Emily every success in her forthcoming role as chairperson of your network. I have no doubt that she will be as successful in her international role as she has been in her domestic role here. I wish you all the very best of success in your discussions here in Dublin, and renewed energy for the return home to your daily work at the frontline of child advocacy and child protection in Europe.

Thank you.

Remarks at the Launch
of the 'Forum on End of Life in Ireland'

Royal Hospital Kilmainham, Dublin, 11 March 2009

Tá an-áthas orm bheith anseo libh inniu agus muid ag céiliúradh an ócáid mor seo. Ba mhaith liom bhuíochas a chur in iúl daoibh as an gcuireadh agus as fáilte a bhí caoin, cneasta agus croiúil.

Occasionally I get to launch things that are truly life changing. This is one of them, and ironically its ambition is to be death changing. The Irish Hospice Foundation's 'Forum on End of Life in Ireland' is about the business of ratcheting up a nationwide debate on dying and death so that, just as we have seen big advances in our quality of life in recent decades, so too we will see big advances in our quality of death. The hospice movement has championed this debate. It has showcased the huge benefits that flow from a much more holistic approach to dying, death and bereavement. It has been the conduit for a whole new and evolving science of palliative care that does not begin and end with medication but begins and ends with the needs of the person and the family as they face death – the one sure part of life, the one we all prefer not to face, yet the one on which we have remarkably strong and clear opinions when we are encouraged to share them. This forum will help us to open up the worries, fears, desires and ambitions about the end of life that we often keep firmly locked up. Most of us would admit to hoping for a 'good' death. How many of us in the past heard our parents and grandparents pray for the gift of a 'happy death'? In their day, when the drugs and treatments we take for granted were not available, they knew a silent thing or two about suffering and deaths that were hard on the dying and hard on those left behind. Behind that prayer was a world of dread.

Yeats captures the human condition elegantly and movingly when he says:

Nor dread nor hope attend

A dying animal;

A man awaits his end

Dreading and hoping all …

Yet we have a wealth of experience to help us illuminate the path to a 'good death', a careful death. Many have watched loved ones face serious illness and death. They saw them die in hospitals, in hospices, at home. They know the strengths and weaknesses of institutions, individuals and families when confronted with dying and death. There is a reservoir of experience that tells us what works well and what does not, what hurts and humiliates, what encourages and supports, what exacerbates the dread and what takes it away. From this forum and the debate it is carrying forward, will come the insight necessary to help us face into this great cultural taboo.

Your work will help construct a plan – or a series of plans – from which will come the tools, the infrastructure and the practices which will reduce our fears, grow our confidence and help us individually and collectively take on dying and death with hope. Death is always going to overcome us but dying does not need to defeat us or overwhelm us. Thanks to the hospice movement, more and more people are finding that out. For it has broadened the science surrounding dying far beyond the realm of the medical, vital though that is, and it has put the patient and his or her complex needs, rights and fears at the very centre, not as a person who needs treatment alone but as a person who is entitled to live life to the full, with dignity, comfort and space for joy right to the last breath.

Most people say they would prefer to die at home. It's a very telling ambition. To be among those we love, in the place we feel most comfortable – it's understandable. It is also very telling that most of us will not achieve that ambition. We will die in a busy general hospital among strangers who, with the best will in the world, will have us and a hundred other things to focus on. Our families and loved ones will be unsure of their place there, privacy may be hard to find and all the kindness in the world from medical staff will not dispel the feeling that somehow this was not the way we wanted death to come. Through hospice care, hospice in the home and, more recently, the mainstreaming of hospice culture in general hospitals, a much better range of options is opening up for those who face the dying process. Hospice characterises dying as a sacred space, to be cultivated with enormous care, compassion, sensitivity and focus. In the aftermath of a death, the traditional coping skills go into gear almost automatically and we Irish organise wakes and funerals with a sure-footedness that is commendable and designed to offer support and solidarity to the bereaved. That whole matrix of deep acts of kindness that magically click into place – the making of the sandwiches, the preparing of the house, marking out the local field as a make-shift car park, the arrangements for the funeral, the flowers for the church, the digging of the grave – all just seem to materialise without anybody asking, simply out of everybody caring, partly because it is what you do and partly in the knowledge that when your family's turn comes, the same will be done for you. But that is after death. Now we want that same, effective, coping system to snap automatically into place around dying. We have good reason to believe we can do just that.

We are already among the most advanced nations in the world in terms of the development of palliative care, yet even here this discipline is in its infancy and still has a long road to travel. It is helped by the world of technology and treatments which now help manage the dying process in ways unimaginable a short time ago. But it is underpinned by a care for things that lie beyond the world of tubes and technologies. There is a determination that the dying person is a living person whose life is going to be made as good as it possibly can be until life is extinguished. It carries a commitment to a dying that will be free of needless emotional trauma and physical suffering, that will be sensitive to the opportunity it presents for healing of regrets or resentments, getting affairs in order, for enhancing and growing personal relationships, for laying the foundation for a grieving process that is healthy. We need this forum and this national debate to get the energy of our hearts and hands behind this culture-changing, life-enhancing, death-enhancing opportunity. We all have a vested interest in getting this right.

When you step out of the daily fray into the calm of a hospice and feel the radiant power of love envelop all who enter that space between fragile life and the certainty of death, there is an immediate reminder that death itself is the constant, the certainty, the one great inevitability. We may not know its mood or mode but we know its outcome. It is mostly treated as an enemy, a superior and ever-triumphant enemy. It does not have to be so. It will, in the end, rob us of life, that is true, but as it dances around us it does not have to rob us of hope, dignity, peace, love, ease and comfort. These human things we can get right; we can do better. With the help of the Irish Hospice Foundation, its supporters and friends and this Forum, we will. My thanks to Paul Murray for the kind invitation on behalf of the Foundation to be here and my thanks to each of you for being here to invest in this debate and to help bring end-of-life palliative care to a level in Ireland that we can be justifiably proud of – a place of death without dread.

Thank you.

REMARKS AT AN EVENT FOR SURVIVORS OF INSTITUTIONAL ABUSE

Áras an Uachtaráin, 28 June 2009

Dia dhíbh go léir, agus céad míle fáilte romhaibh chuig Áras an Uachtaráin. Good afternoon everyone, and on behalf of Martin and myself, let me offer each one of you a warm, heartfelt welcome to Áras an Uachtaráin.

There are moments in a life when words simply fail as a means of expression. No amount of them, no matter how heartfelt, can seem adequate to the moment. The publication of the Ryan Report was one such moment in the life of this nation. The horrible lives endured by thousands of our children, over so many years, as a result of abuse inflicted by those who cared for them in the name of the State and often in the name of the Christian gospel, were laid out graphically in that report. It calls for responses at many levels, official and unofficial, and I know that many of you are actively involved in discussions on those responses. There is an important human response to overwhelming grief and that is to gather as community, to rally around one another and simply be together in solidarity.

The invitation to Áras an Uachtaráin today is an expression of the massive public wish to let you know how deeply your stories have struck a chord. For so long your suffering seemed to make strangers of you in your own land. Today, we simply seek to be family to each other, to assert our common care for one another and to acknowledge that what was done to those of you who are survivors of abuse in institutional care not only damaged your precious lives but diminished our society. Those who switched off the light of love and hope in your lives plunged our country into a terrible darkness. I know that one day in the Phoenix Park cannot hope to restore to your lives all the things that were taken from you. There is no magic potion to put right the things that were made so deliberately to go wrong. Nor is it possible in one event to reach out to everyone affected. I hope this day, though, does send a message that your lives and the lives of all those damaged by such abuse are our care, and that most important of all we stand together in our determination to ensure that our country will honour the ambition set out in the Proclamation in 1916 to be a Republic which cherishes its children equally. Your experiences are monuments to our failure to cherish our children. Our most precious monument to you has to be our determination to be that Republic where children are cherished equally, not just in lofty words but in everyday deeds.

The people of Ireland are desperately sorry for the many ways in which you were not cherished; in the abuse itself, in the silence, in the failure to act, in the failure to listen, hear and believe in time. In their name I offer everyone here and all those whose little lives were robbed of the joys of childhood our heartfelt sorrow.

I want to read you a short extract from a book called *Crime and Punishment*, edited by Sean McBride and published following an unofficial report into the Irish Penal System in 1982:

> Our low minimum age of criminal responsibility, seven, the lowest incidentally in Europe, ensures that the trivial activities of little children come under the censorious scrutiny of the criminal justice system ... precipitated by truancy from school or home or family break-down ... There was an incredible pathos about the submission which began, 'When I was seven I was sent to Clonmel ... I was in it for nine years.'

I wrote that particular section of the report and as a member of the commission had sat through the hearings at which many people spoke of leaving those institutions with little education or skill, often graduating straight into the adult penal system. It was less than thirty years ago but even then there was a silence and a fear, a huge taboo that stopped those men and women from telling the worst, the deepest secrets of their stories, even to a sympathetic audience. Today, thanks to the courage of the children who were abused and grew into an adulthood from which they took a stand against abuse, the veils of silence, authority, deference, pretence, power, powerlessness and impunity are pulled aside and we see what so many tried to ensure we would never see. It has all been at such a dreadful cost to the abused – their childhoods lost, their families scattered, their adult lives and relationships so often deeply affected by their early suffering. From that suffering, however, you have created a force that will in time bring much good to Ireland's children, for you challenge our society to hold to account all those who engrave on their innocent and dependent little lives. What's learnt in childhood is engraved on stone. You met bad engravers; the children of today and tomorrow rely on us to engrave well.

I hope you know how anxious so many people are to share your journey today. You have seen the turnout of Ireland's best entertainers, each of whom immediately volunteered their services when they knew this day was for you, and, through you, for all those whom you represent. I wish we could have had those many thousands here, but I thank the survivor organisations who nominated their guests for today for their help in making this day possible.

So, for all the birthday parties that that seven-year-old did not get in Clonmel, let us enjoy this day of solidarity and community. There is an old Irish phrase, 'giorraíonn beirt bóthar' – two shorten the road. As you leave here this afternoon, I hope you will feel that the road ahead, while still daunting, has been shortened for each of you in a special way and that where once you were on your own, you now have company that cares.

Go raibh míle maith agaibh go léir.

Remarks at CORI's
50ᵀᴴ Anniversary Conference

Grand Hotel, Malahide, 17 April 2010

Dia dhíbh a chairde.

I am delighted to have been asked to open this Golden Jubilee conference. My thanks to Sr Marianne O'Connor for inviting me.

Such a significant anniversary always invites a certain amount of retrospection. When I look back to the spring of 1960, I see an unsuspecting Ireland that was six months away from the transcendent power of Paddy Doherty's boot when he kicked the penalty that sealed the defeat of the Kingdom of Kerry at the hands of the Kingdom of Mourne. How many Irelands have come and gone since those early days; a welter of change that has impacted on every nook and cranny of life, including the world of religious institutes and congregations. The Irish landscape was then dotted with enormous monasteries and convents, full of life and people – young people. Within a couple of years, the flood of lively debate and discussion that was Vatican II would distil into hopes and expectations for a '*novus habitus mentis*' and a new future for what the Council had termed 'the People of God' – a society or communion of equals, whether lay, religious or clerical, in sharp contrast to the pre-conciliar 'society of unequals'.

It was an era when sharp shifts and changes of gear were expected, but other less obvious intimations of change would shortly reveal themselves. They are best summarised in the story of what is now the Emmaus Retreat Centre near Swords, built, if I remember rightly, around that time by the Christian Brothers to house the many new entrants who were expected but who did not materialise. The building never served the purpose for which it was built, but like so many others in a similar predicament found a new life, recycled as a conference and retreat centre. The religious congregations have been right at the heart of the post-conciliar Church, driving forward the agenda of Vatican II within each congregation at a pace well ahead of other sectors. At the same time you have been deeply implicated, through your work and your advocacy, in the growth and development of modern Ireland.

These fifty years have been a process of adaptation, sometimes to welcome changes but often to unwelcome change. The world metamorphosed from an era of deference to an era of declamation. CORI has been an active part of the process of catharsis and no mere passive spectator as events rang the changes. This conference has the title 'Walking the Way' and while the way forward holds great uncertainty and unpredictability, the way already travelled has much to tell us.

You represent almost 140 religious congregations and some 9,000 religious in Ireland. Between them they represent an unequalled and unrivalled investment in Ireland, her education, health and social welfare, and the physical, pastoral and spiritual enrichment of her people. The story has many good, even great chapters, for you and your predecessors created and sustained, and on a not-for-profit basis, much of the founding infrastructure of today's education and healthcare systems and outreaches to the poor and marginalised. The story, as the Ryan and Murphy reports reveal, also has some dreadful chapters, as the rigid hierarchicalism and powerful clericalism which characterised the preconciliar era created vacuums of vulnerability and unaccountability, where children in particular suffered outrageously. The way that will be walked tomorrow will be a different walk.

Already we see the green shoots that you have nurtured begin to alter the landscape around us. Today there are exciting new trusts and broad-based partnerships involving individual and collectives of congregations, along with the laity and civic society spelling a collaborative and inclusive future, which would have been unthinkable fifty years ago but which honours both the letter and spirit of the Vatican

Council, as well as being a pragmatic common-sense response to the decline in vocations.

CORI's members are entitled to be proud of the positive transformations that they have helped to effect over recent decades. The change management process in all the areas in which you work has been, and remains, immensely sensitive and challenging. The old Irish seanfhocal says, 'giorraíonn beirt bóthar', and CORI has been a place where religious could journey in solidarity with one another across the congregational boundaries and the subtle differences in charism, and forge a deep experience of a journey in common. CORI's existence has been a key enabling condition for the transformation that has been achieved.

The work of CORI's members is also, today, as it has been over generations, a key enabler of the life chances of so many individuals who depend on the roles that you are carrying out each day on the ground in communities across Ireland. Through the important impact you have on each individual, they are changed, families are changed, our communities and our country are changed. CORI is also, of course, probably best known for its championing of a fair and just society and for its advocacy on behalf of people whose lives are blighted by poverty and social exclusion.

Prior to the current economic downturn, Ireland had succeeded in halving the rate of consistent poverty between 2003 and 2008, with particularly noteworthy improvements for older people. Achievements like this do not happen by accident or by one stakeholder working in isolation; rather they are in part thanks to the work of CORI as a member of the Community and Voluntary Pillar of social partnership. The new fiscal climate is about as difficult as it can get, but tough though it is, we still have not altered our Republic's basic founding ambition to work for the achievement of a country which cherishes all its children – all its citizens – equally. Our citizens need the reassurance that comes from having credible advocates who stand in solidarity with them in the pursuit of that fairness and equality – to walk the way and talk the way through engagement in policy-making towards a fully inclusive, fair and ethically prosperous society.

This society has a lot of work to do to set our country on the right way. After the publication of the Ryan Report, CORI said, 'All of us accept with humility that massive mistakes were made and grave injustices were inflicted on very vulnerable children. No excuse can be offered for what has happened.' The millstone of the Ryan and Murphy reports will be carried for a long time on the way ahead, just as the millstone of the massive fiscal mistakes will similarly have to be carried for some time to come into the future. There is a long road ahead to redemption on both accounts, but you meet here to prepare for the journey, as volunteers who are not paralysed by the scale of the difficulties but who have a profound belief that there can be healing, there can be renewal, there can be change for the better. You are here because you have, or want to have, hope. Vaclav Havel says:

> Hope is definitely not the same thing as optimism ... It is what gives us strength to live and to continually try new things even in conditions that seem hopeless.

Those who gave their lives in good faith to religious congregations, who lived good lives and who invested generously and unselfishly in the lives of others – in other words the vast majority of CORI's members – have been hearts-calded by the now clearly documented depravity of those who dishonoured their vocation by abusing children and the denial and inaction which allowed that depravity to continue with virtual impunity. They are also heart-scalded by the righteous rage of those who were abused. They have pledged, through CORI and elsewhere, to do their best to put as much right as can be put right and I am glad to see that there is serious engagement on the level of reparations to be made. They are heart-scalded too by the worries and anger carried by those they meet with in the course of their work each day; those coping with worries over money and jobs and raging disappointment at the reck-less and irresponsible business practices which have brought about such economic problems.

Now that grief has to be distilled into wiser, humbler action. This is the moment when we need people of faith to have faith in themselves and in our country's ability to dig deep, heal its wounded and, with their help, walk the way ahead together, to a better time and a better Ireland. It may look like an unlit path but in fact you know and believe there is a guide. Be not afraid …

I congratulate CORI on everything that has been achieved over the last fifty years. I wish you well as you face up with hope to the challenges in the immediate years ahead.

REMARKS AT THE LGBT DIVERSITY NATIONAL CONFERENCE, 'FOUNDATIONS'

Westbury Hotel, Dublin, 29 November 2010

Dia dhíbh a chairde, thank you for your warm welcome this morn-ing and I'd like to thank Derek McDonnell, Programme Manager with LGBT Diversity for his kind invitation on behalf of the Joint Working Group to speak at this your first national conference – and an important milestone in the story of the full social inclusion of Ireland's lesbian, gay, bisexual and transgendered citizens. The conference is well titled – 'Foundations' – for your work is doing nothing less than building the foundations of a very different Ireland and a very different life experi-ence for lesbian, gay, bisexual and transgender people.

That life experience has been, for many, historically characterised by a deep sense of isolation and exclusion, of being misunderstood and being judged – indeed, misjudged by a mile. The toxic attitudes which were heard in homes, streets, workplaces, even in schools and churches, caused untold suffering and nothing is surer than the fact that those attitudes can have and will have no place in the Ireland we are building, for they belong in the same toxic waste dump along with sexism, racism, sectarianism and all those other contrary forces which would diminish the innate dignity, freedom and nature of the human person, reduce their life chances and opportunities and consign them to half-lived lives.

The organisations represented here today have been strong and powerful advocates, promoting human rights, insisting on equality, and diligently chipping away at the hardened old mindsets and prejudices built up over centuries and which no longer hold the moral high ground. As well as offering support to LGBT people and their families and friends, thanks to you, voices which would otherwise have been unheard are now speaking out, raising public awareness, playing a key role in education campaigns and having an input into the formation of public policy. Thanks to you, Ireland is continuing to make visible progress.

Just over thirty years ago, the first campaign for homosexual law reform began. We have come a long way since those days when the focus was on decriminalisation. Recent legislation on civil partnership will substantially change the landscape for same-sex couples. It had been widely recognised that the absence of any official recognition for same-sex relationships contributed to their invisibility in our society and this much-anticipated development will not only have a direct practical impact for same-sex couples who choose to register a partnership, but it will also give families, friends and wider communities an opportunity to publicly celebrate and support gay and lesbian couples who wish to have formal recognition of their relationships.

We are also filling in gradually the research and information gaps, learning about the grim impact and prevalence of homophobic bullying, the vulnerability to mental ill-health and suicide of young gay people as a result of societal pressures, the need for candid and accessible healthcare information, services, counselling and support. Our school curriculum is now responding positively, our healthcare systems are more engaged than ever and while there is still a distance to travel, it is important on a day like this that we acknowledge with gratitude the investment you and others have made, through tireless months and years of effort, to raise public awareness of the issue and ring the changes needed to ensure that every person in our society is treated with dignity and respect and has their human rights fully protected, fully vindicated.

Those whose views on homosexuality continue to feed an unacceptable culture of exclusion that impacts so dreadfully on the safety, security, health and hopes of our LGBT citizens need to be continually challenged and engaged in a civic discourse about our constitutional commitment to the equality and dignity of every human person and the assertion of our Proclamation that we should be a Republic that cherishes all the children of the nation equally. It is good to see that there is now an Advisory Group appointed by the Minister for Social Protection looking at the issue of legal recognition of the acquired gender of transgender persons, for here is a group which faces very particular difficulties and in a context of considerable lack of public awareness and social isolation.

One of the most distressing human experiences we can have is to feel completely alone, to feel like the permanent outsider. There are still pockets of the country, particularly in rural areas, without support groups and there we can only begin to imagine the aloneness felt by a person who cannot access help. But help is on the way, for this conference has chosen to focus on capacity building so that the organisations represented here can expand and grow their network of care, mutual support and public advocacy. There is a rapidly expanding body of knowledge, experience, wisdom and practice which is feeding into this inaugural national conference.

Your work here will be to share as much of that information as possible and to distil it, so that the next steps of the LGBT Diversity

Programme can be surefooted and channelled in exactly the right direction, so that the foundations you lay over the next three years will be fit for purpose. That purpose is nothing less than creating an Ireland that is a comfortable and happy place to live for all our citizens – gay, lesbian, bisexual and transgender alike. A place where they are free and able to make their fullest contribution to building up our society with their talents and gifts as equal citizens of an egalitarian republic. It is the only future worthy of us as a people and we need you to help us get there by the shortest and the surest route.

Go raibh maith agaibh go léir.

REMARKS AT THE OPENING OF A FORUM ON WORKING TOGETHER FOR POSITIVE MENTAL HEALTH FOR YOUNG PEOPLE

Áras an Uachtaráin, 22 June 2011

Dia dhíbh a chairde go léir agus fáilte chuig Áras an Uachtaráin inniúu.

My warmest thanks to each of you for making the journey, whether long or short, to be with us this morning and for being willing to share your thoughts, experiences, insights and ideas as we gather here to discuss ways of creating the conditions for positive mental health among our young people. I am particularly delighted that the newly appointed Minister for Children, Frances Fitzgerald is joining us today.

We didn't choose the topic for today's forum at random – far from it. Studies and surveys indicate that mental health is the number one issue for young people. Dáil na nÓg and Comhairle na nÓg have already hosted in-depth discussions on this topic. Evidence suggests that adolescence is a time in the lifespan when people are particularly vulnerable to mental health difficulties and when concrete supports for learning resilience and coping skills may be weak. Those problems can arise in economic good times and in bad, for young people are in no way immune from stresses and worries. In their world there are issues to do with awakening sexuality, self-image, exams, shyness, bullying, family dysfunction, prevailing social and cultural attitudes about mental health, about sexual identity – all or any mix of these and more can be a lot to deal with alone and no young person needs to deal with them alone or should be left to deal with them alone. Our young people's mental wellbeing is our responsibility and we already know that the availability of one good adult in a young person's life – one adult who believes in him or her – can make a huge benign contribution to their mental health. Our goal here is not to insulate young people from the realities of life, but to equip them well so that they can deal well with life's realities and its inevitable but often unpredictable ups and down.

A phenomenal amount of good work is being done to encourage a culture of positive mental health and positive attitudes to mental health. Each of the organisations and groups represented here today are engaged in that work, and thanks to you the message is getting out that young people need to take their share of responsibility for their mental wellbeing as much as their physical wellbeing and that there is help available to them. Just as there is help and guidance to become skilled at sport or music or academic subjects, there is help to become skilled at healthy personal resilience.

We are challenged to ensure that young people who are troubled or worried have the insight, confidence and information they need to understand that they may need a bit of help, to seek appropriate help and in good time. As the ad says, young people dealing with stress, anxiety or depression need to let someone know. We are challenged to ensure that when they do seek help that they will find sensitive, accessible, timely and effective support. We already know that most young people who experience serious emotional difficulties are not reaching out for help. We know that if they did get help, good early intervention could prevent those problems from becoming unwelcome lifelong companions. So how to bridge those gaps in which people suffer unnecessarily in silence and put themselves at increased risk by so doing?

Today we are going to listen to some very inspirational people who will generously share their life's experiences with us, as we try to drill down deeper into the question of the mental health of our young people. I am grateful for their contribution and hope that they will provoke a very lively and eye-opening discussion.

We pay an awful price as a society for lives that are blighted by mental ill-health. It is not how we want life to be, nor is it how life should be. Our young people want for themselves what we want for them; healthy, happy, well-balanced lives, faith in themselves, hope in the future and a determination to make their best mark on that future.

How do we make that happen, particularly where circumstances conspire to make life very difficult? You have ideas and experiences that can help us answer that question or help us to keep probing it intelligently until the steps towards a better future begin to form in our minds and then in our practice. Each one of you holds part of the answer like pieces in a jigsaw puzzle. The more of those pieces we reveal through dialogue, the quicker we get to see the full picture and discern the signposts to better mental health for our young people.

My thanks to Áine Lalor for chairing today's proceedings, and my warmest thanks to each of you for the part you will play today.

Go raibh míle maith agaibh go léir.

6

AN IRELAND OF COMMUNITY

Ceád míle fáilte – 100,000 welcomes to our superb special athletes, their coaches, families, friends, volunteers, sponsors and supporters. We have been looking forward to this day for a very long time. Ireland is famous for its warm welcome but never in the history of our country has there been a bigger or better welcome for anyone than the welcome prepared for the world's best special athletes.

We are delighted to be the first country outside the United States to host this spectacular event. For months, thousands of people have been working hard to make sure that wherever you come from in the world, here in Ireland you will feel completely at home. You have also worked incredibly hard to get here. Each special athlete is already a champion and now you are representing your country on the international stage, competing with the best in the world.

We are at the start of a week that none of us will ever forget; a week when you will share with us that magical feeling of participation in the Special Olympics World Games. We know that each of you hopes to win and we know too that whether you win or not, each of you will be brave in the attempt.

Thank you for coming to Ireland. We are very proud to have you here and we are proud of the wonderful way this small island, north, south, east and west has opened its heart to you, our special visitors. We are willing each of you on to great success. We wish you fun, laughter, happy memories and the gift of new friendships. Between us all, may we fulfil our dream of making these the best games ever.

REMARKS AT AN AWARDS CEREMONY TO MARK THE 21ST ANNIVERSARY OF GAISCE – THE PRESIDENT'S AWARD – AND THE 50TH ANNIVERSARY OF THE DUKE OF EDINBURGH AWARDS

National Concert Hall, Dublin, 26 April 2006

Your Royal Highness, Ambassador, distinguished guests, Gold Award recipients, ladies and gentlemen,

A hearty céad míle fáilte – 100,000 welcomes – to the National Concert Hall for what is a very special Gold Awards Ceremony, indeed a unique occasion, when the Duke of Edinburgh Award recipients and President's Award recipients receive their awards in a joint ceremony in the presence of both the Duke of Edinburgh and the President. I welcome the award winners, their leaders, families and friends and I am delighted to offer a warm welcome to His Royal Highness, Prince Philip, the Duke of Edinburgh, and other representatives of the Duke of Edinburgh Award Scheme and the International Award.

Gold Award ceremonies are occasions of great pride and joy for we gather to mark and to celebrate the achievements of young men and women who have freely undertaken and transcended the most testing and revealing of challenges. We know what they are made of. We know their strengths, their resilience and their courage. These are not dormant or latent, waiting for life to test them. They have been tested and they have earned our respect – earned gold – the hard way. In addition to their individual stories of determined self-discovery, of generosity and curiosity about our world, today's ceremony has another very significant dimension, for it consolidates and showcases an important and dynamic element of the exceptional relations that now exist between Ireland and the United Kingdom. Our mutual links in the area of youth work and the empowerment of young people is epitomised by the collegial co-operation between the President's Award and the Duke of Edinburgh Award under the shared umbrella of the International Award.

I am happy to have this opportunity also to congratulate the Duke of Edinburgh Award on celebrating its fiftieth anniversary. As the forerunner of other such awards, it continues to be recognised and respected as a world leader in facilitating and encouraging young people to take on life-enhancing and community-enhancing challenges which deepen and stretch them, rounding them into the most admirable, dependable and active citizens. Similar awards now exist in over 100 countries, among them Ireland's President's Award, which comes of age this year, with twenty-one remarkably successful years now to its credit. Today's ceremony marks a new milestone in our long-standing joint co-operation in the interests of tomorrow's young citizens and it bodes well for their future.

It is also a personal milestone in the lives of the Gold Awardees. Their undertaking of the award was a personal crusade, a journey into the self and into the world that they each had to commit to and stick to. No one could go the journey for them but some did go the journey with them; family, award leaders, teachers, schools, employers, sponsors, funders and the award staff. Those who stayed the course have become role models and we hope their success, their enthusiasm for life itself and all its possibilities will be a life-changing light in the lives of other young people.

Recipients of the Duke of Edinburgh and President's Gold Awards do not need to explain to prospective employers or to the world at large that they are people of courage, persistence, dedication and determination – the award says that for them. Their communities know they are people of sensitivity, of conscience, generosity and responsibility, for the award bears witness to those qualities too. Every country needs young citizens like these, whose creative energies are harnessed and focused so enthusiastically on things that build up the human person and human society. It is very reassuring to see that the overall participation rate in the President's Award continues to increase and that the cross-cultural dimension is strengthened as we continue to work closely with the Duke of Edinburgh Award in a spirit of mutual respect and co-operation in Northern Ireland.

It is important to emphasise that the young people we honour today and their leaders embarked on their challenges on a purely voluntary basis. No one said you must – no law demanded it. There were many things which could have distracted them, but together they kept faith with the challenges and so today they share the glory that achieving gold brings. Their investment in the individual is also a huge investment in family, community and society. Each strong individual makes our countries strong and we owe a huge debt of gratitude to those whose work sustains and grows these awards.

I acknowledge with sincere thanks the hard work of both Award Councils, under the enthusiastic chairmanships of Dr Laurence Crowley and Gordon Topping. Please excuse a special mention of the President's

Award Chief Executive, John Murphy. John retires this year, leaving the soundest of legacies, so many lives changed, so much good invested in Ireland's young people. I wish him well in his retirement and thank him resoundingly for all he has accomplished, from the days when this award was just a good idea, to the strong organisation he masterminded, with great assistance from colleagues in the Duke of Edinburgh Award. To all the mentors, teachers and award leaders, donors, supporters and friends, a big thank you for your faith in these awards and your enormous contribution to their success.

Your Royal Highness, your presence is greatly appreciated by everyone here today and it has added a unique and inspirational dimension. I am sure you join with me in offering congratulations to today's Gold Award recipients, whose hard-earned day this is. Enjoy the moment and know that we are proud of each of you, we respect you and today we honour you. Congratulations to you all.

Comhghairdeas libh inniu. Go raibh maith agaibh – Thank you.

REMARKS AT A GARDEN PARTY
HELD TO MARK THE 125TH ANNIVERSARY OF THE GAELIC ATHLETIC ASSOCIATION

Áras an Uachtaráin, 6 July 2009

Dia dhíbh go léir, agus céad míle fáilte chuig Áras an Uachtaráin inniu.

Good afternoon and welcome to this special day of celebration to mark 125 years of Cumann Lúthchleas Gael. Many of you have togged out behind a hedge on a wet winter's day and anyone who has ever been a spectator at Clones is no stranger to a bit of rain, so as a group we have all plenty of experience of enjoying ourselves no matter what the weather is doing.

This is a big group for the Áras but just a small representative sample of the hundreds of thousands of GAA members, past and present, who grew this great national sporting organisation into the most successful amateur sporting organisation anywhere in the world. Your hearth is the magnificent stadium that is Croke Park but your heartland is anywhere in the world where Gaels gather to puck a sliothar or kick a ball. From Derry to Dingle, from Dublin to Dubai, from San Francisco to Hong Kong, day after day, week after week, an army of volunteers cares for this organisation and keeps it full of effort and imagination. In parishes, townlands, villages, suburbs and cities there is nothing to match it and nothing that comes close to matching the GAA. That it remains an unapologetic amateur organisation, rooted deeply in the local, national and international life of the Irish family at home and abroad, is its enduring strength.

This organisation has given to millions memories to last not just one lifetime but many. It has created opportunities, seeded ambition, honed skill, galvanised the individual, harnessed the team. It has brought days of massive pride and occasional broken hearts to the parish, the club, the school, the county, the province and the country. Such a debt as we owe to the GAA could never be repaid, but today we gather to say a heartfelt thank you.

It would be impossible to name all the great GAA leaders on and off the field of play who have earned our respect and gratitude. They are legion and they are legendary. Martin has hinted that I should make an exception and mention the great Antrim players of the past but actually our sights are on the great Antrim players of the present. I do, however, want to make a special mention of the Artane Band, who are here with us today. They are synonymous with the GAA and especially with those wonderful All-Ireland days in Croke Park. They are about to embark on a major tour of the United States and I would like to wish them the very best of luck; travel safe and have a great time.

As you look around the room, there may be many old friends and familiar faces, so enjoy the company, the craic, the caint and the ceol. The winners and competitors of Scór have been showcasing their talent and we'll hear more from them shortly.

On your behalf and on that of Martin and myself, thank you to the wonderful Áras staff, the entertainers, Civil Defence, the Gardaí, the tour guides and everybody who has helped to make the day very special. But most of all, thanks to you for being with us. Have a great afternoon, and return home safely.

Go raibh míle maith agaibh go léir.

REMARKS AT THE CIVIC SOCIETY: RESILIENCE IN TOUGH TIMES FORUM

Áras an Uachtaráin, 29 January 2010

Dia dhíbh a chairde go léir agus fáilte chuig Áras an Uachtaráin inniu.

I am grateful to each one of you and especially those of you who have travelled long distances to be with us today; you're all very welcome. This forum is discussing resilience in tough times, and most people characterise these times as particularly tough. They are disappointing times, for we have lived through a period of virtually full employment and strong economic and social development. The surging confidence of those days has given way to a time of worry. Our coping skills are being tested. Just how resilient are we?

As President, I have the privilege of regularly seeing at firsthand the quiet, life-changing, life-enhancing, hope-generating work that is being done by individuals and all sorts of community and voluntary groups throughout this island. The floods and big freeze gave us a very public insight into the great resources we have in the solidarity of our communities and the culture of volunteering. Nature did its worst and human nature did its best. Today, with your help, we hope this forum will look at the resilience and coping skills we have at work already within us as individuals and as communities, and how we can galvanise that spirit of resilience to help get us through these times. There are literally thousands of volunteer organisations at work in Ireland each day, helping us to cope better and more effectively with a massive variety of issues and problems, and we are going to hear from some of them today. Organisations like SpunOut and Jigsaw, which, as we will hear, are doing their best to encourage people under pressure to focus positively on their mental health wellbeing. Or the St Vincent de Paul, which knows intimately the economic pressure people are facing, because it is right there with them, trying to hold back the tide of fear. Social entrepreneurs are encouraging greater imagination and innovation in solving problems to do with poverty, under-achievement and marginalisation. We'll hear from the Civil Defence, who have a unique insight into what goes on in communities in times of need, and from the academic sector we'll hear about the vital importance of upskilling and getting involved in ongoing education and training.

Within these four walls we have people of great experience, expertise and proven resilience. When times were good, they were not always good for everyone, and these people worked to include everyone. When times got tough, these people got tougher, and the vast majority of the newly unemployed who came to their doors came, ironically, not just as people seeking help but as people offering their help. The desire to help, to make a difference, is the hallmark of the volunteer, and faith in our ability to change things for the better is the seed corn of hope. Our speakers and audience are just a tiny fraction of Ireland's army of weavers and spinners of resilience and of hope.

No one of us has all the answers, but by putting our experiences and insights together we have a better chance of putting together the pieces of the jigsaw that will show how we can face today and tomorrow fired by new possibilities, new ideas, new challenges and above all real faith and hope in ourselves and in our country. Thank you for taking time out from your busy lives to play your part here today.

Go n-éirí go geal libh agus go raibh míle, míle maith agaibh.

Remarks at a Reception to Mark the 30ᵀᴴ Anniversary of the National Adult Literacy Agency

Áras an Uachtaráin, 28 April 2010

Dia dhíbh a chairde,

I am delighted to extend the traditional welcome of the house, céad míle fáilte, as we celebrate the thirtieth anniversary of the National Adult Literacy Agency.

For men and women with literacy problems, life can be a very lonely, private journey. I have met many of them over the years that I have been Patron of NALA and they have told me over and over again, in unforgettable stories, that NALA became their friend, teacher and guide and, through NALA, they were introduced to themselves all over again, but this time with confidence in themselves and hope in the future.

I am regularly asked who is the person who has most impressed me since I became President and I am sure the audience expect me to name someone well-known nationally or internationally. But I always give the same answer that the most impressive people I have ever met, I met through NALA, one a woman and mother who left school without the ability to read or write, reared her children without ever being able to read them a bedtime story or help with their homework and who experienced dreadful levels of shame, unemployment and lack of confidence which made her life secretly and silently miserable. Then she got the courage to seek out NALA. She started like a junior infant with the alphabet and by the time I met her she was doing postgraduate studies in Trinity College. I cannot even begin to imagine the courage she had to find in order to start all over again. What I remember most, though, is her radiance, her joy in life and her restless curiosity to see just who she truly is and could be.

Close behind her was a man who had a job but could never join his colleagues at the coffee break, where they would be talking about the things in the newspapers, for fear he would reveal his inability to read. I met him the night he read his first poem, in which he described the sheer thrill of being able, with the help of NALA, to write the name of his wife and daughters on a blank page.

One woman told me that before NALA, she lived her life as if she was inside a matchbox. Another told me of bringing home what she thought were yellow pack baked beans only to discover she had bought dog food. She said every last vestige of self-belief evaporated on that day but then it became the thing that propelled her into NALA. And when those men and women cross the door of NALA, the story changes from dark to light, from a problem endured to a problem solved.

NALA's professional and volunteer team has, for thirty years, been a source of liberation and encouragement to thousands of people. In their homes and communities they have each been powerful witnesses to the way that education can open up a life. Some were brave enough and generous enough to share their stories on television through the programmes made with RTÉ. Those programmes reached huge audiences and gave a lot of people the inspiration they needed to seek out NALA and start their own life-changing journey to literacy.

Thanks to NALA, we are all more clued in to the kind of problems people have with literacy issues, including things like financial literacy, dealing with banks, building societies or credit unions, or jargon literacy – dealing with filling out complicated forms. All of these things help people to take control over their own lives and to ensure their fullest talents and skills are blossoming as they should.

To Inez Bailey, Director of NALA and all her team, to the many tutors and volunteers around the country, to the sponsors and supporters and particularly to the past and present students of NALA, I congratulate you on your wonderful, inspirational, life-enhancing work of the past three decades. I am so proud of what you have achieved. Enjoy every moment of the thirtieth anniversary celebrations and I look forward to seeing what NALA and its graduates can achieve in the next thirty years.

Go raibh míle maith agaibh go léir.

REMARKS AT THE OPENING CEREMONY OF THE EUROPEAN YEAR OF VOLUNTEERING

Royal Hospital Kilmainham, Dublin, 12 February 2011

Dia dhíbh go léir inniu. Tá an-áthas orm bheith anseo libh ar an ócáid speisialta

It is my great pleasure to join you this afternoon to celebrate the launch of the European Year of Volunteering 2011. Thank you to Elaine Bradley for the invitation and to each of you for such a lovely welcome. Can I in turn welcome you to this special ceremony and extend a particular cead míle fáilte to Minister Alex Attwood, the Minister for Social Development in Northern Ireland.

Mother Teresa once said that volunteers are unpaid not because their work is worthless but because it is priceless. We know how harsh the world has become in this time of recession, as the flow of money through the economy and people's purses dries up. We have no idea how unbearable our country and our world would be if the flow of volunteering generosity stopped coursing through our lives. It would spell nothing less than a psychological ice age. That is how essential volunteers are, how critical they are to our civic wellbeing, our civic resilience and our civic strength.

The kind of volunteers we are celebrating here are people who enhance life by doing good things that could not happen but for the volunteer.

It would be impossible to enumerate what volunteers add to the quality of our lives, for they have a vast reach and unlimited imaginations. Our national games that bring so much fun, skill, memories and friendly disagreements into our lives rest almost entirely on the passion of volunteers who keep on turning up like clockwork, week in and week out. There is a sophisticated volunteer-run web of practical care that makes life better for young, old, disabled, bereaved, addicted, illiterate, lonely, abused, suicidal, sick, poor and unemployed. There is a weft of support for international, national and local charities, voluntary agencies, self-help groups, fundraisers, community, neighbourhood and parish initiatives, schools, hospitals and hospices, care of the environment, our cultural heritage, local economic development, and – so many things volunteers do that to start to list them is to be defeated, because it would be impossible in a short address to adequately cover the infinite ingenuity and reach of the volunteer. But what they do matters to us enormously as individuals and as a common human family.

Right now, this minute, kids are turning up to scouts or sports training and volunteers are there faithfully to look after them. A family is sitting around a fire and has food on the table thanks to the St Vincent de Paul. A homeless woman is dropping into Simon or Focus Point or

Trust and they are there for her. A cancer patient is pouring out her fears to a counsellor. A group of senior citizens are on a fun outing, a man with literacy problems is in class with a tutor, a class of schoolchildren are bag-packing to raise money for an AIDS orphanage in Zambia, a cross-community group in Northern Ireland is working to maintain the hard-won peace, a Civil Defence unit is practising the drill for an emergency or disaster. Each one is investing, quietly and unobtrusively, in our civic strength and in the quality of our civic life.

The Presidency has given me a unique opportunity to see at firsthand the massive range and strength of voluntary effort that is part of Irish life and culture. Though we are apt to characterise the Celtic Tiger years very cynically right now, as we cope with the difficulties and disappointments of the recession, it is worth remembering that in 2003 volunteers showed the world what Ireland was made of when we were able to host the Special Olympics World Summer Games only because of a phenomenal mobilisation of volunteers nationwide. People dug deep into their pockets to raise the huge amount of money needed, they opened their homes to host international competitors and thousands joined the volunteer army that made the event not simply an outstanding success but a showcase of all that is good, positive, enduring and hopeful about our country.

Time and again I encounter voluntary groups which started with literally nothing but a good idea for a needed social initiative, developed around a kitchen table. Each has a story of how, against the odds they delivered their idea, a crèche, a senior citizen housing complex, a youth club, an immigrant support group, a national organisation ... and there are many such stories. I think of the Irish Wheelchair Association, which started fifty years ago when eight people, frustrated by how wheelchair users were confined to their homes and to limited life opportunities, each threw a 10s note into a plastic bucket and started an association that has grown into a wonderful success story with a strong professional pillar still supported by and reliant on a national band of volunteers.

Many voluntary groups which deal with poverty and mental health problems are, we know, under intense pressure as a result of the economic downturn which is causing such hardship. Many volunteers are themselves under those same pressures, with pay cuts, job losses and financial worries casting shadows over their innate optimism and 'can-do' attitude. Yet we also see in these times an increase in volunteering that is reassuring and commendable, for it tells us that we still firmly believe in the truth of the old adage 'ní neart go cur le chéile' – our strength comes from our unity, from facing into problems together and pulling together so we muster the communal strength that becomes the resource of mutual support.

There is a saying that 'He who gives when he is asked has waited too long.' Volunteers are people who see a need and say, 'Let me help.' That offer of help is made without thought of any personal reward beyond the fulfilment that comes from giving. But in this year which focuses on volunteering, I take this opportunity to warmly thank Ireland's volunteers and to encourage them to keep on volunteering and to encourage others to get involved, to volunteer and to discover the hidden treasury of fun, friendships, insight, wisdom, experience and personal wellbeing that comes from being of service to others.

I wish the National Committee every success in its exciting plans for the year ahead. It is great that those plans include collaborative activities with our friends and colleagues in Northern Ireland.

I know of no other country which has such a dynamic volunteer ethic at work enriching everyday life. In this year, I hope we all learn never to take the volunteer for granted and never to pass up the opportunity to be a volunteer. The bad news is that volunteers don't qualify for redundancy but the good news is that they are never likely to be made redundant – for where two or more are gathered there is work for volunteers. Bail ó Dhia ar an obair!

Thank you.

..

7

A CREATIVE IRELAND

Dia dhíbh a cháirde go léir.

Hello everyone. You are very welcome to Áras an Uachtaráin this afternoon. Martin and I hope you will enjoy your visit and we thank you for coming.

This afternoon is a celebration of your work as individual artists and of your collective power as a body in showcasing to Ireland and to the world the artistic imagination and genius of our people in each generation. It is a small thank you for the riot of ways in which you enrich and delight us, the ways in which you evoke vicarious pride in Irish culture, the ways in which you stimulate and challenge, lead and compel, reveal and revel. Just as those who have never read *Ulysses* nonetheless are delighted Joyce was an Irishman, so the many who will never themselves be publicly acclaimed artists, and who may never fully explore your entire canon, still care deeply that you pursue your vocation as artists and that your creativity works as a leaven at the heart of our society. It matters that we have not just an historic reputation for producing talent but that we replenish that cohort of genius in each generation. It matters that this small nation stands tall throughout the world on the shoulders of its writers, poets, painters, dancers, musicians, actors, filmmakers, set designers and all the rest who make up this extraordinary band.

It is through the arts that we share with the world many of the things that make us distinctively and uniquely Irish. It is often only through the arts that we have any significant point of intimate, upfront and personal contact with the citizens of the rest of the world, just as it is often only through the arts that we meet ourselves, and in particular meet those parts of the self only the oil of art can reach.

In a Republic which has set its face against a national honours system, Aosdána is itself a rare and uniquely Irish way of recognising and encouraging artists without in any way compromising their independence and integrity. Your membership is not dependent on political patronage or State approval. You elect your own members, choosing by purely artistic criteria which of your peers you deem worthy of the honour of membership. And membership is a very real honour indeed, precisely for that reason. Can there be any more critical audience than your peers, any more difficult audience to impress?

Aosdána is fundamentally about the State, the people, acknowledging the outstanding contribution the arts make to our lives in Ireland and acknowledging too the difficult road the artist has to travel in pursuit of the levels of excellence which alone bring the accolade of membership of Aosdána. This afternoon is a small way of saluting your achievements, of simply saying thank you. Enjoy the day and long may you continue to be inspired and fulfilled by your individual vocations as artists.

I would like to thank our MC this afternoon, Eugene Downes, for the excellent job he is doing as always and the wonderfully talented Mary Kelly, Teadaí and Patrick Collins for entertaining us so well this afternoon. My thanks also to our friends from Civil Defence and the staff at the Áras for all they have done to make today enjoyable for everyone.

I hope you will take the time to get to know the Áras, to wander through the State Rooms, our visitor centre downstairs and the Hyde Room, with its splendid collection of Hughie O'Donoghue paintings.

Go raibh maith agaibh.

REMARKS AT A RECEPTION FOR SPORTSPERSONS FROM THROUGHOUT IRELAND

Áras an Uachtaráin, 7 July 2004

Dia dhíobh a cháirde. Is cúis mhór áthais dom fáilte a chur romhaibh go léir chuig Áras an Uachtaráin inniu. Fearaim fíor-chaoin fáilte roimh na pearsana spóirt atá i láthair anseo, agus rompu siúd uile atá bainteach le cúrsaí spóirt.

Martin and I are delighted to welcome you all to Áras an Uachtaráin this afternoon. We have sporting heroes here today from all over the country, so a warm céad míle fáilte and a heartfelt thanks to each of you for your contribution to sport in Ireland.

In this room are gathered men and women representing the full spectrum of sport – sport that plays such a huge part in Irish life, our culture and in our collective imagination. We love it; some would say we live for it. It is hugely important to us.

With the Olympic Games almost upon us, we are reminded that, for the ancient Greeks, physical culture was not a separate activity from the rest of life. It was a part of culture as a whole and was valued as much for the way it developed the mind as for the way it developed the body. It was an inseparable part of their civilisation. They were not right about everything, but they were certainly right about sport. The modern Olympic Games are a product of that great civilisation and a continuing lesson for us all.

A great thing about sport, and athletic competition, is that it brings people together even while it fosters competition between them. Sporting occasions stir people with the shared feeling of belonging to a shared enterprise and a shared understanding of what it is to struggle against one's limitations and overcome them; sometimes by individual effort, sometimes in teams determined to create a whole which is greater than the sum of its parts.

Up until recently, sport's educational functions have sometimes been underrated. The obesity epidemic alone argues that sport must be encouraged. The people of the earliest times recognised that sport develops character as well as health. For both competitors and specta-tors it is inspiration to excellence in their own lives. Athletes learn the values conveyed by sport. They develop their physical capabilities and strengthen their motivation to personal excellence, as well as the broader human skills required for teamwork, solidarity, tolerance and fair play. They increase their knowledge of themselves in addition to learning the skills of their chosen activity.

We know that in sport there is never real certainty about the outcome – there are no sure-fire winners – and this is a part of the thrill and excitement for the spectator. It is also part of the lonely journey each sportsman or woman must embark upon, part of the wall they have to face and surmount. But the buzz of victory is not a taunt to those who do not win. Not winning does not make anybody a loser. For us, there is only the trying. Sport takes our failures and teaches us to go on, only next time try to fail better. And better again the next time, and always to the best of our abilities.

And yet, for all the great good it does, it is also a valuable end in itself. The only thing quite like watching someone set a new record or win a competition is doing it yourself. To play in an All-Ireland Final, to represent Ireland at games of international standard, is a spiritual experience as magnificent as any of the great works of art.

But you don't need to be told of the enchantment which involvement in sport works in our lives. From the simple but profoundly important things like the friendships, the loyalty to team and to club, county, country, the commitment, the discipline, the exhilaration of being the best, the humbling acceptance of not being number one, the wellbeing that comes from participating, from feeling alive, from feeling included.

It does not come easy. It takes hard work. I applaud your endeavours in all their manifestations: the training, day in day out, year in year out; the time spent away from home and family; the relentless and determined effort to be the very best; the hardships and injuries suffered; the sacrifices in terms of careers or income or time for other things.

Today is my chance to salute your contribution, your hard work and your commitment to sport. Thank you for the scrapbook of memories you have given to the rest of us – the shared memories of the whole community. This is a happy occasion for everyone. However, on occasions such as this we should also remember all those other sporting heroes who are no longer with us. Dreadfully tragic has been our loss earlier in this year of Cormac McAnallen and John McCall. They had already achieved so much in their young lives and would have undoubtedly achieved a lot more in their sporting careers. Ar dheis Dé go raibh a anaim.

I hope that you will enjoy the afternoon and that you will leave the Áras with a new memory or two, some old friendships renewed, some new ones just beginning.

On occasions such as this I like to invite people to stroll through the gardens – weather permitting, that is! Please take the opportunity to stroll through the formal rooms in the house and the very fine visitor centre downstairs, which tells the story of the Áras – a house which is the veritable story in stone of the people of Ireland and of our relationship with our nearest neighbour, Britain. It embodies all the traditions and cultures which this island shares.

For your entertainment this afternoon we had the very talented Mary Kelly playing the harp in the entrance hall as you arrived.

I would like to thank our Masters of Ceremony for the afternoon, Mr Jimmy Magee, Mr Brian Carthy and Mr Micheal O'Muircheataigh; the delightful Teadaí, who you have just heard; the superb Comhaltas Ceoltóirí Éireann. I would also like to thank our friends from Civil Defence and the staff here at the Áras, who have spent many long hours and days preparing for today.

Go raibh maith agaibh go léir.

REMARKS AT YOUTH FORUM
'A VISION OF 2020'

Áras an Uachtaráin, 27 February 2007

Dia dhíbh a chairde go léir 's fáílte chuig Áras an Uachtaráin inniu.

You are all so welcome here to Áras an Uachtaráin this morning. I am grateful to each one of you and especially those of you who have travelled long distances to be with us today. I know that some of you have travelled from as far as Kerry and Donegal. Cork is represented, as are Longford, Waterford and Kildare, and our capital city, Dublin, is also well represented.

You are representatives of our future in this country – you will carry the flame forward to 2020. You, by then, will be employers or employees, mothers, fathers; members of a society which I hope will be a place you are proud of and happy to live in. What will it be like, this Ireland of 2020? How do you see it? We are here today to explore that question. So, apart from this brief welcome, I will mostly listen, because I want to hear your views. Each one of you brings a unique perspective and this forum, 'A Vision for 2020', is your opportunity to voice the proposals and the vision which you believe will benefit people throughout Ireland.

About eighty of you, from all around the country, from all walks of life, are here, representatives of the many thousands of young people whose adult futures are already well in the making. You are the most exciting generation ever – the best educated, the most informed, the one with the most peace and the most freedom and, in particular, the freedom to stay in Ireland and make a huge contribution to your own and your country's future.

Your views matter, for they will inform your actions, your lived lives, and it is out of those things will emerge the Ireland of 2020. This forum here at the Áras provides a public platform to present your views publicly and to listen to the views of your peers. What you are doing here today is a crucial form of active citizenship, of taking responsibility for the world around you, and in particular for setting its agenda, solving its problems, making it the humanly best that you can between you.

Ireland has a dramatic history – it has cast long shadows over many generations – but this generation is largely free from those shadows and empowered to do things other generations could only dream of. I, and many others, am fascinated by the possibilities and the opportunities open to you, and even more fascinated by how you will use them. Here today you will start to fill in the blanks, to reveal where it is you want your generation, your genius to take this country.

George Bernard Shaw once said, 'You see things and say "Why?" But I dream of things that never were and I say "Why not?"' We, in the twenty-first century, need you to dream of the things that never were so that some day you can bring them into being. You are Ireland's dream team of tomorrow, the most confident, most ambitious generation ever, growing up in a prosperous, multicultural Ireland, respected in Europe and in the world, and with a role to play at home on this island, in Europe and in the world. Good doesn't just happen. Good people make it happen. And you are good people. You answered the challenge to come here and I hope your visit will be a memorable one. Enjoy yourselves, make new friends and leave fired by the possibilities that lie in front of you and by your chance to shape them.

I thank Derek Mooney for agreeing to take the Chair and Jarlath Burns for agreeing to act as Rapporteur; I wish them all the best in their labours. A word of thanks also to Aonghus McAnally and his staff. A great amount of effort and work by your teachers has gone on behind the scenes and I would like to say a sincere 'Go raibh míle maith agaibh' to all of you for that.

My thanks to the Áras crew, and also to our friends from Civil Defence for all their hard work in preparation for today.

Go n-éirí go geal libh agus go raibh míle, míle maith agaibh.

REMARKS AT THE CONFERRAL OF AN
HONORARY DOCTORATE

Dublin City University, 29 March 2008

Chancellor, President, fellow graduands, ladies and gentlemen,

I am grateful to the university for this day, when Martin and I have the honour of being admitted together to honorary degrees.

Today we join a gathering of graduating students and their families, each one filled with pride at the individual efforts, sacrifices and achievements which have led to this day of celebration. The graduands are entitled to feel pride in their accomplishments, to have confidence in their abilities, but the context in which those things will be showcased over a lifetime will of course be in relationships, in families, workplaces, communities, organisations and societies, all of which will be enriched, deepened and strengthened by that mix of intensely differentiated talents and personalities that we celebrate today. They will also be showcased in the social and historical context that accident of birth has placed you in.

For so many past generations, that context was homogeneity, poverty, under-achievement, mass emigration and the menace, north of the border, of political and sectarian conflict. For this generation, the context is growing prosperity, inward migration and developing heterogeneity, multiculturalism and a new political dispensation which has already substantially recalibrated relationships between Great Britain and Ireland and between North and South. There is much to be grateful for when we look at that changed context. The peace we mark in this anniversary year of the Good Friday Agreement did not happen by coincidence. Its cost in human terms was outrageous and it took the combined efforts of people at every level of society, as well as considerable help from abroad, to effect the changes of head and heart that led eventually to the Good Friday Agreement and beyond it to a sustained peace-building process.

The prosperity which Ireland enjoys today also did not happen by coincidence, but is rooted in the widening of access to education which began in earnest with the provision of free second-level education at the end of the 1960s. Not until then did we start to harvest our best natural resource – the brain power of our people. It is still our biggest and best asset, and here in this university you have always believed passionately in education as the surest pathway to revealing and releasing the potential of both the individual and the nation. We know that every extra year spent in education galvanises that potential and that third-level education, in particular, gives to graduates a unique traction in their adult and working life. Your innovative outreach and access programmes have opened up the realm of opportunity offered by third-level education to many people who thought it beyond their reach, beyond their hopes. You became their champion and friend while they were in school, encouraged and supported their often complex pathways to and through university, listened to and responded to their needs and enjoyed with them days of triumph and transcendence like this.

Education altered our country's destiny, slowly at first, but now at a pace which is simply astounding, making this once-poor country the economic success story *par excellence* of the European Union and a cultural powerhouse. This experience, if it has taught us anything, must surely have made us deeply curious and hopeful about what we could accomplish if we harvested and harnessed effectively the talents of all our people and put them at the service of the individual and the common good. We are a people with a vision for our future. It is set out both in the Proclamation and in the Constitution. It speaks of a nation of equals, a place where the children of the nation are cherished equally, a place where there is a true social order where the dignity of each human being is honoured and vindicated. It calls us to build our prosperity and share it wisely. Our common vision is set out too in the Good Friday Agreement, where we work, as John Hewitt would say, 'to fill the centuries' arrears', building up good, neighbourly partnerships in place of wasteful enmity. It is set out in our membership of the European Union, where our futures are twinned with those of the citizens of twenty-six nations whom we are now befriending in ways that were impossible only a short few years ago. It is set out in our global outreach to the world's poor, our membership of the United Nations, our ratification of the Charters and Treaties that champion human rights, our determined policy of military neutrality and our equally determined civic global leadership in peace-building and the elimination of poverty and disease.

That is your context and mine. This is the teamwork that needs your skills, talents, hearts and hands to make things better, to heal what history wounded, to consolidate the peace, renew and refresh the prosperity, to make Ireland the best it can be and to generate in our ill-divided and sometimes savage world a relentless momentum for the full social, political and economic inclusion of each human being.

Here in DCU, you have been well prepared by your own efforts and those of the staff for the journeys and challenges ahead. Tus maith is leath na hoibre. The good start has given you both a great degree and a strong value system. The other half of the work is now up to you; how you use them both to bring fulfilment to your own life and the fulfilment of our shared ideals to the world around you. We are very proud of you this day. Enjoy the day and the promise it holds out for you and, through you, for all of us.

I renew my thanks to the Governing Authority, through you, Chancellor, for this great honour, and of course your President, my former student Professor von Prondzynski, who is such a dynamic force in the world of Irish education.

Thank you all very much, and enjoy your day.

Remarks at the UCC Conference on Ireland and Europe

University College Cork, 22 January 2010

Dia dhíbh a chairde.

It's a great pleasure to be back in University College Cork, where it is now 'business as usual' after a very unusual and unwelcome spell under water. I would particularly like to thank Dr Michael Murphy for the kind invitation to join you here today and to compliment him and the UCC community for the way in which they coped so effectively with the recent floods. They were devastating for the college and the city, but those floods provoked a matching tidal wave of mutual support and community spirit which were inspirational in helping people to cope, to clean up and to face the future with hope and determination again.

Today's conference invites us to take a broader look at that future. It marks the culmination of three years' hard preparatory work by Professor Dermot Keogh and his team, and its timing could not be better, for it invites us to interrogate the relationship between Ireland and Europe just as the European Union enters a new phase with the coming into effect of the Lisbon Treaty after a bumpy journey to ratification in some Member States, among them Ireland, where an initial rejection was, after some adjustments, followed by a decisive endorsement of the Treaty. The outcome of the second Lisbon referendum seemed to answer comprehensively those who saw in the earlier rejection a fundamental Irish malaise with membership of the European Union rather than simply unease with specific aspects of the Treaty as applied to Ireland. Post Lisbon, it is clear that Ireland is, as it has been from the beginning, an enthusiastic participant in the great European project. It is where Ireland's future lies. Already the transformative potential that the then EEC offered when we joined in 1973 has more than begun to manifest itself, vindicating Jack Lynch's signature on the Accession Treaty exactly thirty-seven years ago yesterday and vindicating those founding fathers of the Union who believed that collegial action between Member States would be an epic and historic game-changer in advancing the economic and social progress of Europe.

In this recessionary phase, with its high levels of unemployment and indebtedness, its anger and disappointment that processes heralded as wealth creating carried the virus of poverty creation, it is important to remember just how much has been accomplished and changed for the better since we first joined the Union. This conference will help us contextualise Ireland's relationship with Europe in its broader historical context and to see how important that context is, and will be to us as we try to find a renewed momentum towards prosperity.

The transformation of our economy over the past three decades could not have been achieved without the European context. Corkonians, coming from a port city that has a centuries-long role in our international trade, will particularly appreciate the benefits that exporting to the massive, high-purchase-power European market have brought. Today, as we seek to stabilise our domestic economy and reposition for the upturn, participation in the European Single Market and in the Eurozone are essential conduits to sustainable economic growth. We have seen clearly and in chastening circumstances in recent months, the reassurance that membership of the Eurozone provides in these difficult economic times, even allowing for currency fluctuations which have until now impacted negatively on exports and helped to encourage the bargain-hunting kind of cross-border shopping which is a downstream consequence of freedom of goods and services.

However, as the Irish experience around the Lisbon Treaty reminds us, the European project is about considerably more than trade and I know that this weekend's conference will be an opportunity to reflect on other aspects of its influence, including in the social, employment and equality-related areas.

Since its foundation, the European Union has had a unique set of structures; these evolved and developed over time into something of a patchwork quilt of arrangements, which began to look frayed as it enlarged from Six to Nine to Twelve to Fifteen, and then to the Twenty-Seven of today. Looking back at a Union which expanded not just its membership but its remit, it is perhaps not surprising that so much time and effort were invested in creating an effective and efficient, fair and accountable institutional framework.

The process that began with the Maastricht Treaty and continued with the Convention, the Constitutional Treaty and finally the Treaty of Lisbon, now gives the Union what the European Council recently described as 'a stable and lasting institutional framework'. Importantly, the huge effort required in drafting and ratifying the treaty is no longer needed, freeing up time and effort for investment in the things which preoccupy Europe's citizens – from jobs to climate change to conflict resolution, development aid and disaster relief, and many more issues which impact on our daily lives. It is worth pointing out that following the failed 2008 Irish referendum, significant insights into Europe's wide import were gained from the research into Irish attitudes and opinions on Europe and on the provisions of the treaty. The wide national debate in Ireland, both in the political domain and especially in civil society, was absolutely essential. Essential, too, was the process of listening and responding by our European partners when it became apparent that the problems Irish voters had with the Lisbon Treaty were real and could be addressed with the right goodwill and in compliance with the spirit of consensus and collegiality which is the hallmark of the Union.

It was especially important in the debate in both the political and civic spheres that there was input from leading thinkers and experts which could steer the discourse towards information and analysis which was scholarly, informed and accurate. Our institutions of higher learning, not least among them UCC, were essential sources of credible views and voices. It was also important, for not just Ireland but for the Union itself, that the concerns of the Irish people were taken seriously and accommodated as far as they could be. The European Council's provision to Ireland of legally binding guarantees in relation to taxation, neutrality and ethical issues, and its revised provision for a Commissioner per Member State, was as much a vindication of the European project's fidelity to consensus as it was to Ireland's insistence on being taken seriously as a fully equal sovereign member of the Union.

Now a new, yet to be ratified Commission and a Council headed by a new President head out boldly into the post-Lisbon landscape. Among the strategists who will help guide the Union's future steps is our own Máire Geoghegan Quinn, whom I congratulate on her nomination to the new Commission-in-waiting. I am sure we all wish her well in developing Europe's research and innovation, for these are areas of key importance to the future prosperity of Ireland and Europe as a whole. In the light of the debate in Ireland about the proposed reduction in Commissioners, it will be interesting to see how a Commission with continuing participation from each Member State will function. Although the Commissioners act on behalf of the Commission and not their own homelands, there is, at some deep and inchoate level, an issue here to do with sovereignty and I see that sovereignty will be among the issues that you will address at this conference, though it will span a wide agenda indeed. The exercise by Member States of their sovereignty in pursuit of consensus around the Union table has been the lifeblood of Europe's strength, and its internal and external solidarity. For Ireland, that exercise of sovereignty has given us the opportunity to contribute on the European and world stages in much more ordered, consistent and powerful ways than would have been the case had we stayed outside the Union. However, there can be little doubt that sovereignty remains, and will likely always remain, a potential source of neuralgia throughout the Union as part of the healthy checks, balances and tensions that inevitably arise where equal partners, each in possession of 100 per cent of their own sovereignty, though unequal in size, different in identity, history and perspective, and moving at different paces, gather around a table of equals and a shared agenda which includes some things and excludes others. In many ways, the miracle is that issues to do with sovereignty have not been much more problematic than they might have been. Cumbersome though processes may appear, it is evident that the entire process of participating in and contributing to the EU project has been accompanied by a growth in experience and confidence in our dealings with our partners.

A particularly significant transformation has been effected in our relationship with our nearest neighbour, the EU providing a wider, safer and better structured framework for the development of Anglo-Irish dialogue across a range of issues, including issues which were historically divisive. That transformed relationship created a wholly new and fresh dynamic which was essential to the eventual partnership approach between Dublin and Westminster to the Peace Process and which led to the Good Friday and St Andrew's Agreements. It should be noted, as well, and with the deepest appreciation, that the EU has been persistent in its absolute commitment to peace and prosperity on the island, in particular through providing meaningful financial and practical support for the patient, often tedious, but very necessary work of reconciliation at community level. That is where, in the words of Ulster poet John Hewitt, 'we build to fill the centuries' arrears'. It is surely no accident that the peace which had eluded all past generations over centuries was eventually constructed by the generation which volunteered to partner each other in a Union which itself defied the judgment of history by making partners of enemies and equals of winners and losers.

In a world where so many difficult and dangerous issues can only be meaningfully faced down through shared, consensual global action, the European Union stands as witness to the massive potential that can be unlocked by truly respectful partnership and the pooling of specific elements of sovereignty in order to advance the good and the wellbeing of all.

Allow me to close by recalling the celebrations late last year marking the twentieth anniversary of the events which ended the Cold War and tore down the Iron Curtain. Those events of 1989 reshaped contemporary Europe, liberating many people from the stranglehold of imposed communism and opening up the space through which a democratic future could enter those parts of Europe for whom the Second World War had effectively never ended. Was it inevitable, in that giddy moment, that there would or could be a smooth transition to democracy, the rule of law and peaceful co-operation? The stories are very different if one is talking about Slovakia or Serbia, Kosovo or Slovenia. History will show, I believe, that the decisions made by political leaders at the time and the policies adopted, in particular by the European Community and by those countries that set their faces firmly towards membership of the Union, were utterly vital in delivering the peace and stability that the European continent enjoys today. The colourful ceremony of welcome of ten new Member States which took place at Áras an Uachtaráin on a gloriously sunny afternoon in May 2004, was a relaxed, happy and emotional affair which very few pundits, historians, political scientists or analysts could have believed humanly possible just a few short years before. It did not happen by accident or clatter together by some cosmic coincidence. It happened because the Union had made itself a strong credible centre of gravity, had made itself a place of welcome and homecoming to Europe's estranged nations and a place unafraid of taking risks in order to secure a peaceful and prosperous new egalitarian Europe.

In his poem to mark that very special day, Seamus Heaney juxtaposed the myth of the phoenix as a symbol of rebirth with the Gaelic name Fionn Uisce. In so doing, he not only marked the occasion as a new departure for the European Union, but also reminded us of the great overlap between the past, the present and the future:

Move lips, move minds and make new meanings flare
Like ancient beacons signalling, peak to peak,

From middle sea to north sea, shining clear
As phoenix flame upon fionn uisce here.

Today's European Union is an entirely new type of entity; a *sui generis* model for co-operation and the most successful peace project in the chequered history of our continent, indeed our globe. It is still only in its infancy and so in the absence of familiar landmarks or clear precedents it is natural to look for guidance from the beacons of history. They are almost all, if not all, entirely a case of negative education, a wasteland of greedy imperialism, miserable dictatorships, endemic conflict, poverty, dissipated energy and cruelly wasted lives. The European Union distilled all that barely digestible wisdom and from it charted a pathway out of the savagery of a long-standing conflict-centred, competitive model of international relations. Forged out of death, the Union chose life, oxygenated by shared democratic values and an unshakeable belief that the dreams of all for equality, prosperity and opportunity could be achieved by working together to an agreed agenda. It is no perfect place, that is true, but as earthly places go, membership of the Union has given us a better Ireland than any Ireland known to our forebears. It is still a work in progress, which is why such a conference as this is so important. The potter's wheel is ours; the clay that shapes the Union is in our hands. Only with the best help, insight and guidance will we shape it to the best it can be.

In closing, I wish you the very best for this weekend's conference and look forward to your collective wisdom guiding our hands and shaping our Ireland our Europe to a future of equally cherished European children.

Remarks to the Price Waterhouse Cooper/ Institute of Directors 'Business Leadership in Ireland of Today' Event

Spencer Dock, Dublin, 4 March 2010

Dia dhíbh a chairde.

It is a great pleasure to be here this evening. I'd particularly like to thank Rónan Murphy of Price Waterhouse Cooper and Ann Riordan of the Institute of Directors for the kind invitation to join you here today.

You certainly didn't pick an easy time to talk about business leadership in Ireland, but maybe you chose the right time, for business leadership is currently being interrogated and is interrogating itself in an unfamiliar language that is more searching and censorious than it is affirming and reassuring. A sensible woman once said that the only safe ship in a storm is leadership, and we are surely in a severe economic storm. This is when we discover the skills, wisdom and resilience of those who are out front and their preparedness for this spell of bad weather. Some jobs diligently prepare people for the very worst eventualities, even though the odds of them happening are minimal. That is how Captain Chesley Sullenberger, who retired yesterday, was able to safely land an Airbus A320 on the Hudson River after it flew into a flock of geese on takeoff. Among the many questions he was asked after the so-called 'Miracle on the Hudson' was whether he prayed during the thirty seconds he had to decide on a course of action now that his plane had no functioning engine. His reply was interesting. He said, 'No, I hoped the people down the back were doing that.' In other words, he was utterly focused on bringing every bit of nerve, creativity and skill to bear on the worst and most potentially devastating moment in his flying career.

There are a lot of people down the back in Ireland praying that the crew of our economic ship have just such a reservoir of nerve, ingenuity and skill to bring Ireland safely through this very exacting time of trial. The middle of a storm would be a bad time to discover that the ship has only a fair-weather crew. What it needs are people who have a depth of experience and distilled wisdom and the courage to give leadership. Napoleon memorably said that 'A leader is a dealer in hope.' But as his subsequent career, marooned in ignominy on St Helena proved, hope has to be soundly rooted. Mock bravado won't do. Pollyanna and Micawber won't do either. The hope offered has to be credible. The leadership offered has to be credible.

A few short years ago, our business leadership was in strong, self-congratulatory mode, but those giddy highs of the Celtic Tiger era rapidly gave way to the chastening lows of a national and global recession, the baleful effects of which soberingly swift. We have had to change register very dramatically and every single thing we do in this hole that is largely of our own making will impact significantly on the next chapter in the story of Ireland. Will it be a story of a remarkable bounce back from adversity? I believe it can be and will be if we see Ireland as the ship in which we all sail and not as a scattered convoy. Our business leaders are a very important part of the ship's crew. For you are key to developing a successful, wealth-creating, sustainable, equitable economy that translates into jobs and opportunities and hope for Ireland's citizens.

Your leadership is a crucial enabler of recovery. Research has shown that CEO leadership style has a direct impact on the profitability of an enterprise. It also tells us that the more uncertain the environment, the more important the leader. Nothing shapes an organisation's culture more than the 'visible behaviour' of its leaders. Your positive influence is especially crucial at a time when many are paralysed by negativity. It's a mood that is fully understandable, given what we now know of unacceptable and reckless business practices in some quarters. However, rather than conducing to a draining fatalism, it should provoke an energising determination within the business sector to rapidly restore trust and get momentum back into our economy.

Finding the energy to be the generators of momentum in this crisis is, I know, far from easy, for the business environment is currently very cruel. But everything is relative. We could be the generation facing civil war, or either of two World Wars; we could be the generation that faced economic isolation, or mass emigration, or high infant mortality, or that couldn't afford universal primary education or that depended on remittances from its scattered children. We are the generation that benefited from free first-, second- and third-level education, from good healthcare, from membership of the European Union, from the growth of human rights and democracy. We are the generation which turned history on its head by ending widespread endemic poverty, reversing the tide of mass emigration, attracting massive inward investment, especially in the high-tech sector, creating an indigenous entrepreneurial sector, a multi-cultural Ireland and constructing a peace which had eluded every other generation. We were racing two steps forward, rewriting Irish history at a feverish pace when we were shoved unceremoniously one step backwards. Not three steps backwards, not back to Ireland of the ceann faoi, but one step backwards to that new can-do Ireland which had the confidence that comes from having greatly improved its quality of life, the wisdom that comes from having made mistakes and learnt from them, and the determination that comes from wanting to be defined by how we got out of this mess and not how we got into it.

We know that things will have to change. We have to become competitive again. We have to be ideas driven, knowledge and innovation driven; not greed driven but rather people centred. Our economy has to be greener, more sustainable, infrastructurally advanced, technologically sophisticated, entrepreneurial, problem solving not problem generating, capable of upping our game globally and upping our quality of life locally. It's a big ask but it's the only ask we can make of ourselves and of the coming generation.

The young people in our schools and colleges have grown up during the heady days of super-confidence and linear growth. They anticipated fair weather ahead and have been ill-prepared for the adversity they are facing. Every generation before them knew little else except adversity. Every generation before them faced into it and faced it down as best they could. There are legions out there who, like Captain Sullenberger, have in their deepest being the experience and the courage to cope, to adapt and innovate when things go badly wrong. We are not as badly prepared as we fancy. What is more, we have many pluses and potentials that are yet to be fully harvested, most notably in a youthful, well-educated and ambitious population, a strong presence in the global marketplace and a historic peace with its growing scope for new partnerships. Our Government has taken strong action and our people have taken considerable personal financial pain to help stabilise our national finances. Notwithstanding these sacrifices, our traditional resource of community and social solidarity remains as strong as ever.

If ever there was a time for sound strategic leadership and for excellence in management, it is now, as we work to develop the smart economy and the sensible, competitively priced economy and to ensure that Ireland is optimally placed to benefit from the global upturn. It is important to remember that not all the news is bad; falling costs make our businesses more competitive, recent months have seen an increase in our export orders, productivity is growing and we remain one of the easiest countries in the world in which to do business. High-calibre management and leadership are the key skills that will bring companies through the current economic difficulties and, equally importantly, will prepare companies to take advantage of the new opportunities which will emerge.

As strategists – people who look to the future – one of your key concerns has to be the next generation of business leaders. It has been said that leaders don't create followers; they create more leaders. We have suffered from a culture of unquestioning followers, an altogether different phenomenon from intelligent communal solidarity, and that has huge implications for the next generation of leaders and for all here this evening, for you are uniquely placed to ensure measuredness, integrity and ethics are embedded deep within our business culture and its future ambassadors.

There is truth in the saying that if you want the crowd to follow you, don't follow the crowd. Leaders have to be prepared to maintain lonely vigils, to be sole voices, to be misunderstood, to be tough enough to stand up to the second guessers, carpetbaggers, the corrupt and the armchair experts.

At a time when we are confronted with the daily litany of business failures, it is worth being reminded by you that the vast majority of our businesses are successes, that they are holding on through hard times by their ingenuity, resourcefulness and adaptability, and that they are every day showing the leadership that is already guiding us through the storm to calmer waters. When we have weathered this storm, as we will, and when we have defied the odds to become the most talked-about small successful nation again for all the right reasons, you will be able to tell your children that you were among the people who stepped up and did their best, not among the people who sat back and sneered cynically at those who tried to make things better.

I wish you well with this and I hope that this evening's event is an opportunity to combine your collective wisdom to help chart our course to recovery. I congratulate all those involved in bringing this event together.

Go raibh míle maith agaibh go léir.

REMARKS AT THE ANNUAL MEETING OF THE IRISH SENIOR CITIZENS' PARLIAMENT

26 March 2010

Dia dhíbh go léir inniu. Tá an-áthas orm bheith anseo libh ar an ócáid speisialta seo. Míle bhuíochas dibh as an gcuireadh agus an fáilte a thug sibh dom.

Thanks to each of you for the warm welcome to the Irish Senior Citizens' Parliament and to President Sylvia Meehan for inviting me.

This parliament is one of a number of Senior Citizens' Parliaments across the EU, providing access to political decision-making at the highest level and enhancing the co-ordinated and collective voice of older people, in particular those at risk of social exclusion. It only exists because you care about the quality of life of our senior citizens and care enough to get involved, get organised and insist on being heard. Thanks to your individual sense of responsibility and collective efforts, this Parliament has become a recognised and necessary centre of gravity right at the forefront of representing the distinctive needs and perspectives of older people at local, national and international levels. I thank you for giving older people such a structured and effective opportunity to engage actively on the many issues that affect your day-to-day lives.

They say that with age comes wisdom. A lot of other things come along too, things that can change a person's context and priorities considerably. Among the images I have from my teenage days is the memory of the rehabilitation of a small local park into which benches were specially put for the first time for seniors. It was a kindly, well-intentioned thought but it carried a subliminal message that those of advancing years were expected to be sedentary and to be spectators. A more recent image points up the changed expectations and ambitions of Ireland's seniors – that is the opening of the first Tone Zone, a public outdoor gym for seniors in Dunshaughlin, thanks to Meath County Council's Tom Dowling and the redoubtable Mary Nally. That good idea has caught on all over Ireland so strongly that the equipment once manufactured in China is now manufactured here. The 'grey pound/euro' and 'grey ambition' are showcasing their collective power and their intention to use their lives to the full in new and imaginative ways that enhance their quality and their opportunities.

You have issues that are of special pertinence to seniors, from mental and physical healthcare to financial and physical security, education, access to social life, the demands of being carers, the demands of being cared for, housing, travel, pensions, the vulnerability to suicide of elderly males in particular, and a host of other matters that require a response customised around the changing needs of your constituency. They require careful and insistent advocacy and you have helped bring fresh focus to many of them. However, your remit extends way beyond issues that are of immediate and intrinsic interest to seniors, and reaches to the wider sphere of civic and political life, where your contribution is needed more than ever.

Living as we are through these humbling days, when we see the ghastly consequences of mistaking a culture of speculation for enterprise, we need wise counsel and determined voices to rouse us from the pit of paralysing fatalism and spur us on to finding and implementing solutions. Who better to be involved in the national discourse we need right now than those who know from the deep wells of lived lives just how essential individual initiative is and how powerful civic spirit can be in moving through and beyond difficult times.

Our young generation are the best educated we have ever produced, the healthiest, the most ambitious and sophisticated, but they face a landscape of diminished returns that they never contemplated having to face. Most of you, by contrast, faced little else over a lifetime but struggle against tough and implacable odds. You remember many different Irelands in which lives were constrained and even wasted by poverty, lack of access to education, the drain of emigration, the recurring misery of conflict, the attitudinal barricades that held back the potential of women in particular, the narrow biases that kept heads and hearts down. You also remember the leaders who emerged in homes, schools, communities and politics to galvanise the fresh energy and vision that brought Ireland from 'ceann faoi' to 'can do'. You know that we face difficulties, not impossibilities, and through these times your guidance and encouragement are utterly essential.

Already many seniors are filling the gaps in childcare, in economic support to the next generation. They are the backbone of the massive volunteer effort that deepens and enriches civic life in every corner of Ireland through sports clubs, charities, choirs, drama groups, self-help groups, parish teams, adult education, youth clubs, homework clubs and all the rest. For social entrepreneurship, our seniors cannot be beaten. It was they who responded to the needs of immigrants to Ireland for befriending and language tuition with the Fáilte Isteach programme. It is they who are filling the childcare gaps and helping their families through economically vulnerable times. They are the carers for the infirm, even at times when they are infirm themselves.

We are extremely fortunate in Ireland to have so many active senior citizens investing in our families, community and country, whether through organisations or on their own initiative. They are an often taken-for-granted social asset; a backbone and reliable network of endeavour which adds hugely to our individual and collective coping skills.

The Irish Senior Citizens' Parliament is a stellar example of older people working for older people and for Irish society, infusing it with their vitality, vision and distilled wisdom. Sylvia Meehan is a classic example of the surging energy and potential of Ireland's seniors and it was great to see her recognised in 2009 when she was presented with the 'People of the Year Award'. Sylvia's belief that change is possible with focused effort has been vindicated time and again and I wish her well in her future endeavours.

I congratulate all the members of the Senior Citizens' Parliament for being the persuaders for change and the catalysts for change. Life has changed for Ireland's seniors beyond all recognition. There are wide and accessible horizons now that would have been unthinkable a generation or two ago. There is greater longevity and greater ambition to live life to the fullest possible, to be fully of these times and no mere spectator. They are texting, Skyping and blogging. They are learning new skills and sharing old ones. They are running marathons and running homes, multi-tasking in retirements that put a whole new gloss on the concept of retirement.

Benjamin Franklin once said, 'We do not stop playing because we grow old; we grow old because we stop playing.' The Irish Senior Citizens' Parliament is a repository of irrepressible joy in life, curiosity about life, faith in life and faith in one another. It is about people helping people to live better and to flourish, no matter how many miles are on the clock. I wish you well with this annual meeting and continued success in the future.

Go raibh míle maith agaibh go léir.

REMARKS AT AN EVENT TO CELEBRATE POSITIVE AGEING WEEK 2010

Georgian Museum, Dublin, 28 September 2010

Dia dhíbh go léir inniu a chairde. Tá an-áthas orm bheith anseo libh ar an ócáid speisialta seo.

It is good to be back again in the lovely setting of No. 29 to mark Positive Ageing Week 2010 and to visit the Positive Ageing Week Photographic Exhibition. I would particularly like to thank Robin Webster, CEO of Age Action Ireland for his invitation and to thank each one of you for committing with such enthusiasm to this festival of celebration that Positive Ageing Week has become. Thanks to Age Action and their sponsor, ESB Customer Supply, this week has become well established in the annual calendar of national awareness-raising events. It brings an important balance and focus to a public space that is more often than not oriented towards younger age groups and their interests and where the older population can feel relegated to a second division. But thanks to Age Action Ireland and many other organisations and groups across

Ireland, the interests, concerns, needs, contribution and potential of older people is getting a more engaged hearing than in the past, and the axis of interest is beginning to shift in their direction.

There are things on the agenda today that were simply absent a short time ago: an emphasis on positive ageing, on ongoing social, physical and intellectual activity and lifelong learning, on volunteering with fresh new ideas, on harnessing the phenomenal skills base represented by our retired citizens, on greater scrutiny of the experiences of vulnerable older citizens with more accountability and access to help, and on more research and insight into the needs and desires of the chronically and terminally ill. There has been a relentless and successful assault on the simplistic assumption that discussions about ageing should jump immediately into issues to do with passivity, decline, increased infirmity and dependency. These are certainly part of the spectrum of issues that ageing gives rise to, but they are a long way from being the whole story, and at a time of severe economic retrenchment, as we count our remaining blessings, foremost among them is an older generation with lived experience of resilience and survival through tough and turbulent times. Grandparents are already the backbone of childcare, of elder care, of voluntary organisations. Our older citizens have their shoulder to the wheel of national progress in millions of seen, but more often unseen, ways.

What is more, this is a generation with time and talent, skill and wisdom in abundance. The organisations and projects which are already tapping into that huge, under-used resource are revealing to us a capacity for infusing into all our lives a stabilising energy and a dynamic creativity with considerably wider application and potential. In the past few months alone, I have seen some of that work in action and it is inspirational. DCU's Intergenerational Learning Project, which I saw earlier this year, has created a rich learning environment for young third-level students and older learners, many of whom had never before been over the door of a third-level institution. Each participant was simultaneously both tutor and learner, and crucially, all felt they had not only benefited from the shared learning environment but that they had tapped into something very worthwhile. The GAA's Social Initiative aimed at the social inclusion of older people is building both on the caring culture of the GAA and its national yet local network. The very encouraging and successful pilot phase is over and now, with the appointment of a new national director, the initiative is set to really make a difference across the country. I was hugely impressed by the work of Muintir na Tíre, particularly in community safety initiatives for the elderly, and of course I got to see firsthand the transfer of skills from the Irish Senior Citizens' Helpline to their newly established New York counterpart. Week in and week out, the Áras hosts groups of seniors from rambling clubs, active retirees associations, day care centre users or nursing home patients. I got a letter from Meath County Council telling me that their Tone Zone initiative has now been rolled out in thirty other places nationwide and that a local supplier is now making the exercise equipment for older people. And of course, who will forget the pictures of Micheal O'Muircheartaigh's eightieth birthday, as he strode to the top of Mount Brandon. The evidence is mounting rapidly that the Positive Ageing movement has, over the past two decades, turned the tide of thinking about ageing and how we actually experience ageing. Thanks to your determination, ageing is no longer seen as an endgame but as an opportunity for new challenges and new beginnings.

Thoreau once said, 'None are so old as those who have outlived enthusiasm.' The photographs from the 'Generations Together' photographic competition are a showcase for the truth of that statement, for they depict exuberance and joy in life that transcends the wrinkles and lines that mark our advancing years. Each one is a powerful statement about how much more important attitude is than age. Age is just a number we cannot change. Positive attitude is a power we can use to make changes.

The changes we want and need are about the business of creating an age-friendly, age-dynamic Ireland, and thanks to this week and to the year-round work of Age Action and others who champion the causes of our senior citizens, we are getting a glimpse of what an age-friendly Ireland could be in the years to come.

I would like to thank you again for giving me the pleasure of being here on this wonderful occasion and I wish every success to Positive Ageing Week 2010.

Gurb fada buan sibh 's go raibh míle maith agaibh go léir.

ADDRESS AT THE 2010 NEWMAN LECTURE, 'RE-IMAGINING OUR UNIVERSITIES FOR THE TWENTY-FIRST CENTURY'

Newman House, St Stephen's Green, Dublin, 19 October 2010

Dia dhíbh a cháirde.

President, Chairman, Revd Fathers, ladies and gentlemen,

To deliver the 2010 Newman Lecture in the month after Newman's beatification is a particular honour and where could be more appropriate than here in Newman House, UCD, the successor institution to the Catholic University of Ireland, which first opened its doors in this very building on 3 November 1854. I thank President Hugh Brady for the kind invitation to be here with you this evening and for the most cordial welcome which he and his colleagues have afforded me.

In common with most universities of the time, Newman's university was an elite, largely male establishment for the wealthy and no bigger than many second-level schools today. However, his backdrop was the convulsive industrial revolution and his legacy to us was a university which was to become UCD and a massive contributor to the political, social, economic and intellectual development of Ireland. It is entirely appropriate, therefore, to gather in his name during this, the equally convulsive 'knowledge revolution' and to contemplate, as he did, the role of the university in this century.

Newman, we know, was strongly sceptical of an approach to education that focused exclusively on preparing people for the job market. He saw education as a means to cultivating the mind and, in particular, what he described as 'the philosophical habit of mind' – a habit he believed had an intrinsic and fundamental value whatever one's career choice or walk of life. Importantly, he saw it as a habit of broader reflection, a meta-discipline which brought or sought a degree of order, harmony and reconciliation to a baffling world in which education was increasingly characterised by a plethora of disciplines and forensic differentiation within them, as well as external pressures to conform education solely to the prevailing needs of the marketplace.

In Newman's view, university was 'the *alma mater* of the rising generation' and a place where 'inquiry is pushed forward, and discoveries verified and perfected, and rashness rendered innocuous, and error exposed, by the collision of mind with mind, and knowledge with knowledge'. For Newman, the purpose of education was not to 'load the memory of the student with a mass of undigested knowledge' but instead to be able to perceive 'many things at once as one whole, of referring them severally to their true place in the universal system, of understanding their respective values, and determining their mutual dependence'.

Newman famously said that 'to live is to change, and to be perfect is to have changed often'. We have certainly changed a lot, though obviously not yet enough to have attained anything close to perfection. UCD itself has lived through convulsive social and political changes, pushing itself from modest origins to its contemporary status as one of the world's leading universities. The secret of your success here has been precisely that ability to change and adapt to new realities. In fact, if we look at our university sector it has a resilience and adaptability that is almost unique when compared with other institutions and structures.

It will need all that strength and more to navigate the unmapped terrain of tomorrow's world. While every generation has probably fancied that it alone has lived through the most complex of times, in truth the exponential growth of knowledge, and the means of its dissemination and analysis, is now squeezed into tight and testing timeframes as never before. As quickly as we are amazed by what we now know and what we can now do, we are confounded not alone by the realm of mystery that remains but by the unpredictability and caprice of things we thought we had mastered.

In our own time, the unnoticed frailty of the building blocks of global economics and revered institutions that were household names for solidity and predictability has revealed itself to us rather alarmingly. Helping to fix those problems is now added to the list of challenges that face our universities, for we look to you to educate and train the brain power that is our most important natural resource, the key to problem-solving and the bridge to our progress and prosperity. We have a dependence on the intellectual lifting power, the ideas-generating power, the creativity and commitment of educated men and women. And we are fortunate that, more than in any other generation, we have huge numbers of school leavers entering third-level education, as well as a more educated population generally than at any time in the past. Their brain power fuels the engine of our nation's economy, our culture, our politics and our community life.

Ours is a sophisticated society and highly diversified economy that requires available cohorts of talent, skill and expertise in a wide range of areas that sweep broadly across the worlds of science, technology, the arts and humanities. From poets to nanotechnologists, from geneticists to theologians, from expertise in sign language to Chinese language, our universities are under pressure to ensure Ireland is ready for what the future will require. That Ireland is not the same place it was ten years ago. It is now home to people of many ethnic identities, languages and cultures. It is home to a computer-literate and instantly socially connected generation who will push pedagogical methodologies to new limits relentlessly. It is home to a challenging public who demand levels of professional competency and accountability that impact down the line on already crowded university curricula and a rapid-fire media that works to a considerably shorter analytical timeframe than the hallowed halls of academe.

As a global smart economy, we have a need for the competitive edge that comes from the innovation, research and development conducted in and through our universities, especially through their team work and national and international collaborations, which nowadays promote multi-disciplinary and interdisciplinary partnerships and require strong academic leadership as well as facilitating bureaucracies. There is an expectation that our universities, as public service enterprises, will engage directly with the contemporary needs of our society and, as sites of universal knowledge, will also be engaged globally in solving the bigger universal problems of disease, hunger, climate change and clean renewable energy, to name just a few.

However, since our society is considerably more than an economy and our graduates much more than potential employees or employers, the Newman focus on an education that addresses the whole person, living fully and not just working in a complex universe, remains a live issue. Few institutions know more about the problem-solving skills of the individual and the team than universities, for universities are fuelled by the belief that, for all the avoidable and unavoidable fragility of our world, the curious, probing, interrogative intellect is capable of producing the solutions that help us transcend our problems.

Such a short time ago we seemed to have a roaring confidence about our national problem-solving capacity and, despite the ambient disappointment and economic retrenchment, it is important to acknowledge that we have much to be proud of and reassured about, even in this glum time. No other generation has had such success in peace-building, in attracting high-quality foreign investment, in growing a strong entrepreneurial indigenous sector, in developing a high-end export economy that is currently doing very well, in globalising Irish culture and in strategically harnessing the energy of the global Irish family. These things eluded other generations and they remain centres of strength and gravity for us as we stabilise our economy and plough through these painful times to better times ahead.

There was a time when virtually all education involved a transfer of not just knowledge but wisdom and skill, when students did not labour alone in libraries but learnt their craft by trial and error, by practice and repetition direct from the experts with the intimacy of apprentices. Graduation was the beginning, just the beginning of experience, and caution was more advisable than over-confidence. Numbers have now comprehensively overwhelmed that model of educational delivery. Yet recent experience has taught us that, along with encouraging confidence, entrepreneurialism and leadership, we also need to encourage prudence and risk awareness so that the common good is never compromised again by a blindness to consequences.

Are we capable of constructing a universal bulwark against the threat of recidivist foolhardiness? Will it be enough to construct such safeguards by official oversight and regulation of institutions and institutional practices without also addressing, at a much more intimate level, the everyday human bulwark constructed by the kind of common sensibility that comes from what Newman calls the 'philosophical habit of mind' – a habit of mind that actively looks out for ways of thinking and doing that promote a holistic and integrated view of the individual, society and humanity.

Somehow it seems to me that before we can re-imagine our universities we have to re-imagine our society and our world, for all of our universities are placed foursquare in the public space. They manage a plethora of relationships, from those with the applicant student to Government, from alumnae to philanthropists, from professional bodies to representatives of industry and commerce, from their staff and trade unions to the media and the taxpayer. They have to teach, to research and to serve the cause of knowledge, which is the cause of humanity. They have to face into problems that seem intractable and break them down so that they can become manageable. They have to manage scarce resources and try to do more with less. They have to manage the tensions between specialisation and meta-thinking, create opportunities for lifelong learning and on-line learning, contemplate the possibilities of the virtual university, create partnerships with competitors and, alongside their core education, provide high-quality recreation, sports facilities and support services for students. How many workplaces are as complex as today's and tomorrow's university?

The second Glion Declaration recognises that universities have an indispensable role in fostering innovation in the leaders of each new generation; it is in universities that 'boundaries to our existing knowledge are explored and crossed; it is there that unfettered thinking can thrive and unconstrained intellectual partnerships can be created. It is there, within each new class, within each new generation that the future is forged.'

To me, this speaks powerfully to the role with regard to discovery of the twenty-first-century university. However, Newman's words are a reminder that universities will have a responsibility, not just for creating and disseminating new knowledge, but for distilling the previous wisdom gained from both human failure and success into tools for the formation of tomorrow's well-educated citizens. Universities have been the incubators of many life-enhancing ideas. They have been the platform from which has been launched the potential of individuals and nations. Without them, Ireland's rapid jump from poverty to remarkable progress could not have happened. In them, we have precisely the institutions fit for the purpose of critiquing, analysing and interrogating the kind of re-imagined education they need to deliver – what Newman calls 'the intercommunion of one and all'. If we are to effectively re-imagine the university for the twenty-first century, our challenge is to carry out a creative and critical retrieval of those elements of Newman's ideal that best align with our contemporary aspirations for economic stability, sustainable prosperity and social justice which is both local and global in its sensitivities.

In the poem 'From the Canton of Expectation', Seamus Heaney describes the transformative power of widened educational opportunity which took a community that lived under 'high, banked clouds of res-ignation' to 'banked clouds edged more and more with thunderlight'. In the final lines, he says something that could so easily be a plea for the educational integration – between the old wisdom, new knowledge, between the functional and the holistic – that Newman had the audacity to imagine and which could yet be our hope:

> I yearn for hammerblows on clinkered planks,
> the uncompromised report of driven thole-pins,
> to know there is one among us who never swerved
> from all his instincts told him was right action,
> who stood his ground in the indicative,
> whose boat will lift when the cloudburst happens.

The development of an educated instinct for all that is 'right action' sets a tough and controversial agenda. We have laws and a Constitution that shape the notion of what is right action. We have public criticism to mark the territory of what is wrong action. Our current context is a compelling and also disturbing mix of historic, outstanding, meteoric success and discouraging but hopefully passing disappointment. Our task is to build on all that was good in our success and to make our disappointments a springboard to re-imagine ourselves and our society.

We cannot do it without fresh thinking, by which I mean something beyond the superficial or anecdotal, which is always readily to hand with its morbid drumbeat but which may prove a false friend. We need the earnestness, the tried and trusted-ness of scholarship of the place dedicated to serious, forensic intellectual endeavour; the place Newman describes as 'a seat of wisdom, a light of the world'. That place is the university; where learning and unlearning go hand in hand, where there has been heresy and heterodoxy, partisanship and openness, but where there has also been an uncanny ability to re-imagine itself effectively from generation to generation.

If our twenty-first-century Irish universities can re-imagine themselves as successfully as they have done to date, then Ireland itself will be more than re-imagined – it will surely be reborn.

Go raibh míle maith agaibh go léir.

REMARKS AT THE IRISH BOOK AWARDS AND PRESENTATION OF A LIFETIME ACHIEVEMENT AWARD TO MAEVE BINCHY

25 November 2010

Dia dhibh go léir a chairde.

Ladies and gentlemen,

Thank you for that very warm welcome. Thank you also to Madeleine Keane and the *Sunday Independent* for their kind invitation to the Irish Book Awards for this celebration of the very best of Ireland's creative writing talent.

Somerset Maugham once said, 'To acquire the habit of reading is to construct for yourself a refuge from almost all the miseries of life.' There are plenty such miseries and we certainly have need of refuge from them, for the mood of the nation is about as far from celebratory as it is possible to be. But rather than concede to Maugham that what we are engaged in here is some form of escapism or avoidance, or diversion from life's hardships, maybe we should ponder first the contribution to our lives made by those whose genius with words and stories can enthral us, educate us, perplex us, engage us, challenge us, impress us and, importantly, reassure us that in each generation Ireland continues to produce outstanding writers of national and international distinction, in whose reflected glory, recognition and respect we take pride. That pride is an important resource at a time of low national self-confidence.

While fully respecting the nature of my role, I want to acknowledge the understandable distress and dismay being experienced by people all around the country who feel fearful about their future. We are confronted by massive problems and while so many of our people had no role whatever in creating these problems, each one of us does now have a role in resolving them. In facing up to the present difficulties, there needs to be candour, accountability and debate to ensure that the grave failures of the past are never repeated. I firmly hope that our people, despite their anger, will constructively support one another through this torrid time to renewed confidence, economic growth and prosperity.

Throughout our history, the Irish people have been tried and tested in all sorts of grim ways. We have proven ourselves to be extraordinarily resilient and now we need to draw on that resilience more than ever. We are more than capable of overcoming our present difficulties, and it is surely in our best interests to lift our hearts, minds and voices beyond mere recrimination to confronting the stark realities and consequences so that we can put them behind us as quickly as possible.

We need to do that for all the individuals, families and communities who are so deeply affected in their daily lives, through losing their jobs, reduced household income, renewed emigration, negative equity and the cumulative draining weight of coming to terms with these crisis events. The quicker we can stabilise our finances and return our economy to growth, the sooner we will be able to relieve the distress being experienced on the ground.

Let no one claim that Ireland is anything less than a great country. Our people are entitled to be defined by much more than this period of economic turmoil. This is a country where community matters to our people, where social inclusion and social justice matter to our people, where people invest their very best in a kaleidoscope of endeavours that build up to a life rich in civic spirit that is the envy of others. In a fragile world where uncertainty is easy to find, I am certain of one thing – the Irish people will rise to this challenge. They will face it down and in a time shorter than we dare to imagine right now, we will be able to say: it was difficult, it hurt, but Ireland got through it.

We also know that more than once in our history we have gone from mess to meitheal to miracle, not simply thanks to the richness of our often overlooked community solidarity, not simply because of our innate resilience as a people, but thanks to the original thinkers, the creative minds, the innovators, the polemicists and provocative intelligences that have sustained a culture of the written word in which this small island has produced some of the world's greatest writers, among them four Nobel literary prize winners and a litany of others whose widely acclaimed work has staked our claim to a prominent place on the global stage. Our pride in them consoles us. It fuels our common sense of identity – for this is a public and a civic gathering and, as such, an important acknowledgment that we are not decoupled from community or from a shared and strong commitment to the common good.

Those nominated tonight are a mix of renowned writers and those soon to become renowned. Each has a personal story to tell of their career as a writer – the odyssey of effort, of times of buoyant success and crushing disappointment, of occasional self-doubt and the miracle of renewed confidence in the integrity of their vocation as writers. I congratulate each of them on the fine achievements which have brought them here tonight and thank them for providing us, not just with a refuge, but with the hard evidence of the reservoirs of ability we have, the capacity for mutual encouragement we possess and the future we are capable of crafting between us.

Occasionally in life you meet a person who has the capacity to make you smile and feel good no matter what the mood. If the world is divided into radiators and drains, this lady is one of life's most natural radiators of all that is best in the human condition. Maeve Binchy is known and loved throughout the world as a writer and as a person of humour, humanity, empathy and endurance.

Someone remarked recently that what we could do with right now is 'Maeve on tap'. That is quite an accolade in itself and it is also an accurate summary of how Maeve is regarded as a writer and an Irishwoman here at home. Maeve exemplifies a way of being where success and keeping your feet on the ground are not mutually exclusive, where hope is not artificially inflated with hubris, where to encourage the talent of others is more important than precious one-upmanship, where the glass is always half full rather than half empty.

Ernest Hemingway once said that 'A writer should create living people; people, not characters.' Maeve's writing takes that to heart, for her stories are populated by everyday folk, and their lives are explored, revealed and relayed with a craftswomanship that elevates them way beyond the ordinary. In her inimitable way, she bravely sets before us a philosophy of life that is itself not cynical, embittered, narcissistic, rootless or ungenerous, though some of those who people her stories are capable of all sorts of meanness, petty prejudices and small-mindedness. There is no false nostalgia or rose-tinted lens but here is an empathetic and honest telling of lives lived inside a tight community solidarity.

We know when we read Maeve that here is someone with a passionate interest in other people, a profound curiosity, the eavesdropper of others' conversations, the observer of others' lives, the nosey parker who is not up to mischief but up to good. If people all over the world take refuge in the stories she spins out of the lives of men and women coping with life's ills, then the good she does is considerably more than the quantum of books she sells or of the audiences who watch her films. There is unquantifiable comfort, fun, company, entertainment, relaxation, excitement, insight, intrigue and absorption. They justify many times over this lifetime achievement award, which it is my privilege and honour to present to a much-loved Irishwoman and author, Maeve Binchy.

Comhghairdeas agus gura fada buan tu a Maeve uasal. Go raibh maith agaibh go léir.

Remarks on
International Women's Day

Burlington Hotel, Dublin, 8 March 2011

Dia dhíbh a chairde and thank you for the welcome to this gathering. Thank you in particular to Mark Ryan for inviting me to this special centenary celebration of International Women's Day.

On this day 100 years ago, there were thirty-three female doctors registered in Ireland, of the 5,000 members of the legal profession there were a mere sixty female clerks, of the 3,000 working in banking, seven were women and in the world of accountancy there were 100 and eighteen female accountants.

A hundred years ago, university education was available only to a very privileged and mostly male elite. UCD was then the size of a modest second-level school, with only 500 students. Those women who had salaried employment paid the same taxes as men but they had no vote. About this time, 100 years ago, Irish suffragettes were organising a boycott of the national census planned for 2 April in protest at their exclusion from the franchise. You won't find a census return that year for Hanna Sheehy-Skeffington, but you will find that, thanks to her and others like her, the momentum for change was generated that would in time lead to full civic equality for women. I am here, you are here, not simply by virtue of our own efforts but because in past generations, when the rights of women and opportunities for women were outrageously restricted, there were brave and inspirational people, both men and women, who refused to accept such discrimination and who pitted themselves against the government, the establishment, the law, and the powerful cultural consensus which would, if it could, have kept women as second-class citizens. With the creation of an International Women's Day 100 years ago, the focus on the negative impact, the injustice and wastefulness of gender-biased patriarchy began to impact on more and more countries and cultures, including our own.

We acknowledge with pride the considerable changes in attitudes, opportunities, experience and legislation which have resulted from the long battle for the emancipation and equality of women. We have women Presidents, politicians, chief executives, soldiers, police officers, entrepreneurs. Many professions that were once dominated by men have now become substantially feminised. Women can work and raise a family simultaneously if they choose to. They have maternity pay and leave rights today which would have been unthinkable a couple of generations ago. There is an understanding of and response to domestic violence that is growing more sophisticated and effective all the time. But if anyone in this audience thinks the work begun a century ago is over, you are not tuned in to the real world.

In most parts of the world, women still continue to live in the kind of conditions and with the kind of restrictions that were familiar to

Irish women in 1911. So there is the challenge to us of international solidarity with those women whose lives are still only half-lived, for their education, health, life prospects, civic participation are all much lower than those of their male counterparts. In our own country, we still face the wastefulness and the skewed outcomes that arise from the fact that women still earn less than men and participate numerically way below their potential in the political, business, economic, spiritual and intellectual life of our country.

So while today we are right to celebrate with enthusiasm all that has been accomplished these 100 years, today is also a day for committing to the work that lies ahead in the next century.

We have at our disposal much more help with the heavy lifting than was available to Hanna Sheehy-Skeffington and her colleagues. We have the confidence and independence that each of us garnered from our education, experience and personal success, but today we also have the support of our national legislation and our Government and our political parties. We have an international architecture that underpins women's rights and that is championed by the European Union, the United Nations and the Council of Europe. In the overseas development field, our country's official overseas aid programme particularly targets women through a focus on maternal health and lists the promotion of gender equality and the empowerment of women as one of its main goals.

And on the home front there is a growing realisation that to the extent that we fail to fully harness the complete range of talents, input and potential of women, our country will fly on one wing instead of two. Their contribution is essential to economic growth, to the problem-solving capacity of our civic society and to the ethical and moral input into the spiritual and secular intellectual wells from which we draw our ideas and values.

Encouraging individual women to step up and develop their fullest potential is an imperative for our society, for it is an essential element in developing our national potential. It is reassuring to see leading employers, among them Accenture, offering programmes specifically designed to encourage the advancement of female staff. None of us can fully measure the paralysing effects of centuries of biased attitudes to women, to their roles and their aptitudes. But we can be sure that those effects continue, sometimes overtly and sometimes very subtly, particularly as women struggle to be mothers, carers and homemakers as well as employees or employers. Our challenge is to keep on building a culture of good practice so that women share positions of influence with men across all key sectors, so that their voices are listened to carefully and sensitively and so that our society shifts from the lopsidedness of inherited patriarchy to the organic balance of gender equality.

We, as women but also as a society of men and women, owe a huge debt of gratitude to all those who helped change the landscape of opportunity for women: the religious orders and other schools which offered women education long before it was politic to do so and whose alumnae became the women with a new ambition for themselves and their country; the men who championed equality for women; the women who made the best of lives frustrated by rules they had no way of changing; women who were our mothers and grandmothers, described by W.R. Rodgers, as the 'Watchers and the Wakeners' (from the poem 'Resurrection') and whose sacrifice paved the way for our opportunities, and the women who, a century ago in this city, not far from here at 52 Pearse Street, then Great Brunswick Street, without violence or the threat of it, used their imaginations to draw attention to the injustice that enslaved them.

As each of us leaves this celebration today, we take with us that same challenge of 100 years ago, of how can we as women, help women, help our country and our culture to become more family friendly, more sensitive to the things which inhibit women's full civic participation and which reduce the fullness of our shared civic life.

Back in 1911, the idea behind International Women's Day was 'women helping women'. It is still a good idea. In fact it is still necessary and we are the hands of the work of the next century.

Go raibh míle maith agaibh go léir.

REMARKS AT THE 'DUBLINSWELL' EVENT TO CELEBRATE THE DESIGNATION OF DUBLIN AS UNESCO CITY OF LITERATURE

The Conference Centre, Dublin, 18 March 2011

Dia dhíbh go léir. Tá an-áthas orm bheith anseo libh ar an ócáid speisialta seo.

Ladies and gentlemen,

I'm delighted to join you here this evening to mark and to celebrate our capital city's designation as a UNESCO City of Literature. Dublin's literary credentials need little rehearsal, if any, either at home or abroad, for this is the city mapped and immortalised in one of the greatest literary masterpieces of the twentieth century.

It is the city in which three great Nobel Laureates in literature first saw the light: William Butler Yeats, George Bernard Shaw and Samuel Beckett. It is the adopted home of our most recent Nobel Laureate in literature, Seamus Heaney. It is home to a litany of world-class writers and to an educated audience of readers of literature, and after yesterday's St Patrick's Day parade through O'Connell Street, we all know, thanks to Roddy Doyle, that Dublin and Ireland are quite simply 'brilliant'.

Stories matter to the Irish. Our literature probes without ever exhausting the experiences and imagination drawn from our dramatic past and present, our landscape so ridiculously diverse and marvellous for such a small island, our centuries-old culture of scattering across the world and planting Irishness of one sort or another in so many places, our emerging new culture of integrating immigrants into Ireland, the endless well of the Irish language, the unique fluency we have in its younger sister, the English language … the sources and streams that fill Dublin's literary imagination are so phenomenally diverse that they are reminiscent of the sage who said that you never step in the same stream twice and the even greater sage who remarked that, in fact, you never step in the same stream once.

This evening we are privileged to step into the stream in the company of some of the most exciting exponents of Dublin's literary tradition and we are doubly privileged that we do so in celebration of UNESCO's recognition of Dublin's love affair with literature.

I congratulate everyone concerned and look forward to the many good things that will be accomplished through this focus on Dublin as a member of the UNESCO Creative Cities Network. With the sun shining on O'Connell Street yesterday and all day today, it was tempting to believe that maybe literature, maybe DublinSwell can after all teach us to believe how brilliant our city and our country truly are.

Comghairdeas libh arís agus go raibh maith agaibh go léir.

REMARKS AT A CONFERENCE ON
'CHILDREN: THEIR LIVES, THEIR LEARNING'

Marino Institute of Education, Dublin, 4 May 2011

Dia dhíbh a chairde, tá an-áthas orm a bheith in bhúr láthair inniu ag an gcomhdháil speisialta seo: 'Children: Their Lives, Their Learning'. Is ábhar fiorthábhachtach é ó thaobh leasa agus todhchaí ár bpáistí agus sochaí na hÉireann de.

I'd like to thank Dr Anne O'Gara, President of Marino Institute of Education, and Dr Anne Looney, Chief Executive of the National Council for Curriculum and Assessment, for their kind invitation to address you today.

My grandmother, who had eleven children and sixty grandchildren, used to remark, 'What's learnt in childhood is engraved on stone.' I didn't get the full import of her words until a tiny misspelling on my grandfather's granite headstone led to a conversation with the stonemason as to whether it could be easily corrected. He said no; the only way the problem could be corrected was to take the faulty headstone down and put up a new one. Those of us who are the engravers on the unwitting lives of innocent children do not get that option. We get one go around – one chance to get it right, so that we engrave well, scrupulously, carefully and leave an imprint that does not skew a lift or blight a life long after childhood has passed. It is a solemn responsibility, a sacred trust and it is right that at a conference like this we should reflect on those precious, all-important childhood years and ask in particular what primary education must bring to their lives.

It's an important time in our country's educational history, for debates are afoot which have the capacity to radically change the structure and the experience of primary education.

Those who are the engravers on children's lives need to be deeply implicated in those debates to ensure that primary education, which is the very bedrock of our educaobnal system, is customised to the needs of our children. Five hundred years ago, Erasmus observed that the main hope of a nation lies in the proper education of its youth. It was true then and it is true now.

A good education is crucial to the life chances of each child. Life circumstances are not scientifically or equitably distributed. Poverty, family dysfunction, disability or ill health can conspire to make a childhood much tougher than any of us would wish for a child. In an unequal equation it is often education which offers a cantilever and a transcending conduit to fulfilling a child's potential. Our society needs citizens who are active, engaged problem-solvers; people who are confident, creative, resilient, adaptable. The journey towards that kind of citizenship begins in childhood.

We enter this debate from a position of strength, for Ireland has long had a deep commitment to learning. How many of us in this room can tell of fathers and mothers who made huge sacrifices so that we could have educational chances that would have been like lottery wins to our parents? A respect for education is deeply embedded in our psyche and we have witnessed the formidable transformative power of widened access to good education, particularly in the final quarter of the twentieth century.

It was Yeats who warned that education is not about filling a pail but about lighting a fire, and in this era of rapid technological and scientific change, the world we are preparing our children for is very different from the world we were prepared for. The old Irish proverb tells us, 'doras feasa fiafraí' – an enquiring mind is the door to knowledge. Feeding and encouraging the natural curiosity of the child is one of the most important jobs anyone – whether a parent or a teacher – can undertake. Yes, we need our children to be literate and numerate, for these are essential minimum pathways to their own potential, but we also need them to believe in their own creativity, to develop their own critical, analytical and forensic skills, to grow emotionally, metaphysically, psychologically and socially.

A good curriculum and good teaching are two prime ingredients of any successful educational experience. Here at Marino Institute of Education, the programme of teacher education is continually developing in response to fresh insights and research into the needs and responses of the child learner. The NCCA promotes a culture of scholarly interrogation of pedagogy and curriculum that will ensure that our primary education system is soundly based and is responsive to research and to best international practice.

I have been very fortunate to visit a large proportion of our primary schools – big, small, urban, rural, Catholic, Muslim, Protestant, Educate Together, Gaelscoileanna. I have seen the tremendous work that goes on in them every day, been amazed at how seamlessly they absorbed thousands of immigrant children, how they have integrated special needs children and those with disabilities who in past times had only a limited choice of educational opportunity. I have seen the walls decked with the children's work, heard their singing and their musicianship, watched their drama, dance and sports, congratulated their Trojan efforts to win green flags, strolled around their organic gardens, been amazed at their fundraising efforts for poor children in developing countries, sat in on the classes they share via the internet with students from all over Europe, listened to them explain how they deal with bullying, how they promote a value system of mutual care and respect … and I have marvelled at the busyness of their lives, the embedded multifaceted opportunities they have for a rich daily lived educational experience, thanks to men and women who make primary teaching their vocation and who delight in making school a happy, fun, exciting, participating place to be. Our teachers are strong academically and pedagogically. They are trained and tested, tested and trained so that their ability and empathy for this vocation are sure and well validated, well vindicated by the time they graduate. They know they are partners with parents in each unique child's education and that the parents are the primary educators of their children. So they know that their focus has to look to the child's context, to his or her parents and family situation. They know that fairness and even-handedness to all children is essential, but that ironically, a one-size-fits-all approach is inimical.

Many of us can point to a teacher who made a difference in the very trajectory of our lives – the teacher whose intuitive eye, whose professionalism and humanity lit in us that self-possession and intellectual curiosity that opened us up to our own abilities and to the contribution we could make to our families, our communities and our country. What a phenomenal privilege it must be to know you are the one, the person who lit that fire, the teacher who engraved so expertly on the life of a child that you brought out the sparkling diamond in him or her and helped them on their life's journey to rewarding, fulfilling lives. Every child is entitled to a teacher like that and to an experience of school that is the best we can make it.

Days like this allow us to take the time to think about what has been achieved, to understand the wisdom gleaned from things that work well and things that need to be looked at anew.

This is a good opportunity to share what you have learnt and what you know so that the roadmap to doing things even better still can reveal itself through your deliberations.

I wish you well with your hugely important work.

Go raibh míle maith agaibh.

REMARKS TO THE ENVIRONMENTAL PROTECTION AGENCY

Johnstown Castle Estate, Wexford, 15 June 2011

Dia dhibh a chairde. Tá an-áthas orm bheith anseo libh ar an ócáid speisialta seo.

Ladies and gentlemen,

I am delighted to be here with you today. Thank you to Dr Mary Kelly for her invitation and to the IT team for organising video conferencing facilities which allow us to communicate between here and the regional offices.

There is a very familiar and true saying that 'We do not inherit the earth from our ancestors, we borrow it from our children.' It is not just a smart, pithy phrase; it is a philosophy which, once we get its meaning, insists that we tread this earth with a respectful vigilance, with an abiding duty of care to those who come after us and who depend on us to act honourably, intelligently and thoughtfully.

Yet we live in a world of conflicting demands and with many, many examples, both historically and in contemporary times, of decisions made, of things done which have brought so-called benefits to one generation at an appalling cost to the next. In our own time, prosperity, complex modernity and technological sophistication have run in tandem with – and often at odds with – great debates about effective environmental protection. The tensions can lead to difficult decisions and competing needs. Navigating through the chaos of so many voices, we need the strong, scholarly, steady, persuading influence of bodies like the Environmental Protection Agency. Thanks to your work, we know and accept that, as a society, we all have a collective responsibility to ensure that the future development of our economy is proofed so as to contribute to the sustainability of the environment in which we live and work.

Our country has changed phenomenally in a relatively short period, from a predominantly rural lifestyle to large-scale urbanisation, from low-tech industries to high-tech or added-value industries and services. Our consumer-driven growth and globalised industrial base have created dependencies around imported oil which we are trying to offset with moves to renewable sources of energy, many of which are still in the relatively early or mid-stages of full development. We have become accustomed to thinking more strategically, both personally and communally, in terms of recycling and reusing, in terms of reducing our carbon footprint and our energy consumption.

We buy energy-efficient appliances and bulbs, insulate our homes, change our behaviours and work practices as part of a national effort to transform old wasteful ways of working and living into dynamic modes of sustainable working and living.

A change in attitudes like that does not happen overnight. It happens because of people who have the determination, the passion and the foresight to effect change, people who have the vision to look to the future and see how it should be shaped and people who have the energy and courage to drive an important message home, even when it is often not what others might wish to hear.

Somebody once said that 'There are no passengers on Spaceship Earth; we are all crew.' Our behaviours affect each other across geographic borders and so environmental protection is a global issue and responsible environmental education and practice are global imperatives.

But responsibility starts locally, and your work helps us in our task of being exemplars of good practice and in garnering the national spirit of social responsibility which can truly ring the changes we need to see. It is no surprise that the National Economic and Social Council recently cited you as one of Ireland's best agencies and one with a high international standing. No surprise – but something each and every one of you should be very, very proud of.

Because of your work in research and development, environmental education and guidance, policing, monitoring, licensing, assessment, regulation and all the many other things you do, the children of today's Ireland and tomorrow's Ireland have a chance to breathe pure and healthy air in a green and environmentally secure place – a country where our greenhouse gas emissions will be reduced, our water and soil will be of high quality, our resources will be used efficiently, and environmental considerations will play a central mainstreamed role in policy-making at every level, from the national to the local, including in the home.

There are both very sophisticated and very simple weather vanes which point to your success. Among the simplest and the most pleasant is the welcome increase in the number of Irish beaches that have been awarded Blue Flag status this year. That did not happen by accident but by the persistent driving towards excellence and refusal to accept anything less.

The Environmental Protection Agency has a broad and constantly evolving remit that is more than a task; it is a mission. I would like to thank each one of you for making this mission your own personal vocation and your life's work. You promote a culture that protects and conserves our environment. You engage with all the partners you need to bring on board to make sure that 'Crew Ireland' are helping steer the good ship Earth in a direction that is sensible and good for all of humankind.

I congratulate you on the high standards you constantly set yourselves and achieve; standards which are admired internationally and which make me very proud to be in your company today.

Go raibh míle maith agaibh go léir agus comhghairdeas libh arís.

8

A SHARED PAST
AND FUTURE

I very much welcome this historic breakthrough. It is a momentous day which heralds a new phase in developing relationships between the peoples of these islands. It is a great tribute to everyone involved in this difficult process – a process involving the building of trust and the taking of risks. I would like to commend the Independent Chairmen led by Senator George Mitchell, the two Governments, the politicians and the officials. We are all grateful to them for their endurance, courage, vision and commitment. I would also like to pay tribute to the many people abroad, and particularly those in the United States of America who nurtured the process and helped to bring it so a successful conclusion.

It offers a new beginning – a chance for everybody to reach out and accommodate those with whom we share this unique part of the world – an opportunity to build bridges and partnerships based on mutual respect for all traditions, cultures and creeds on this island.

STATEMENT ON THE OMAGH BOMBING

15 August 1998

I am deeply shocked to learn of the appalling bombing in Omagh which has left so many dead and injured. My heart goes out to the bereaved families who are now left to mourn their loved ones. The bombing has obliterated the hopes and dreams of so many families in one cruel afternoon of purposeless terrorism. We must do everything in our power to ensure that those responsible are brought to justice quickly and that they face the full rigour of the law. The families who have so grievously suffered in Omagh this afternoon must have the hope and certainty that the perpetrators will be brought to justice.

The promise of the Good Friday Agreement cannot be frustrated by those responsible for this cowardly act. This appalling bombing must bond us all together to redouble our efforts to foster the consensus and reconciliation which so many throughout this island have been working to achieve.

REMARKS AT A RECEPTION ON THE OCCASION OF THE INAUGURATION OF THE MESSINES PEACE TOWER

Messines, Belgium, 11 November 1998

Governor, Burgomaster, aldermen and citizens of Mesen, ladies and gentlemen,

Thank you sincerely for the warmth of your welcome, both at the Island of Ireland Peace Park and at this beautiful Countess Adela House. I deeply appreciate the work of the people of Mesen and the members of A Journey of Reconciliation Trust who together made this momentous day possible. We are all especially grateful to those whose hands built the Peace Tower and landscaped the Peace Park.

Today's ceremony at the Peace Park was not just another journey down a well-travelled path. For much of the past eighty years, the very idea of such a ceremony would probably have been unthinkable.

Those whom we commemorate here were doubly tragic. They fell victim to a war against oppression in Europe. Their memory, too, fell victim to a war for independence at home in Ireland.

In the history of conflict which has blighted my homeland for generations, respect for the memory of one set of heroes was often at the expense of respect for the memory of the other. As former Taoiseach (Prime Minister) Sean Lemass, himself a protagonist in the Irish people's fight for independence, said thirty years ago:

> In later years, it was common, and I was also guilty in this respect, to question the motives of those who joined the new British armies at the outbreak of the Great War, but it must, in their honour and in fairness to their memories, be said that they were motivated by the highest purpose ...

Today, we are keenly aware that if we are to build the culture of consensus promised by the Good Friday Agreement then we need to create a mutually respectful space for differing traditions, differing loyalties – for all our heroes and heroines.

Men of the 36th Ulster Division and the 16th Irish Division died here. They came from every corner of Ireland. Among them were Protestants, Catholics, unionists and nationalists, their differences transcended by a common commitment not to flag but to freedom. Today we seek to put their memory at the service of another common cause expressed so well by Professor Tom Kettle, an Irish nationalist and proud soldier who died at the Somme:

> Used with the wisdom which is sown in tears and blood, this tragedy of Europe may be and must be the prologue to the two reconciliations of which all statesmen have dreamed, the reconciliation of Protestant Ulster with Ireland and the reconciliation of Ireland with Great Britain.

I do not think that it is too bold to suggest that this day has been a day of historic significance.

The problems we face in building a culture of consensus are difficult but not impossible. We can draw strength from the collegial partnerships built in Europe this past forty years between once bitter enemies and the enormous goodwill towards Ireland from our friends around the world, not least here in Belgium.

None of us has the power to change what is past but we do have the power to use today well to shape a better future. The Peace Park does not invite us to forget the past but to remember it differently. We are asked to look with sorrow and respect on the memory of our countrymen who died with such courage far from the common homeland they loved deeply. Their vitality, genius, youth and commitment was lost to Ireland. In this generation we redeem their memory, acknowledging their sacrifice and the pain of those who loved them. We pray that just as this park has changed the landscape of Belgium, so too it will help to change the landscape of our memory. These, too, are Ireland's children, as those who fought for her independence are her children and those who fought against each other in our country's Civil War, and of course the dead of recent decades – their children's children – who have not known the peace for which they yearned. To each, let us give his or her acknowledged place among our island's cherished dead.

In the Irish language I wish God's blessing on their souls:

Ar dheis Dé go raibh a n-anamacha uasal.

We hope that the goal of peace promised by the Good Friday Agreement will be our gift to the next generation. I wish to thank you most sincerely for affording me the opportunity of commemorating the memory and honouring the sacrifice of those from the island of Ireland who died in the Great War.

REMARKS AT A RECEPTION FOR PEOPLE FROM OMAGH, BUNCRANA AND BALLYMONEY

Áras an Uachtaráin, 25 November 1998

Martin and I would like to extend a very warm welcome to all of you to our house this evening, in particular the injured and bereaved who have come a long way to be with us – from Ballymoney, from Buncrana and from Omagh. I would like to welcome His Excellency, the Ambassador of Spain, who is representing families of the Spanish victims of the Omagh bombing, and His Excellency the Ambassador of Austria who is with us also.

I am delighted also to welcome the representative of the Omagh District Council and the emergency services – the police, the fire service, the ambulance service, the hospital medical teams and assistants – indeed the many services and people who had essential roles to play in helping people to cope on the terrible day in Omagh. Our MC this evening is the very accomplished actor Gerry McSorley, who is himself from Omagh, and I would like to thank him for making this evening such a success. To all of you, let me say how delighted we are that you have accepted our invitation to come to Áras and Uachtaráin.

We are very privileged this evening to have the world-renowned Vienna Boys' Choir with us, and I would like to thank them for agreeing to come along to provide a suitable seasonal flavour for the evening. A little later, we expect to welcome Prime Minister Tony Blair and his wife, Cherie. They are on their way as I speak and will arrive closer to six o'clock.

Our main reason for inviting you to be with us this evening is to have an opportunity to show our solidarity with all of you as this unforgettable year draws to a close. It has been a mixed year, with our optimism and high expectations in the wake of the momentous Good Friday Agreement and the referenda that followed shattered by the awful happenings at Ballymoney and at Omagh. In that respect, it was a painful year for all of us – particularly for you whose lives have been so terribly affected in a year that, with God's help, will never be repeated in its pain and its suffering.

I know, however, that your hurt, your loss, and your suffering will remain with you for your lifetime. You have been through some terribly difficult days and weeks, and you face a daily struggle in the months and years ahead as you try to come to terms with what has happened in your lives. Too much loss, too many hopes obliterated, too many people asked to carry burdens of grief and physical injury. Yet you are not alone. Everywhere I have gone – Australia, Canada, America, New Zealand, Liverpool – complete strangers told me of their prayers for you and for our homeland. By bringing you to our house this evening, it is our way of giving you a hug of love and friendship, and of saying how we want to share your burden with you in whatever way we can, all the while being painfully aware of how inadequate our efforts are to restore what you have lost or even to lighten that burden.

As this fateful year closes, it is perhaps appropriate that we should look ahead – however difficult we may find it at times. While our expectations suffered so terribly during this turbulent summer, our hopes were not destroyed by those who thought the Peace Process so fragile that it could be bombed to extinction. They were so wrong. The spirit of Omagh – of the sacrifices of the little Quinn boys – bolstered and strengthened our resolve and determination to move forward from the chaos and suffering that we have had to endure, to move towards a time and a place that cherishes human life in all its diversity.

We have been given an opportunity to build a new future for ourselves and for the coming generations, so that they will not have to know the kind of suffering and destruction that has brought so much hurt and misery to this small island. We owe it to all those whose lives have been blighted – to those who have experienced pain and loss over the last thirty years in Ireland – to take lessons from the dead, the injured and our grieving, and to prove that we too can transcend our differences, that we can debate and dialogue our way through the issues we disagree on and that we can create space for all based on mutual respect for our traditions, creeds and cultures.

This house was once the home of the British Viceroys in Ireland. For them, Dublin was, after London, the second jewel in the Empire's Crown. History has made it my home and I want to make it a place where we, the children of our troubled history, can all feel at home. It is a repository of hundreds of years of British history and Irish history – and the intertwined histories of our two islands. All the stories – whether of Viceroys, Governors General or Presidents – are told here respectfully in our visitor centre. No one who comes here – whether from the Shankill or South

Armagh – should feel uncomfortable. This home tells the story of our shared history. It has a store of shared memories. We really look at them differently, care about them differently – but they are now ours to share.

Thank you for taking the time to join us and for giving us this opportunity to offer some hospitality. Martin and I wish you well in the years ahead and we would like to assure you that you are in our thoughts and prayers – especially at this approaching Christmas time, which we know will not be easy for you. We pray that you will have the strength to continue to recover and overcome the personal difficulties that have been cast in your way. My renewed thanks to you and the Vienna Boys' Choir.

May we together create a new and a happy shared memory here in Áras an Uachtaráin. On the day that Martin Luther King was shot, Bobby Kennedy quoted this piece from the poet Aeschylus:

> … in our deep sleep, pain which cannot forget falls drop by drop upon the heart, until in our own despair, against our will, comes wisdom through the awful grace of God.

STATEMENT ON
IRA DISARMAMENT

26 September 2005

President McAleese has welcomed today's announcement by the Independent International Commission on Decommissioning that the IRA has decommissioned its entire armoury.

The President said:

'Today's announcement will remove a major obstacle to the search for a lasting and peaceful solution to the problems which have beset Northern

Ireland for so long. I hope that these developments will help to bring about a better climate in which trust between the two communities in Northern Ireland can flourish in the years ahead and that it will herald a speedy end to all ongoing paramilitary activity.

'We are indebted to both the Irish and British Governments and the many individuals and organisations who have worked tirelessly to bring about today's developments in order to help create a much better climate for political progress in Northern Ireland.'

STATEMENT ON THE STORMONT AGREEMENT

26 March 2007

I welcome in the warmest terms today's historic agreement at Stormont. The decision to restore the devolved institutions on 8 May marks a profoundly important milestone on the journey towards lasting peace and reconciliation. I congratulate everybody involved in bringing us to this extraordinary day. The Good Friday Agreement promised a new beginning in relations within Northern Ireland, between North and South, and between Ireland and Britain. Today's landmark agreement clears the way for us to fulfil that promise in an unprecedented way and opens up before us a great horizon of hope. The challenge for all of us now is to ensure that this golden opportunity is grasped to the full.

Remarks at the 16ᵀᴴ (Irish) Division Exhibition

Somme Heritage Centre, County Down, 10 September 2007

It is an honour to be here at the opening of this exhibition commemorating the Battles of Guillemont and Ginchy, part of the heroic struggle of the Battle of the Somme fought over ninety years ago. Congratulations to Dr Ian Adamson, Carol Walker and all the members of the Somme Association for this labour of love which allows the stories of those who fought and died to be honoured and respected and better known by a new generation.

Last year, two very significant events in the history of this island – the ninetieth anniversary of the Battle of the Somme and the ninetieth anniversary of the Easter Rising – were the subject of elegant and moving official commemorations in Dublin. Both events shook and shaped the destiny of this island. In the generations since, Irish men and women have often looked back at those times through very different prisms, so different and so riddled with conflicting viewpoints that the sheer reconciling power of this remarkable platform of shared memory was overlooked and neglected.

This exhibition is part of that platform – a place to stand together in shared respect and a place to help us grow in understanding of those difficult times. Here, in recalling these battles of Guillemont and Ginchy, where the 16ᵗʰ Irish division fought so bravely in the most outrageous conditions, we recall the courage and generosity of so many young Irish men, from every background and belief, from Antrim to Cork, whose sacrifice forged our shared history, our shared memory. They showed us that there is no contradiction between working together collegially, in friendship and good neighbourliness on missions of common concern and interest while continuing to hold differing views and identities.

Many personal histories that should be better known, and could have helped us to better know ourselves and our commonalities, were swept away in the tumultuous events that engulfed Ireland immediately after the First World War and the Easter Rising. Thinking of Guillemont and Ginchy, I remember in particular two men: Tom Kettle and Emmet Dalton; one a wise philosopher and poet at thirty-six, the other half that age; one who died and one who lived; two who fought with great heart.

Tom Kettle fought, in the words of his widow Mary, for 'Ireland, Christianity, Europe … [and] a reconciled Ulster'. Dalton fought out of patriotism also, but partly, as his innocent words reveal, for 'the glamour of going to war. I mean at eighteen years of age what do you know?'

Back in June, on the ninetieth anniversary of the Battle of Messines Ridge, in the company of Mr Edwin Poots, the Northern Minister for Culture, Arts and Leisure, I visited for the third time the Irish Peace Park at Messines in Belgium. The Park was opened a few years ago by Her Majesty Queen Elizabeth, His Majesty King Albert and myself to honour the memory of the men of the 36th Ulster Division and the 16th Irish Division who fought shoulder to shoulder at Messines and Wijschate in a cause they saw as bigger than themselves and their divisions. Those who worked so hard to create that memorial knew that this troubled and conflict-ridden generation needed to be reintroduced to the voices of those who fell at Guillemont, at Ginchy, at Messines and Wijschate, because their voices would exhort us to use our best endeavours to build the peace, the reconciliation, the better world that they dared to dream of.

This year we saw the welcome re-establishment of the devolved institutions in Northern Ireland under the First and Deputy First Ministers. The First Minister summed up what many of us were feeling on that historic day when he said, 'How good it will be to be part of a wonderful healing.' Since then, we have seen and felt a fresh and energising new spirit of hope grow, exemplified by the visit of the First Minister along with An Taoiseach, Bertie Ahern to the site of the Battle of the Boyne.

The First Minister has long had an association with this museum and with championing the memory of those who fought and died at the Somme and other battlefields of the Great War. It is an interest we have in common and I am sure he shares my great satisfaction that over recent years more and more people have found it possible to acknowledge the full reality of what happened and to take pride in the comradeship and courage of the men of the 16th Irish and the 36th Ulster Divisions. And in so doing, we have taken those tragic memories, those names of grand-fathers and fathers, brothers and uncles, husbands and sweethearts out of the shoeboxes in the attic where they had lain in restless uncertainty for decades. We have restored them to the light of respect and of pride so that they have become a powerful, recovered, shared memory and indeed a wonderful healing.

First Minister, I congratulate you and the Deputy First Minister and all your colleagues in the Executive for the tremendous start you have made on your journey of partnership towards a new society in Northern Ireland and a new mood of good neighbourliness across this island.

There could be no better monument to the brave men of Guillemont and Ginchy.

STATEMENT ON
UDA DECOMMISSIONING

6 January 2010

President McAleese has warmly welcomed the announcement today that the UDA has completed decommissioning. Following this announcement and the related press conference given by the Ulster Political Research Group (the UPRG), the President said:

'Today's announcement represents a very positive milestone on the journey of peace. The decommissioning of weapons by the UDA, which follows a similar move on the part of the UVF last year, is further testimony to the reality that we are witnessing the deconstruction of a culture of paramilitarism in Northern Ireland and that it is being replaced by a culture of consensus, democracy and good neighbourliness. This is a deeply important and welcome development in terms of consolidating the new beginning heralded in the Good Friday Agreement and the St Andrew's Agreement.

'Violence and the weapons used in dispensing it have left a deep legacy of suffering and hurt, and on this significant day our thoughts and prayers are also with the victims of that violence. The challenge now is to ensure there is no return to that cycle of despair that was the hallmark of the Troubles. Part of that journey is ensuring that the dividend of peace is real on the ground in the lives of people. Hard to reach communities in Northern Ireland have been vulnerable to the influence of paramilitary groups and the ongoing challenge is to ensure that these communities are included more and more in the sharing of that dividend of peace.

'The Office of the President remains strongly committed to a process of real engagement with loyalist communities in Northern Ireland and I look forward to seeing continued progress in the development of a new era of peace and reconciliation.'

STATEMENT ON THE HILLSBOROUGH CASTLE AGREEMENT

5 February 2010

In responding to the agreement reached today involving the Irish and British Governments and the Northern parties, President McAleese said:

'This is a deeply significant day in the evolution of the Peace Process. Indeed, history may well record this agreement as the moment when the Peace Process transitioned from potential to reality. After many years of negotiation and inching forward at an often cautious and painstaking pace, a decisive move ahead has been made and, critically, it has been made by the parties themselves. As always, the facilitation role played by the two Governments has been crucial and I congratulate the Taoiseach, Brian Cowen, Prime Minister Gordon Brown, Minister Martin, Secretary of State Woodward and their dedicated officials on their great work. But they will be the first to agree that the centre of gravity of this agreement rested with the Northern parties themselves, led by the DUP and Sinn Féin. That is why this development augurs so well for the future. Peace-building is a long haul and a long road and we are still at a very early stage of its journey, but after today's agreement we can have more faith than ever that there is no turning back and that the most crucial ingredients for its long-term success – mutual respect and trust and a real sense of partnership – have at last begun to take root. In this, the first week of spring, it is clear that the new beginning promised in the Good Friday Agreement is becoming real and we can all take great hope and heart from that.

'Our gratitude and admiration go to the representatives of the parties who negotiated this agreement and for the leadership and courage they have shown. The critical task now is to use the powerful platform that has been created by this agreement to give full life to the devolution project and to ensure that the dividend of peace is experienced in real terms on the ground in all communities.'

Inaugural 'St Patrick's Day Lecture at Armagh'

19 March 2010

Dia dhíbh a chairde tráthnóna. Tá gliondar orm bheith anseo libh ar an ócáid speisialta seo agus ba mhaith liom mo bhuíochas a chur in iúl díbh as an chaoin-chuireadh agus an fháilte.

Where better to be in this week of St Patrick than in the ecclesiastical capital of Ireland? I thank Councillor Thomas O'Hanlon, the Mayor of Armagh City and District Council, for the kind invitation to give the inaugural 'St Patrick's Day Lecture at Armagh'.

In divided communities, particularly where the divisions are bitter and where memories are often invoked only to sharpen the division, the calling to mind of a shared heritage, a shared memory, can be an important bridge to reconciliation and to recognition of one another as brothers and sisters rather than strangers. Gathering here as we do in the name of St Patrick, across borders of history and of hearts and minds, we acknowledge that whatever our politics or perspective, we are each one a child of St Patrick; his story is our story, his legacy our legacy. Patrick created for us a platform of shared inheritance strong enough to help us to share more, to share better with one another in the days and years ahead.

It is always going to be difficult to interrogate thoroughly a life lived over a millennium and a half ago. Patrick's life has gathered legends and contradictions in the generations between his day and ours, but there is neither mystery nor legend about the fact that he came among us as a stranger, that he was a passionate ambassador for the Christian faith and that the message he espoused left an enduring impact and indeed an enduring challenge on this island that he came to love so much and to be identified with in every corner of the known world.

The man who came as an immigrant slave to these shores became by sheer force of principle and personality, a powerful catalyst for change. He was a victim of violence, a child kidnapped, held captive and abused. He was one of the downtrodden, the overlooked, the disregarded. He knew the cruelty of loss and loneliness for he was taken away from those he loved and who loved him. He knew well the inhumanity of which his fellow human beings were capable, for they visited enough of it directly on him to leave him in no doubt that almost all the unnecessary suffering in the world is inflicted by human beings on one another.

Seamus Heaney's poem 'The Cure at Troy' says tersely, 'Human beings suffer, They torture one another, They get hurt and get hard.' And there is truth in those words, as this country has cause to know. But not everyone gets hard. There are some who refuse to become hardened and bitter, who do not, through their acts, add more to the pile of human misery but instead commit their lives to softening, to reducing the mountain of hurt, to ending the cycle of misery. Patrick was one of those rare human beings; a man whose righteous frustration and indignation, his anger and his pain, distilled not into more hatred but into a loving forgiveness that stopped the toxin of hate dead in its tracks.

Sometimes we remember only Patrick the bishop, striding through Ireland, powerful, persuasive and compelling, but there is another Patrick more pertinent to these times. He is the slave boy, herding sheep on Slemish, frozen to the bone, realising the sheep were regarded more highly than he was and wondering was there ever to be a life for him – would he ever know freedom to live life on his own terms.

In this city and county and around Northern Ireland, there are men, women and children who feel that they too have been left out and left behind. They have been demoralised and drained by the conflict, they feel their youth and potential was robbed by forces beyond them and though peace is gathering momentum, consolidating day by day, the benefits of this great historic shift are not yet evenly distributed. That will take time. It will also take the same kind of courage, focus and commitment that was demanded of Patrick. The seemingly wasted years of his youth distilled into a passion that would make his name resound a millennium and a half later. Instead of letting victimhood and vengeance consume the rest of his life, he used the present not to dwell on the past or in the past but to fix what he thought needed to be fixed so that the future would be a place of hope – a place where all could safely belong. There are more and more people doing just that here in Northern Ireland. They are trying to build a reconciled society and at the same time trying to address the underlying tensions and problems which helped fuel the conflict. They are searching for ways to deal effectively and sensitively with the many deep traumas of the past. The fresh new momentum they have gathered into this phenomenon we call the Peace Process has offered such a new vista that more and more people have become peacemakers, including many who once sought to advance their cause through violence. The transformation in their thinking and their lives is the very thing that gives us such hope that real change is possible, that love can indeed transcend hatred and help heal hurt. The conversion to peace is not unlike the conversion of Ireland to the vision of St Patrick, for he too knew the wonder and the miracle of persuading sceptics and enemies to give up their old ways of thinking and join his mission. Patrick also knew what it was like to make hard choices, to put the common good before his own safety and wellbeing, to put his life in the service of others. He had escaped from captivity after six miserable years. He had gone home. He was safe. He was free, but a voice called him back to Ireland and he surrendered to that voice very reluctantly, as he said in his *Confessio*, 'I did not proceed to Ireland on my own accord until I was almost giving up.'

Had he given up, there would be much more than a big vacant hole in the March calendar. In every generation, whatever its circumstances, there has been a part of St Patrick's story to inspire, to comfort and to engender hope. In this once deeply fractured Ireland, which is on the journey to healing, there is his capacity for forgiveness of those who hurt him and his great love of this island. His status as an emigrant lodged deep in the hearts of the many millions of Irish who left their homeland driven out by poverty and politics. His arrival as a nonentity of a stranger who was to leave a massive imprint on the country of his adoption, reminds those of us who live in post-Plantation Ireland and who live in multicultural Ireland that the stranger is a repository of new energies, ambitions and perspectives that can make a rich contribution to our society. So Patrick teaches the stranger to have faith in the contribution he or she can make and he teaches the native to see inward migration as an opportunity.

A key element of Patrick's success was that he respected and worked alongside the old pagan culture so that his form of Christianity was absorbed easily and fluently into Irish life, growing side by side with the old pagan culture, with no anxiety to obliterate it. As a result. Ireland was transformed into something new, a place with a distinctive psychological identity, capable of seamless yet radical change.

When we speak of radical change, it is easy to miss the import of the cumulative changes we ourselves have lived through. Perhaps we are as yet too close to these events to see their true magnitude. But who could ever have imagined that an Irish Government would purchase the site of the Battle of the Boyne and develop there a heritage site for all the people of the island of Ireland? Who could have imagined a government in Northern Ireland with Sinn Féin Ministers working side by side with Democratic Unionist colleagues? It is only when we pause and take a step back to look at the bigger picture, over a longer perspective of time, that we truly appreciate how momentous this process of change really is and how much closer it brings us to Patrick's vision for the people of this island.

We are no longer the one-time island of saints and scholars that illumined all of Europe with scholarship, erudition, literacy and the great commandment to love one another. But that Ireland is still embedded in our DNA, just as the memory of those wandering monks is still to be found in the street names all over the European mainland. Centuries later, the children who had grown up on those European streets and who had slaughtered each other in their millions in two devastating World Wars would, out of the craven wreckage of those times, create the European Union, a most unlikely partnership of old enemies. They put war behind them and a future of friendship in front of them, and it was our membership of that Union, along with the United Kingdom, that set the scene for the development of one of the most crucial dynamics in our Peace Process. Shared membership of the Union allowed the relationship between Ireland and Britain to metamorphose rapidly from lukewarm and distrustful to fulsome and warm. A new collegiality opened up the space for a joint endeavour to bring peace to Northern Ireland and to put all the fraught relationships of history on a fresh and healthy footing.

This city was to become associated with the recalibration of those relationships in a very special way, for appropriately, the city where Patrick established his See is now home of the North South Ministerial Council and the Centre for Cross-Border Studies. Here the new culture of consensus and good neighbourliness is being incubated each day and rolled out across the island. North–South co-operation has replaced the wasteful days of living with 'back turned to back'. So much potential, for everything from simple friendship, safety and commerce, leached away into the sands of time because of the embedded culture of conflict. We are the first generation to know the joy of a future to look forward to, one that is humanly decent and uplifting. The politics that deliver this new horizon are not always pretty or straightforward but they have a visible forward momentum and importantly they result from democratic dialogue, plain speaking and compromise.

Now we have Ministers from the Irish Government and the Northern Ireland Executive co-operating regularly across a range of issues of common importance. We share North–South bodies like InterTradeIreland and Tourism Ireland. We harmonise our plans for building roads together, we share our precious natural resources and provide cancer and GP services on a cross-border basis. These things show what happens when our energy and initiative are liberated to be a positive force that makes a real difference to the lives of people on both sides of the border. There is no better place to observe that force at work than here in Armagh.

Last month, with the agreement reached on the devolution of policing and justice powers, we witnessed a moment when the Peace Process transitioned from potential to reality. It was a lumpy, awkward and difficult business. All of us on this island know that politics is at times a painstaking business, but in the end something inspirational did occur; the two traditions began to look more and more like one community and they spoke more and more convincingly with one voice. The politicians answered the call of the people for leadership just as St Patrick answered the voice that called him to leadership in Ireland.

He wrote in his *Confessio*, 'I am the sinner Patrick. I am the most unsophisticated of people, the least of Christians'. He was an ordinary man who found in himself the capacity for extraordinary, heroic things. Every community needs such people – the simple and the sincere who don't follow the giddy crowd, but who give remarkable leadership in their families, streets, communities, workplaces, clubs and country. They are the men and women who stop the toxin of hatred by refusing to laugh at the sectarian or racist joke. They are the men and women who make friends across the fractures of history's making. They are the men and women who teach their children to respect all others and to expect difference as well as to respect it. They are the backbone of the Peace Process and they have always been true to Patrick's call to love one another, forgive one another and to see each other as brothers and sisters.

We have rounded the cusp of change and now need to gather the momentum which will build, grow and consolidate this new emerging culture of good neighbourliness. That momentum is being quietly gathered in so many corners of this island by the persistent but largely unsung transformational work that is being done by individuals and all sorts of voluntary groups. They are unobtrusively fixing things that are or were wrong; they are filling in the 'centuries' arrears'.

The Peace Process went through many a wobble – some of them of seismic proportions – but today its robustness is a cause of real hope. The economy is going through a considerable wobble and history teaches us that we will find a way out of it – and this time we have on our side the resource of a peace, a resource denied to so many other generations over the centuries.

In his great poem 'From the Canton of Expectation', Seamus Heaney described the grim psychological hinterland inhabited by the generations before us, 'We lived deep in a land of optative moods, under high, banked clouds of resignation.' Not any more we don't. Today there is a lovely stanza from 'Station Island' that describes this moment better:

> As little flowers that were all bowed and shut
> By the night chills rise on their stems and open
> As soon as they have felt the touch of sunlight,
> So I revived my own wilting powers
> And my heart flushed, like somebody set free.

There is the touch of sunlight in this hard-won peace. And in this week we think of the littlest flower of them all, the shamrock, so beloved as a teaching tool by St Patrick.

In his poem 'The Shamrock and Laurel', the Revd William McClure points the way to our coming future:

> As the Lily was the glory
> Of the olden flag of France;
> As the Rose illumes the story
> Of Albion's advance –
> In the Shamrock is communion
> Of all Irish faith, and love …

STATEMENT ON THE VOTE IN THE NORTHERN IRELAND ASSEMBLY IN FAVOUR OF TRANSFER OF JUSTICE AND POLICE POWERS

9 March 2010

President McAleese has warmly welcomed today's cross-community vote in the Northern Ireland Assembly approving the transfer of justice and policing powers from Westminster to Stormont.

'Today's vote in the Northern Ireland Assembly represents an eloquent statement of confidence in the political institutions established under the Good Friday Agreement. It demonstrates that partnership politics are firmly taking root in Northern Ireland and that the devolved Assembly and Executive are courageously facing up to the challenges of delivering good government for all of the people they represent.

'The achievement of the devolution of policing and justice also represents a major milestone in the transformation of policing in Northern Ireland and will further assist the PSNI in carrying out their duties with the full support and confidence of all communities.

'I strongly commend all of the parties who have played an enabling role in taking forward the implementation of the Hillsborough Agreement and creating the political space for this afternoon's positive result in the Assembly.

'While the devolved institutions still face many challenges, today is a very good day for Northern Ireland. It shows that power-sharing politics is working; the elected representatives are working together in partnership for the benefit of all, and everyone can now look forward to the Assembly and Executive delivering even more on the full potential of the Good Friday and St Andrew's Agreements.'

An Opinion Piece for the *Irish News*

August 2010

Those who contributed to the special edition of *The Irish News* on Monday 23 August come from very different community, political and religious perspectives. There are many things they disagree on but they are resolute in their support for the Peace Process and the shared future it alone is capable of creating. So they have a simple message for those who think they can achieve their political objectives by violence and who are attempting to destabilise the peace we are successfully building on our island. That message is: your violent campaign will not succeed and it is long past the time to stop.

As President of Ireland, I wholeheartedly endorse this appeal to the few who remain on the paramilitary path to join the rest of us on the humanly uplifting path of peace.

My life introduced me early to the horror of sectarianism, division and violence and, over many years, including my time as President, I have met too many people who bear the scars, visible and invisible, of conflict on this island. The human devastation has been appalling. We are capable of so much better and we are proving it, despite the last gasp efforts of those who remain wedded to the use of violence in order to further the ambition for a united Ireland.

The crass methodology of the so-called dissidents has been overtaken by a radical and intelligent new dispensation which fully acknowledges the legitimacy of the aspiration to a united Ireland but crucially recognises that it can only be brought about 'by peaceful means with the consent of a majority of the people, democratically expressed, in both jurisdictions in the island'. These words, which find expression in Article 3 of the Irish Constitution and the Good Friday Agreement, are representative of the clearly and unequivocally expressed will of the people. Paramilitaries are not. What is worse, everything they do sullies that legitimate objective of uniting Ireland in the eyes of those who most need to be persuaded of its merits and makes its achievement less and less likely.

Since 1998, huge progress has been made in creating a more positive, egalitarian and pluralist Northern Ireland. A power-sharing government, a representative and accountable police service and a legal infrastructure to defend the civil and human rights of all have evolved rapidly, thanks to hard negotiations and the beginnings of a culture of consensus. Relationships within Northern Ireland, and between North and South, have improved considerably and many of those who were actively involved in violence or who supported paramilitarism have become convinced champions of the Peace Process and of our collective power to build a society that cherishes peace, justice and diversity.

The momentum behind this new dispensation is manifest. It is not easy or straightforward but it is markedly better than anything which has preceded it. It offers hope and it offers that hope to everyone. The children of today and tomorrow are entitled to the fruits of that hope and the peacemakers are utterly determined that future generations will not endure the misery that past generations experienced. In fact, the people of this island, whether they live North or South of the border, are already united in their shared determination that the days of the old, wasteful, embedded culture of conflict are over. Paramilitarism is the past.

My predecessor and Ireland's first President Douglas Hyde said, 'Hatred is a negative passion; it is powerful – a very powerful destroyer; but it is useless for building up. Love on the other hand is like faith; it can move mountains, and faith, we have mountains to move.'

Achieving a united Ireland is a mission that challenges us all, in a spirit of love, mutual respect and peaceful dialogue, to move mountains, but then again, who could have foretold the extent of the positive shifts in the political landscape that have already happened since the Good Friday Agreement? However, one thing is dismally clear – unity will never be achieved by the powerful destroyer of hatred and violence.

We are now well on our way to a positive future of peace, equality and good neighbourliness. Anyone who claims to be passionate about this island's future should be doing what they can to build the trust, the reconciliation, the mutual respect and acceptance which make people comfortable with one another, even where profound differences exist. Those who still think they can drag us back into darkness should take serious note of the fact that, despite a litany of gruesome acts of violence, the seed of peace has taken root strongly in many hearts once estranged from one another. Love is stronger than hate. It is as simple as that.

REMARKS AT THE RECEPTION FOR SURVIVORS AND FAMILY MEMBERS OF THOSE KILLED ON BLOODY SUNDAY

Áras an Uachtaráin, 17 September 2010

Céad míle fáilte.

We are delighted to have you here with us today and extend a very warm welcome to all of you.

Thank you for making the long journey from Derry to be with us today. But then, you are well used to long journeys, for thirty-eight years ago you started a journey for justice that only reached its destination on that momentous day of 15 June 2010, when the Saville Report finally told the world what you had always known – that those who were killed on Bloody Sunday were utterly innocent people who were not only wrongfully killed but whose reputations were distorted and sullied until Saville's detailed and forensic enquiry officially set the record straight.

The British Prime Minister has offered a welcome, sincere and contrite apology for what he described as the 'unjustified and unjustifiable' events that took the lives and health of those you loved. A dark cloud that had been hanging over Derry lifted that day, as the truth shone brilliantly over Ireland and the world. Without your fidelity to the truth and to justice there would have been no Saville Report. It took all of your patience, resilience and determination to get truth across the line and, at the same time, to carry as you did unbearable personal heartache and loss. Your resolve and dignified determination have inspired all those who heard your story.

I know that Derry is proud of you, and Ireland is proud for your dignity and your unshakeable resolve, for your support for one another through those awful days and years, for your magnanimity when finally vindicated and for your care for all those who suffered during the Troubles, no matter what their religion or politics. It was great to see you receiving the 'People of the Year' award last weekend.

I hope that each one of you has an easier heart than you had before that day in June this year and I hope, too, that in the years ahead we will all be reassured by the new culture that is emerging of peaceful good neighbourliness, partnership, mutual respect and tolerance, where the dignity of every individual and their equality of citizenship are recognised. You have led the way. You showed what had to be done and what could be done. You prized truth and honour, justice and integrity enough to sacrifice almost forty years of your lives in their service.

Thank you for your vital and outstanding contribution to that process; thank you for the dignity and generosity with which you sustained your long campaign; and thank you for your unwavering insistence that the truth be upheld and the innocent vindicated.

Remarks at the Launch
of 1641 Depositions Exhibition, 'Ireland in Turmoil: the 1641 Depositions'

Long Room, Trinity College Dublin, 22 October 2010

Provost, Lord Bannside, ladies and gentlemen,

For all our economic preoccupations, I think this is a better Friday 22 October to be alive than that other Friday 22 October, 1641, which we are recalling in this exhibition.

Ireland was then a powder keg of highly combustible political, ethnic and sectarian passions in the wake of the Elizabethan conquest, subsequent plantation and effective dispossession of large parts of Gaelic Ireland. With war in Scotland and the authority of Charles I under threat in England, and fearful for their increasingly fragile future, the Irish and Old English made a fateful bid to wrest back political control of their country. What was intended by the instigators as a conservative coup, spun out of control and Ireland descended into a bitter politico-sectarian conflict that in the following years visited appalling human suffering, culminating in the violent reconquest affected by Oliver Cromwell and casting long, brooding shadows from which we, 350 years later, are only beginning to emerge.

The events of 1641 have been the subject of considerable dispute and controversy, with wildly divergent accounts in both the Catholic and Protestant historical narratives. Facts and truth have been casualties along the way and the distillation of skewed perceptions over generations have contributed to a situation where both sides were confounding mysteries to one another. That is why, in these more chastened and reflective times, as we try to understand more deeply and generously the perspectives which have estranged us and as we try to reconcile, to be good neighbours, friends and partners across those sectarian divides, it is such a valuable thing to have access to this unique collection of witness testimonies from some of those who experienced the terror and horror of those tragic times.

The stories recorded in the 1641 Depositions, though they come largely from the Protestant communities, include some from Catholics, from people of all social backgrounds, from the illiterate – so often completely written out of history – and, poignantly, from a disproportionately high number of widows. They bring us deep into that dysfunctional and insane world, where neighbour killed neighbour and where a ferociously harsh winter ensured that many more were to perish from the cold as they fled from the encircling violence. Let us hope that their voices and their suffering, far from driving us deeper into our sectarian bunkers, do the opposite and inspire us to keep on working to ensure an end forever to such suffering, a profound, embedded, respect for one and all and an egalitarian, just, democratic society where peace prevails.

This exhibition is aptly placed in the wonderful jewel in Trinity's crown, the Long Room, at a university which itself predates these events, lived through them, was part of them and indeed was a partisan player in seventeenth-century Ireland, but is now a comfortable yet challenging intellectual meeting place for the forensic examination of facts and perspectives. Although housed here in the College Library for centuries, it is only now that these documents are open to us and to the world. That is largely thanks to a formidable partnership starting with teams in Trinity College Dublin and the universities of Aberdeen and Cambridge, who have just completed a major inter-institutional research project which has allowed the digitisation, transcription and online publication of the 1641 Depositions. They were helped by funding from the Arts and Humanities Research Council in the UK, the Irish Research Council of the Humanities and Social Sciences and Trinity College Library. I congratulate the multi-disciplinary team of scholars, librarians and IT specialists who worked together with Eneclann and IBM LanguageWare Dublin to produce what is a remarkable and timely resource. The three researchers who painstakingly transcribed every one of those handwritten documents deserve special mention, as does Professor Aidan Clarke, the general editor and a distinguished scholar of the Old English in Ireland.

The on-line publication of the Depositions will allow members of the public and the academic community alike to conduct their respective searches for deponents, and the Irish Manuscripts Commissions will publish the Depositions over the course of the next few years – quite a change from the 1930s, when the Commission's attempt to publish them was thwarted on the grounds that they might encourage divisiveness. The outbreak of the Troubles in Northern Ireland in 1969 made short shrift of another attempt. Third time lucky – and it is no coincidence that it occurs in the context of a peace that, for all its difficulties, is little by little healing history's hurts.

As we head into a period of iconic anniversaries of events about which all sides have very different views, let us hope that we will all endeavour to see these commemorative events as opportunities to practise and perfect the mutual sensitivity and respect which is needed for neighbour to live contentedly with neighbour. If approached in an open, honest and constructive spirit, these anniversaries will allow us transform topics whose taboo status weakened all of us into sources of informed mutual comprehension and strength. We are, even after the publication of the Depositions, unlikely to agree a common version of history, but we can agree that to have a common future, a shared and peaceful future, there is nothing to be gained from ransacking the past for ammunition to justify the furthering of hatred and distrust. There is, however, everything to be gained from interrogating the past calmly and coherently in order to understand each other's passions more comprehensively, to make us intelligible to one another, to help us transcend those baleful forces of history so that we can make a new history of good neighbourliness, understanding and partnership between all the people and traditions on this island.

In that context, it is a pleasure to see Lord Bannside here today, in this place where the technology of the twenty-first century has opened up part of the actuality of the seventeenth century to a generation capable of handling truth, together. I am sure that the exhibition will be a huge success with the public. And I look forward to the online project enhancing mutual respect and understanding on this island.

Go raibh míle maith agaibh go léir.

Remarks at the State Dinner in Honour of Queen Elizabeth II

Dublin Castle, 18 May 2011

A Shoilse Banríon, A Mhórgacht Ríoga, A Thaoisigh,
a Phríomh-Aire, a Chéad Aire, Tánaiste,
Rúnaí Gnóthaí Eachtracha agus a aíonna oirirce, fearaim céad míle fáilte romhaibh tráthnóna go Caisleán Bhaile Átha Cliath ar ócáid atá thar a bheith speisialta ar fad.

Your Majesty, Your Royal Highness, Taoiseach,
Prime Minister, First Minister, Tánaiste, Foreign Secretary, distinguished guests,

It is my pleasure to welcome you to Dublin Castle this evening on this, the first ever State Visit to take place between our two countries. This visit is a culmination of the success of the Peace Process. It is an acknowledgment that while we cannot change the past, we have chosen to change the future.

The relationship between our two neighbouring nations is long, complex and has often been turbulent. Like the tides that surround each of us, we have shaped and altered each other. This evening we celebrate a new chapter in our relationship that may still be a work in progress, but happily, has also become a work of progress, of partnership and friendship.

The contemporary British–Irish relationship is multifaceted and strongly underpinned by the most important connection of all – people and families. Large numbers of British-born people live here in Ireland and many more of our citizens have British backgrounds, ancestry and identity. In Britain, those of Irish birth, descent or identity are numbered in millions.

The two-way flow of people between these islands goes back millennia. This very room is dedicated to St Patrick, whose name is synonymous with Ireland. Yet he is reputed to have been born in Britain. Patrick's life as the man who brought Christianity to Ireland is illustrative of the considerable exchange of ideas and knowledge that there has been between our two nations throughout history.

It has been a fascinating two-way street, with Britain bestowing on Ireland our system of common law, parliamentary tradition, independent civil service, gracious Georgian architecture, love of English literature and our obsession with the Premiership. Conversely, Britain greatly benefited from the Irish genius of the likes of: Edmund Burke, the Duke of Wellington, Daniel O'Connell, Charles Stuart Parnell, Maria Edgeworth, Oscar Wilde, George Bernard Shaw and even Father Ted. Indeed, it was Shaw who wryly observed that:

> England had conquered Ireland, so there was nothing for it but to come over and conquer England.

However, even Shaw might not have dared to imagine that this cultural conquest would come in time to include rugby and cricket.

The Irish in Britain and the British in Ireland, both as individuals and communities, have made an invaluable contribution to both our homelands, while also cementing the links between us.

Today, those links provide the foundation for a thriving economic relationship. As close trade and investment partners and as partners in the European Union, Britain and Ireland are essential to each other's economic wellbeing. It is imperative that we work fluently together to promote the conditions that stimulate prosperity and opportunity for all of our people.

It is only right that on this historic visit we should reflect on the difficult centuries which have brought us to this point. Inevitably, where there are the colonisers and the colonised, the past is a repository of sources of bitter division.

The harsh facts cannot be altered nor loss nor grief erased, but with time and generosity, interpretations and perspectives can soften and open up space for new accommodations. Yesterday, Your Majesty, you visited our Garden of Remembrance and laid a wreath there in honour of the sacrifice and achievement of those who fought against Britain for Irish independence. Today at Islandbridge, just as we did at the Island of Ireland Peace Park at Messines in 1998, we commemorated together the thousands of Irishmen who gave their lives in British uniform in the Great War.

As the First Citizen of Ireland, like my fellow countrymen and women, I am deeply proud of Ireland's difficult journey to national sovereignty. I am proud of how we have used our independence to build a republic which asserts the religious and civil liberty, equal rights and equal opportunities not just of all its citizens but of all human beings.

I am particularly proud of this island's peacemakers, who, having experienced firsthand the appalling toxic harvest of failing to resolve old hatreds and political differences, rejected the perennial culture of conflict and compromised enough to let a new future in.

The Good Friday Agreement represented a fresh start and committed us all to partnership, equality and mutual respect as the basis of future relationships. Under the agreement, unionism and nationalism were accorded equal recognition as political aspirations and philosophies. Northern Ireland's present status within the United Kingdom was solemnly recognised, as was the option for a united Ireland if that secures the agreement and consent of a majority of the people of Northern Ireland.

The collegial and co-operative relationship between the British and Irish Governments was crucial to the success of the Peace Process and we can thank the deepening engagement between us as equal partners in the European Union for the growth of friendship and trust.

The Governments' collaborative efforts to bring peace and power-sharing to Northern Ireland have yielded huge dividends for the peoples of these two islands.

W.B. Yeats once wrote, in another context, that 'peace comes dropping slow'. The journey to peace has been cruelly slow and arduous but it has taken us to a place where hope thrives and the past no longer threatens to overwhelm our present and our future. The legacy of the Good Friday Agreement is already profound and encouraging. We all of us have a duty to protect, nurture and develop it.

Your Majesty, from our previous conversations I know of your deep support for the Peace Process and your longing to see relationships between our two countries sustained on a template of good neighbourliness. Your visit here is an important sign – among a growing number of signs – that we have embarked on the fresh start envisaged in the Good Friday Agreement. Your visit is a formal recognition of what has, for many years, been a reality – that Ireland and Britain are neighbours, equals, colleagues and friends. Though the seas between us have often been stormy, we have chosen to build a solid and enduring bridge of friendship between us and to cross it to a new, a happier future.

Your Majesty, your Royal Highness, it is in that spirit of mutual respect and warm friendship, it is in faith in that future, that I offer you the traditional warm Irish welcome: céad míle fáilte – 100,000 welcomes.

I now invite you, distinguished guests, to stand and join me in a toast:

To the health and happiness of Her Majesty and His Royal Highness;

To the wellbeing and prosperity of the people of Britain;

To the cause of peace and reconciliation on this island;

And to continued friendship and kinship between the peoples of Ireland and Britain.

Go raibh maith agaibh.